Simon Haines
Barbara Stewart

Cambridge English
First
MASTERCLASS

Student's Book with Online Practice

OXFORD
UNIVERSITY PRESS

Contents

Unit		Reading and Use of English	Listening	Speaking
1	Appearance and identity	Part 1 – Multiple-choice cloze p15 Part 5 – Multiple choice p12 Word building p12	Part 1 – Multiple choice p10	Part 1 – Conversation with interlocutor p17 Pronunciation: Sentence stress p17
2	Talents	Part 7 – Multiple matching p22 Part 2 – Open cloze p25 Part 3 – Word formation p30 Phrasal verbs: *turn* p22	Part 2 – Sentence completion p31 Adjective prefixes: *extra, hyper, over, under* p31	Part 2 – Individual long turn p27 Pronunciation: Sentence stress p27
3	Compulsion	Part 6 – Gapped text p38	Part 4 – Multiple choice p34	Part 3 – Collaborative task p41
4	Roles	Part 5 – Multiple choice p46 Collocations with *have* and *take* p47 Part 2 – Open cloze p49 Part 4 – Key word transformation p52	Part 3 – Multiple matching p50 Pronunciation: Stressed syllables p50	Part 2 – Individual long turn p53
5	Travel and culture	Part 7 – Multiple matching p58 Part 3 – Word formation p62	Part 4 – Multiple choice p63	Parts 3 & 4 – Collaborative task (Part 3) & Discussion on topics of collaborative task (Part 4) p65 Pronunciation: Opinion language p65
6	The mind	Part 6 – Gapped text p74	Part 2 – Sentence completion p70 Personal qualities p70	Parts 3 & 4 – Collaborative task (Part 3) & Discussion on topics of collaborative task (Part 4) p73 Pronunciation: Linking words p73
7	Free time	Part 5 – Multiple choice p82 Part 1 – Multiple-choice cloze p88	Part 1 – Multiple choice p89	Part 3 – Collaborative task p87 Pronunciation p87
8	Media	Part 6 – Gapped text p100 *so* and *such* p100	Part 3 – Multiple matching p94	Part 2 – Individual long turn p97
9	Around us	Part 5 – Multiple choice p106 Word building p107	Part 4 – Multiple choice p113 Travel collocations p113	Part 1 – Conversation with interlocutor p112 Pronunciation: Intonation in sentences p112
10	Innovation	Part 7 – Multiple matching p118 Parts 2 & 4 – Open cloze (Part 2) & Key word transformation (Part 4) p121	Part 2 – Sentence completion p124	Part 2 – Individual long turn p122
11	Communication	Part 6 – Gapped text p130	Part 1 – Multiple choice p136	Parts 3 & 4 – Collaborative task (Part 3) & Discussion on topics of collaborative task (Part 4) p134 Collocations with *say, speak, talk* and *tell* p134 Confusing verbs: *hope, wait, expect, look forward to* p134 Showing you are listening p134 Question tags p135 Pronunciation: Sentence intonation p135
12	Society	Part 7 – Multiple matching p142 Crime vocabulary p142	Part 3 – Multiple matching p146	Parts 1, 2, 3 & 4 – Conversation with interlocutor (Part 1), Individual long turn (Part 2), Collaborative task (Part 3) and Discussion on topics of collaborative task (Part 4) p147

Extra material p153   Grammar reference p158   Overview of exam tips p175   Writing guide p178   Audioscript p185

Writing	Grammar	Vocabulary	Review
Part 1 – Essay p18	Modal verbs of obligation p11 Present tenses p14 Adverbs p14	Parts of the body p16 Seeing verbs p16	p20
Part 2 – Email p28 Formal and informal language p28 Meanings of *get* p29	*can / be able to* and other ability structures p24 Comparatives and superlatives p26	Phrasal verbs p29	p32
Part 2 – Article p42 Creating interest p42	Habits and typical behaviour p35 *used to* and *would* p35 Part 2 – Open cloze p36 Countable / uncountable nouns p36	Phrasal verbs p37 Phrasal verbs with *give* p37 Pronunciation: Phrasal verbs p37 Adverbs p40	p44
Part 1 – Essay p54 Linking words p55	The future p48 Part 2 – Open cloze p49 Future continuous and future perfect p49 *bound to / likely to* p49	Phrasal verbs with *bring* p51 Words with several meanings p51	p56
Part 2 – Review p66 Evaluative adjectives p66 Compound adjectives p67 Language of recommendation p67	Past time p60	Travel phrasal verbs p61 Part 4 – Key word transformation p61 Words often confused p64 Extreme adjectives p64	p68
Part 1 – Essay p78	Gerunds p71 Gerunds and infinitives p71 Part 4 – Key word transformation p72	Collocations p76 Part 1 – Multiple-choice cloze p77	p80
Part 2 – Letter p90 Formal vocabulary p91 Word building p91	Passive verbs p84 *have / get* something done p85 Part 2 – Open cloze p85	Sports vocabulary p86	p92
Part 1 – Essay p102 Connecting ideas p103 Avoiding repetition p103	Reporting statements p95 Reporting questions p95 Time references p95 Other references p95 Reporting functions p96 Part 4 – Key word transformation p96	Compound nouns p98 Pronunciation: Stress in compound nouns p99 Word formation p99	p104
Part 2 – Report p114 Impersonal language p115	Relative clauses p108 Part 2 – Open cloze p109	Dependent prepositions p110 Part 4 – Key word transformation p111	p116
Part 2 – Review p126 Evaluative adjectives p127	Wishes and regrets p120 *I'd rather* and *it's time* p120	Adjective suffixes p123 Part 3 – Word formation p123 Compound adjectives p125 Pronunciation: Compound adjectives p125	p128
Part 2 – Article p138	Conditionals 0, 1 and 2 p132 Conditional 3 p132 Mixed conditionals p133 *unless, as long as, provided that* p133 Part 4 – Key word transformation p133	Positive or negative? p137	p140
Part 2 – Report p150 Complex sentences p151	Probability and possibility p144 Articles p148	Part 1 – Multiple-choice cloze p149	p152

Introduction and exam overview

About First Masterclass This fully-updated and revised edition of *First Masterclass* provides material which gives prospective candidates appropriate preparation and practice for the 2015 *Cambridge English: First* exam. The material in this course also provides opportunities for candidates to develop their English on a broader level for success in the real world beyond the exam.

The units in this Student's Book contain practice of exam-type tasks for all the parts of each paper in the exam. Vocabulary and grammar at a B2 level are developed throughout the course, with the latter being supported by the *Grammar reference* section (page 158). The *Writing guide* (page 178) further supports preparation for the Writing paper.

The Online Practice (unique access code on the card at the back of this book) contains exercises which build on and extend the language and skills covered in the Student's Book. It includes:

- skills-training exercises for all the task types in the exam
- exam practice tasks for each part of the four papers in the exam, including speak-and-record tasks
- *Oxford Advanced Learner's Dictionary* search box
- *feedback on your answers.

(*Available if your teacher sets assignments from your Online Practice 'with help' or with self-study use.)

The access code for your Online Practice also gives access to a full *Cambridge English: First* online practice test.

We hope you enjoy using *First Masterclass* to help you to prepare for the *Cambridge English: First* exam.

About the exam *Cambridge English: First* exam tests English at Level B2 on the CEFR scale. The exam consists of four papers covering all four skills and it also tests understanding of the structure of English. The *Cambridge English: First* certificate is proof of the fact that a candidate has a B2 level of English.

For more information about the exam go to www.cambridgeenglish.org

About the papers

Reading and Use of English

This paper consists of 7 parts and takes one hour 15 minutes. In Parts 1–4, candidates are tested on their knowledge of the structure of English with a focus on vocabulary and grammar, while Parts 5–7 include longer texts with related comprehension tasks focusing on reading skills. This paper includes 52 questions in total.

	Task type	Number of questions and marks	What you do	What it tests
Part 1	Multiple-choice cloze	8 questions; 1 mark each	Choose one word from a set of four options to complete the gaps in a short text.	Accuracy with vocabulary including knowledge of phrasal verbs, idioms, and collocations.
Part 2	Open cloze	8 questions; 1 mark each	Think of a single word that best fits each of the eight gaps in a short text.	Knowledge of grammar in context, as well as vocabulary.
Part 3	Word formation	8 questions; 1 mark each	Use a given root word to form another word that fits appropriately in a gapped text.	Accuracy in word building, including compound words, prefixes and suffixes.
Part 4	Key word transformation	6 questions; up to 2 marks each	There are six unrelated sentences each followed by a single word and a gapped sentence. Use the word given to complete the gapped sentence so that it means the same as the first sentence.	Control of a wide range of structures, vocabulary and collocation.
Part 5	Multiple choice	6 questions; 2 marks each	Answer each question about a long text by choosing one option from a set of four.	Understanding of a text, including detail, purpose, opinion, gist, implication, main idea, meaning from context and text organization features.
Part 6	Gapped text	6 questions; 2 marks each	Choose sentences to complete a long gapped text.	Understanding of how texts are structured, including cohesion and coherence.
Part 7	Multiple matching	10 questions; 1 mark each	Match ten prompts to elements in a long text or several short texts.	Ability to locate detail or specific information and understand opinion and implication.

Remember!
- Read and follow all instructions carefully.
- Read each text through quickly before doing the related tasks.
- If there is a question you can't answer, don't waste time worrying about it. Go on to the next question.
- You will not have time to read all texts in detail, and it isn't necessary. Skim and scan texts for answers where possible.

Find more tips for the Reading and Use of English paper on page 175.

Writing

This paper takes one hour 20 minutes and consists of two parts. In Part 1, you must answer the question, which is always an essay. In Part 2, you must choose one of three questions. These may include articles, letters or emails, reports and reviews. Each task carries equal marks.

	Task type	Number of words	What you do	What it tests
Part 1	Write an essay using the ideas given and an idea of your own.	140–190 words	Read the context and task instructions. Write your answer, making sure you use all the notes given and that you give reasons for your opinion.	Ability to give opinions and reasons for your opinion in a clearly structured piece of writing in an appropriate register. The range and accuracy of your grammar and vocabulary, and whether you have answered the question.
Part 2	Choose one question from questions 2–4. These can include an article, a letter or email, a report or a review.	140–190 words	Read the task instructions and write your answer.	Ability to produce a clearly structured piece of writing in an appropriate style for the intended reader. The range and accuracy of your grammar and vocabulary, and whether you have answered the question.

Remember!
- Spend a few minutes making a simple plan for each piece of writing. Decide on an appropriate style, layout and organization. Think about the content of paragraphs and the language you will use, e.g. verb tenses. Keep your plan in mind while writing.
- Don't spend more than half the time on your first answer.
- Make sure you answer all the points in the question appropriately.
- Check your writing by reading it through. Try to hear your own voice and 'listen' for mistakes. Check grammar, spelling, and punctuation.

Find more tips for the Writing paper on page 176.

Listening

This paper consists of four parts and takes about 40 minutes. The recorded texts may include the following:

Single speakers: answerphone messages, public announcements, anecdotes, lectures, news reports, radio programmes, stories, talks.

Two or more speakers: conversations, discussions, interviews, radio plays.

The speakers will have a variety of accents. Background sounds may be included before the speaking begins to provide contextual information. Candidates are given time to read through the questions after they listen to the instruction. They also have five minutes at the end to transfer their answers to the answer sheet. They hear each recording twice. There are 30 questions in this paper.

	Task type	Number of questions and marks	What you do	What it tests
Part 1	Multiple choice	8 questions; 8 marks	Listen to eight short unrelated extracts. For each one, answer a question by choosing one option from a set of three.	Understanding of detail, gist, feeling, attitude, purpose, agreement between speakers.
Part 2	Sentence completion	10 questions; 10 marks	Listen to one monologue and complete each of the ten sentences with a word or short phrase from the monologue.	Ability to identify detail, specific information and opinion of the speaker.
Part 3	Multiple matching	5 questions; 5 marks	Listen to five short monologues with a common theme or link. Match each speaker to one of eight options.	Ability to identify main points, detail, gist, purpose, attitude, opinion and feeling.
Part 4	Multiple choice	7 questions; 7 marks	Listen to an interview or discussion (two speakers) and answer each of the questions by choosing one option from a set of three.	Ability to identify main idea, gist, attitude, opinion, detail and specific information.

Remember!
- Listen carefully to the instructions on the recording.
- Try to predict as much as you can about the recording from the questions on the question paper, before you listen.
- Don't panic if you don't understand much the first time.
- Answer all the questions, even if you are not sure of your answer.

Find more tips for the Listening paper on page 176.

Speaking

This paper consists of four parts and takes approximately 14 minutes. There are normally two candidates and two examiners. One examiner just listens and assesses, while the other assesses, gives instructions and talks to the candidates.

You will be assessed on:
- Accurate use of grammar, and range and use of vocabulary
- Pronunciation
- Interactive communication
- Discourse management

	Task type	Timing	What you do	What it tests
Part 1	Interview	2 minutes	Answer the examiner's questions about personal information	Ability to interact in general and social situations.
Part 2	Individual 'long turn'	4 minutes	Speak individually for one minute about two photographs you are given and give a 30-second response to questions about your partner's photos.	Ability to speak at length, express opinions, describe and compare.
Part 3	Two-way conversation	4 minutes	You are given written prompts to discuss with your partner for two minutes according to the examiner's instructions. This is followed by a one-minute decision-making task.	Ability to interact with another speaker, give and ask for opinions and justify them, speculate, make suggestions and work towards a decision with your partner.
Part 4	Follow-up discussion	4 minutes	Answer questions related to the topic of the Part 3 task that the examiner asks.	Ability to give opinions and justify them, speculate and agree or disagree with your partner.

Remember!
- At first, the examiner will ask you a few general questions about yourself. This is to help you relax.
- In Part 2, when you are given the pictures, don't spend too long talking about the physical details. Move on to the theme of the pictures.
- Don't dominate the conversation. Allow your partner the opportunity to talk.
- In all parts, take the opportunity to show the examiner how good your English is. Do this by using a wide range of vocabulary and grammar, and by speaking fluently and with good pronunciation.
- Keep talking until the examiner asks you to stop, and stay calm.

Find more tips for the Speaking paper on page 177.

Unit 1 — Appearance and identity

Introduction

1 Look at the photos. Which people do you think are being described in the statements below?

She looks rather cheeky.
I'd imagine he's very confident.
She's probably quite easy-going.
I reckon he's really moody.
She could be fairly shy.

2 Underline the adjectives in **1**. Circle the modifiers.
Example: *She looks (rather) cheeky.*

3 Work with a partner. Now, take turns to describe the people in the photos. Use the language in *italics* in **1** and the language below.

Modifiers: a bit   extremely   fairly   not at all   quite   rather   really   very

Adjectives: cheerful   friendly   good-natured   honest   insecure   outgoing   reserved   sensitive   serious   sociable   sophisticated   trustworthy

4 Which people in the photos would you …
- invite to a party?
- lend money to?
- tell a secret to?
- ask for advice?

9

Listening Part 1

Think ahead

1 Complete sentences a–e with the correct prepositions. Say whether you agree or disagree.

a I think looks are important. I take great pride _____ my appearance.
b I don't care what people think _____ me.
c First impressions _____ people are always misleading.
d Don't worry _____ identity theft; it doesn't happen _____ many people.
e Putting personal information on social networking sites leads _____ problems.

Exam practice

Multiple choice

Tip

Before you listen to the recording, read the question and the three options. As you listen for the first time, mark the option which you think is correct.

2 🔊 1.01 You will hear people talking in eight different situations. For questions 1–8, choose the best answer (A, B or C).

1 You hear a man telling a friend about an email he has received. How did the man respond to the email?
   A He gave the information he was asked for.
   B He checked the authenticity of the email.
   C He realized immediately that someone was trying to trick him.

2 You hear someone talking about her first impressions of someone. How did she react when he suggested meeting for a drink?
   A She agreed immediately.
   B She refused.
   C She hesitated but then agreed.

3 You hear a conversation between a young man and an older relative. What does the young man say he's going to do at the weekend?
   A go for a job interview
   B send the company his CV
   C find out more about the company

4 You hear someone describing how he heard about winning a competition for a mobile phone. What does the speaker now regret?
   A going in for the competition
   B giving personal information
   C forgetting to charge the phone

5 You hear two friends talking about tennis. What do we find out about the speakers?
   A They've been playing tennis for the same length of time.
   B They've often played each other at tennis.
   C Neither woman knew that the other played tennis.

6 You hear someone talking about a bad experience on a social networking site. What is the speaker's advice to other people?
   A Don't put personal details on social networking sites.
   B Ignore offensive messages after two weeks.
   C Report offensive messages to the police.

7 You hear a message on an answering machine. Why is the speaker apologizing?
   A She didn't speak to the friend she is calling.
   B She didn't recognize a relative of the friend.
   C She was too busy shopping to call her friend earlier.

8 You hear a politician talking about his appearance. What does he say about the kind of clothes he wears?
   A He wears formal clothes when he is involved in official duties.
   B He wears formal clothes for work and at home.
   C He wears informal clothes when he's meeting members of the public.

Over to you

3 Can you relate to any of the experiences or events described by the speakers?

Grammar (1)

Modal verbs of obligation
▸ *Grammar reference* page 159

1 Look at the words in *italics* in sentences a–g. Match them to the meanings in 1–7.

a I *have to* verify my account information.
b You *must* look smart at the interview.
c You *should* contact them directly.
d You *must* carry ID at all times.
e You *don't have to* give any personal details.
f You *mustn't* wear jewellery at work.
g I *must* get a new suit for work.

1 Rule: I'm telling you to do this.
2 Advice: it's a very good idea to do this.
3 Rule: I was told to do this.
4 Advice: it's a good idea to do this.
5 Not a rule: this is my own personal wish.
6 Not a rule: it's not necessary.
7 Rule: you're not allowed to do this.

2 Look back at **1**. What are the future forms of the language in sentences a, d and e?

3 In the following pairs of sentences is the meaning the same or different?
a There is no need to dress up. / I mustn't dress up.
b I needn't dress up. / I don't have to dress up.
c I must dress up. / I have to dress up.

4 What is the difference in meaning between these two sentences?
a There was plenty of time so I didn't need to hurry.
b There was plenty of time so we needn't have hurried.

5 Read the text below about preparing for a job interview. For 1–12, choose the correct modal verb. More than one answer may be possible.

Appearances count

First of all, clothes. You (1) *must / need to* look smart. You (2) *needn't / mustn't* wear your most formal clothes, but you (3) *don't have to / mustn't* look as if you've just got out of bed.

Arrive on time. You (4) *need to / must* allow more time than you think, in case there are unexpected hold-ups.

You (5) *have to / should* do everything you can to prepare. You (6) *must / should* think of a few questions to ask about the company.

Job advertisements normally say that you (7) *must / should* provide references when applying for a job. If you haven't already sent these, take them to the interview. You (8) *have to / should* have extra copies of your CV with you.

If you are offered the job, you (9) *must / have to* try to find out anything you (10) *need to / needn't* do before you start. For example, I expect you (11) *will have to / should* have a medical examination. I remember I (12) *must / had to* have one for the last job I went for.

Over to you

6 Think about the past. Discuss with a partner what you had to do or didn't have to do …
a as a secondary school student.
b if you went out for the evening when you were under the age of sixteen.
c if you wanted extra pocket money from your parents.

7 Think about a recent event in your life. Complete these sentences.
a I didn't need to _____ .
b I needn't have _____ .

Reading and Use of English Part 5

Think ahead 1 Discuss these questions.
   a What do you understand by the phrase 'identity theft'?
   b In what situations or circumstances can people become victims of identity theft?

2 Quickly read the text on page 13. Answer these questions.
   a Was Mr Bond a fraudster or not?   b Is identity crime increasing or decreasing?

Exam practice

Tip

Read the whole text through quickly before you start the task. Don't stop to think about individual words you don't know.

Multiple choice 3 For questions 1–6, choose the answer (A, B, C or D) which you think fits best according to the text.

1 The writer says that real-life fraudsters
   A are not qualified to do ordinary jobs.
   B live a glamorous lifestyle.
   C are criminals who cheat other people.
   D are not as bad as they seem.

2 In Cape Town, it was difficult for Derek Bond to establish his innocence because
   A his correct details were in a police file.
   B he had a bad reputation there.
   C there was proof that he was a criminal.
   D nobody knew him personally there.

3 Describing something as 'not rocket science' in lines 63–64 means that it is
   A very difficult.
   B incomprehensible.
   C complicated.
   D straightforward.

4 Criminals commonly collect information about individuals by
   A stealing their credit cards.
   B reading their telephone bills.
   C going through things people have thrown away.
   D contacting a credit checking agency.

5 People should be particularly careful about using credit or debit cards because
   A criminals may find a way of stealing them.
   B corrupt staff may pass on their details to criminals.
   C online systems may not be secure.
   D criminals may listen to people giving their details on the phone.

6 The main purpose of this article is to
   A tell the story of Derek Bond.
   B describe the dangers of identity theft.
   C explain how to steal someone's identity.
   D advise readers how to avoid having their identity stolen.

Word building 4 Complete these sentences with a word related to the word in *italics*.
   a We describe a person who has no *qualifications* as _____. (adjective)
   b Someone with a job in *financial* services works in _____. (noun)
   c The activities of a person who commits *fraud* are _____. (adjective)
   d A *retired* person is someone who has taken _____. (noun)
   e Someone who *impersonates* another person is an _____. (noun)
   f A person who commits *theft* is a _____. (noun)
   g The *immigration* officers checked the identity of all _____ as they arrived. (noun)
   h Someone involved in *organized* crime works for a criminal _____. (noun)

Can you prove who you are?

1 Today, we frequently read newspaper stories of unqualified people who are convicted of posing as surgeons, dentists, airline pilots or financial experts. These
5 people are sometimes portrayed as amiable crooks, but in reality, they are not amiable; they are fraudsters who prey on people's good nature. Fraudsters can do more than just trick you or steal your
10 cash; they can steal your identity, too.

Some years ago, Derek Bond, a seventy-two-year-old retired civil servant, found out for himself how dreadful modern fraud can be. As he stepped off a plane at
15 Cape Town airport, he was arrested and put in prison. It was worrying enough that he could have been mistaken for a 'most wanted' criminal, but what made matters worse was that, despite having an
20 impeccable reputation in his hometown, it took three weeks for Mr Bond's family to convince the authorities that they had made a mistake. Away from people who knew him, Mr Bond's reputation was
25 based solely on the contents of a police file. If that file said that Mr Derek Bond, a man of medium height and build, was actually Derek Lloyd Sykes, a conman responsible for a multi-million dollar
30 fraud in Texas, then who could prove that it wasn't true?

Mr Bond was the victim of identity theft, where a thief assumes another person's identity and uses it to steal directly
35 from that person or to commit crimes using that person's name. In the world of organized crime, for those involved in drug-trafficking, money laundering, illegal immigration or benefit fraud, a
40 fake ID is a licence to print money. Even more worrying is the fact that there is now a ready market for stolen identities among the world's terrorists. More and more people are shopping and banking
45 online or by phone these days, so the opportunities for the fraudulent use of credit cards or other personal information are increasing rapidly. In fact, it is true to say that identity theft is booming, and for
50 those affected by it, the consequences are often catastrophic.

Under existing financial regulations, banks and credit organizations are required to 'know their customers' before
55 they are allowed to open an account. This means that they have to request specific proofs of identity before they allow them to start spending: usually proof of name and address and a photo ID such as a
60 passport or a driver's licence.

This sounds satisfactory, but in reality it is far from foolproof. The problem is that stealing someone's identity is not rocket science. In theory, all an unscrupulous
65 thief needs to start using a person's name is a few snippets of information, such as a discarded phone bill or a credit card receipt.

It has been claimed that 'bin diving'
70 is a common way for thieves to get information. In an extensive survey, a credit checking agency examined the contents of 400 rubbish bins. They found that one in five of these contained
75 enough sensitive information to commit identity fraud. Every time people buy or sell goods, individuals are providing information about themselves on paper. Receipts, invoices and bills all contain
80 personal information that is useful to a fraudster. But identity thieves don't even need to get their hands dirty. How often do people hand over their credit or debit cards in shops? How many people buy
85 something over the phone or shop online? All it takes is one dishonest employee and people can say goodbye to their hard-earned cash. Today, sophisticated criminals also use computer software
90 packages to hack into the systems of banks and other organizations to steal lists of their customers' identities, lists which can sometimes run to millions of individuals.

95 There is no doubt that we all need to be careful about who we share personal information with and, without being suspicious of everyone we meet, we should remember that criminals are
100 always looking for an opportunity to make easy money.

Over to you

5 Discuss these questions.
a What precautions do you take to make sure nobody steals your identity?
b What should happen to someone who steals another person's identity?

Grammar (2)

Present tenses
▶ *Grammar reference* page 159

1 Look at these extracts from the text on page 13. Choose the correct verb forms.
  a More and more people *shop / are shopping* online or by phone these days.
  b Identity theft *booms / is booming*, and for those affected by it, the consequences are often catastrophic.
  c Every time people *buy / are buying* or *sell / are selling* goods, individuals provide information about themselves on paper.
  d Receipts, invoices and bills *contain / are containing* personal information.
  e Today, sophisticated criminals *use / are using* computer software packages to hack into the systems of banks.

2 Now, decide which sentences in **1** refer to …
  a current trends or temporary ongoing actions.
  b habitual actions.
  c facts that are always true.

3 What is the difference in meaning between these pairs of sentences?
  a 1 I live in Madrid.
      2 I'm living in Madrid.
  b 1 Shh! Can't you see I'm watching the news?
      2 These days I'm watching a lot of documentaries.
  c 1 They always forget my name.
      2 They're always forgetting my name.

4 Correct any wrong verb forms in these sentences.
  a I'm having three brothers and one sister.
  b She's understanding Spanish very well, but she can't speak it.
  c Can you explain? What exactly are you meaning?
  d Could you phone him later? He's having dinner at the moment.
  e I'm believing we've met before somewhere.

Adverbs
▶ *Grammar reference* page 161

5 Look at the list of adverbs below. For each one, decide if it can be used with the present simple, the present continuous or both. Write two lists.

at present   at the moment   currently   every day   every so often
most weekends   never   now   occasionally   often   rarely   sometimes
this week   today   twice a week   usually

Example: Present simple: *every day*
               Present continuous: *at present*

6 Decide where each of the adverbs in **5** can be used in the two sentences below. Some can be used in more than one position.
  a I wear bright clothes.
  b I'm wearing bright clothes.

Over to you

7 Work in pairs or small groups. Tell each other about …
  a things you do in your spare time, using the language in exercise 5.
  b things you never do if you can possibly help it.
  c ongoing situations or activities that you are involved with at the moment.
  d trends that are currently affecting you, your family or your friends.

unit 1 appearance and identity

14

Reading and Use of English Part 1

Exam skills 1 Collocation is one aspect that is tested in Reading and Use of English Part 1. Complete the following word combinations with the correct part of speech.

adjective + noun — a mutual friend / a fake identity
_____ + noun — a bank account / a sense of humour
_____ + noun — make a mistake / take a photograph
verb + _____ — come into fashion / mistake someone for someone else
_____ + verb — deeply regret something / distinctly remember something

Tip

Read the text quickly for general understanding before you look at the four options for each gap.

2 Make common collocations by combining a word from list A with a word or phrase from list B. There are five words in A that do not combine with anything in B.

A: act   close   conceal   confidential   cover   friend   judge   peer   perform   rank
B: information   pressure   sb by their appearance   suspiciously   your true identity

Exam practice

Multiple-choice cloze 3 For questions 1–8, read the text below and decide which answer (A, B, C or D) best fits each gap. There is an example at the beginning (0).

Should children wear school uniform?

In Britain, the issue of whether or not children should be (0) _made_ to wear school uniform has been (1) _____ debated for many years. Newspapers frequently include reports of children being (2) _____ home for wearing the wrong (3) _____ of shoes or the wrong colour of pullover. Britain has no national uniform (4) _____: it is the responsibility of each head teacher to decide whether their students should wear a uniform, and to (5) _____ down exactly what that uniform should be.

By contrast, Japanese schools are very (6) _____ about the wearing of uniform. Boys in secondary schools wear a dark jacket with buttons down the front, while girls wear a blue and white uniform (7) _____ on a nineteenth-century sailor suit. There is a correct length for girls' skirts, and teachers will sometimes use a tape measure to check this. In Japan, as in many other countries, children find ways of (8) _____ the uniform rules.

0	A encouraged	B allowed	C made	D persuaded
1	A strongly	B hotly	C heavily	D powerfully
2	A sent	B directed	C shown	D lead
3	A fashion	B mode	C model	D style
4	A policy	B principle	C strategy	D procedure
5	A put	B lay	C rule	D decide
6	A heavy	B stern	C strong	D strict
7	A founded	B related	C based	D associated
8	A changing	B adapting	C bending	D twisting

Over to you 4 Discuss these questions.
a How do you feel about uniforms that students and others have to wear?
b Do you think uniforms help to create a strong group identity or crush individuality?

unit 1 appearance and identity

15

Vocabulary

Parts of the body

1 Name the parts of the body A–U in these photos.

2 Complete these sentences with the correct body words.

a When I asked her the time, she just shrugged her _____ and said she didn't know.

b I went upstairs in a hurry and stubbed my _____ on one of the stairs.

c Some fortune-tellers read people's _____.

d I always wear my watch on my left _____.

e Babies crawl around on their hands and _____.

f He sat with his _____ on the table and his _____ in his hands.

Seeing verbs

3 Complete these sentences with the correct form of a verb from the list below. More than one answer may be possible.

gaze   look   notice   see   stare   watch

a She _____ exactly like my sister. I couldn't take my eyes off her. She must have wondered why I was _____ at her.

b Many teenagers spend more time playing computer games than _____ television.

c _____! There's a fantastic rainbow in the sky.

d He's my greatest hero, but when I tried to get his autograph, he didn't even _____ me.

e The couple _____ lovingly at their newborn baby. They couldn't believe he was theirs.

f I could just about _____ the station through the fog.

4 The eyes in some paintings appear to follow the viewer around the room. How do you think artists achieve this illusion? When you have discussed this, turn to page 153 for an explanation.

unit 1 appearance and identity

16

Speaking Part 1

Think ahead

1 Look at this list of possible Part 1 topics. For each one, think of two or three questions you might be asked.

clothes   education   family and friends   free time   work

2 Work with a partner. Take turns to ask and answer the questions you have thought of.

3 🔊 1.02 Listen to two candidates doing a Part 1 task. Does the examiner ask any of the questions you thought of? If so, which ones?

4 🔊 1.02 Listen again. Which candidate, George or Adriana, do you think gives the better answers? Give reasons.

5 🔊 1.02 Complete these extracts from the interview with one or more words. Then, listen again and check.

   a   I am from Patras – it's a _____ town in the south-west of Greece.
   b   I read _____, _____ I'm also _____ keen on all kinds of sport. I play football, basketball and tennis, _____ sport takes most of my spare time.
   c   I have two brothers and a sister and we all get on _____.
   d   We're in the same class at college, _____ we've been _____ friends since we were about twelve.
   e   _____, we have _____ different characters. I'm sociable, whereas Anatol's _____ shy.
   f   When I first met him, he seemed very unfriendly, _____ we get on extremely well.
   g   Yes, _____, for example for special family occasions like weddings.

6 Look at the answers in *italics* to questions a–c. How would you give fuller answers?

   a   What kind of clothes do you feel most comfortable in?
       T-shirt, jeans and trainers.
   b   Are there occasions when you like to wear smart clothes?
       Yes, there are.
   c   When was the last time you wore smart clothes?
       Last weekend.

Sentence stress

7 🔊 1.03 In English, one word in a sentence is usually more stressed than the other words. Listen and underline the word in each candidate's response which is most stressed.

   a   I went to the cinema.
   b   I've been studying English for four years.
   c   I swim quite a lot.
   d   I spend most of my spare time with my friends.
   e   I'd have to say casual clothes.
   f   My best friend is called Antonio.

8 Why are the words you underlined stressed?

Tip

Give full answers to the questions. Don't just answer with a few words or short sentences.

Exam practice

Short exchanges

9 🔊 1.04 Listen to these Part 1 questions. First, make a note of the questions. Then, take turns to ask and answer them with a partner.

unit 1   appearance and identity

17

Writing Part 1

Think ahead

1 Discuss these questions.

a Why do you think the people in the photographs wear special clothes for work?

b Why do you think some people enjoy wearing a uniform for work?

Exam skills

2 Read the Writing Part 1 task below. Answer these questions.

a Who are you writing for?

b What must you include in your answer?

> In your English class, you have been talking about the advantages and disadvantages of having to wear a uniform or other special clothes for work.
>
> Now, your English teacher has asked you to write an essay.
>
> Write an essay using **all** the notes and give reasons for your point of view. Write your **essay** in 140–190 words.
>
> **Essay question**
>
> Uniforms should be worn by people doing certain jobs. Do you agree?
>
> **Notes**
>
> Things to write about:
>
> 1. uniform for identification
>
> 2. uniform for protection
>
> 3. _____ (your own idea)

3 Read these four possible introductions to the essay question above. Decide how interesting or appropriate each one is. Then, choose the most suitable.

A

The main reason people wear uniforms is so that other people, for example the general public, can see what their job is just by looking. This is very important for police officers or firefighters.

B

What is meant by the word 'uniform'? In my opinion, a 'uniform' means special clothes like those worn by a police officer or a firefighter. Typically, uniforms are made of dark material and often have badges. They're very formal and not attractive at all. And people who wear uniforms get very hot.

C

I'd never want a job where I had to wear a uniform. Uniforms are so boring. Anyway, I'd never want to be a police officer or a firefighter or anything like that.

D

In every country, certain people, for example nurses and firefighters, wear uniforms for work. Usually, they have no choice in this.

unit 1   appearance and identity

4 Now read the continuation of the essay. Answer these questions.
  a Do you agree with the writer's ideas?
  b Has the writer answered the question in full?

The most common reason for (1) *this / which* is that uniforms allow wearers to be seen and identified by the public. (2) *For example / Like*, if you are visiting someone in hospital, you need to know who is a nurse or doctor and who is an ordinary member of the public. (3) *Another / Other* reasons include protecting wearers from danger or disease, for example firefighters at a blaze, or nurses working in a hospital. However, uniforms have disadvantages for some people. They make everyone look the same (4) *because / so that* people cannot express their individuality in the same way as if they were wearing clothes they had chosen themselves. A more serious problem may be for soldiers who are fighting. Their uniform gives the enemy a clear target and may (5) *actually / probably* cost soldiers their lives. In my experience, I have found that people in uniform are often given more respect than people in ordinary clothes. (6) *For instance / An example*, it would be difficult for someone in ordinary clothes to arrest another person. (7) *In conclusion / To end with*, I would say that there are certain jobs for which wearing a uniform is necessary.

---

5 Read the essay again and divide it into paragraphs.

6 Choose the correct words in *italics* to complete the text.

Exam practice

Essay
▸ *Writing guide page 178*

Tip
Before writing an essay, make a paragraph plan. This should include an introduction which is as interesting as you can make it.

7 You are going to write an essay. First, read the task below carefully. Then work through stages a–e.

In your English class, you have been talking about whether people should be required to wear smart clothes for work.

Now, your English teacher has asked you to write an essay.

Write an essay using **all** the notes and give reasons for your point of view. Write your **essay** in 140–190 words.

Essay question
Everyone should have to wear smart clothes for work if they come into contact with members of the public. Do you agree?

Notes
Things to write about:
1. jobs which require smart clothes
2. what smart clothes show
3. _____ (your own idea)

  a Discuss these questions with a partner.
   • What is your first reaction to the essay question?
   • What are your first thoughts about 1 and 2 in Notes?
  b Think about the topic. Discuss the following in pairs and make brief notes.
   • What clothes are considered smart in your country? Who wears these clothes?
   • What do clothes say about someone's personality / how good they are at their job?
   • Think of 'your own idea'. For example: clothes and working conditions / respect.
  c Plan each paragraph, using some of the words and phrases you chose in **6** if possible.
  d Write your essay. Refer to your notes. Check you've answered the question in full.
  e When you have finished writing, check your grammar, spelling and punctuation.

Unit 1 Review

1 For questions 1–8, read the text below and decide which answer (A, B, C or D) best fits each gap. There is an example at the beginning (0).

THE HISTORY OF CONVERSE

In 1908, the Converse Rubber Shoe Company began trading in the USA. Initially, the company made simple rubber-soled footwear for men, women and children. By 1910, Converse was (0) _producing_ 4,000 pairs a day. The company's main turning (1) _____ came in 1917, when the red-and-white basketball shoe was introduced. This was a real innovation, (2) _____ the sport was in its infancy. Then, in 1921, 'Chuck' Taylor, a basketball player, (3) _____ the company complaining of sore feet. Converse immediately (4) _____ him as a representative, and he promoted their shoes for the (5) _____ of his career. In 1941, when the USA became involved in the Second World War, Converse shifted production to manufacturing boots, and protective (6) _____ for pilots and soldiers.

Converse shoes were hugely popular with teenagers during the 1950s, and in 1966 the company added a range of new colours. They remained popular until the (7) _____ 1980s, but lost a large proportion of their (8) _____ share during the 1990s with the appearance of trainers.

0	A preparing	B producing	C creating	D constructing
1	A point	B place	C pot	D situation
2	A accounting	B considering	C viewing	D bearing
3	A communicated	B wrote	C contacted	D spoke
4	A employed	B occupied	C worked	D invited
5	A remains	B surplus	C rest	D remnants
6	A dress	B cloth	C attire	D clothing
7	A young	B primary	C early	D first
8	A shop	B sales	C retail	D market

2 Complete these sentences using the verb in brackets and the negative form of a modal verb from the list *have to / must / need*. More than one answer may be possible.

a Children in Britain go to school from Monday to Friday, but they (go) on Saturdays.

b These tablets are very strong. You (take) more than eight a day.

c I wish I'd known the train was going to be late. I (hurry).

d You (tire) yourself out. You've got a busy day tomorrow.

e I had just turned on the computer when she phoned, which meant that I (send) her an email.

3 Choose the correct verb form to complete these sentences.

a Has the post been yet? *I expect / I'm expecting* a parcel.

b Paul *normally works / is normally working* in New York, but this week *he visits / he is visiting* offices in other parts of the country.

c *Do you have / Are you having* a calculator? *I try / I'm trying* to work out how much money I've spent.

d *I don't usually like / I'm not usually liking* horror stories, but at the moment *I read / I'm reading* the new novel by Stephen King and *I enjoy / I'm enjoying* it.

e The Nile *flows / is flowing* into the Mediterranean Sea.

unit 1 appearance and identity

20

Unit 2 Talents

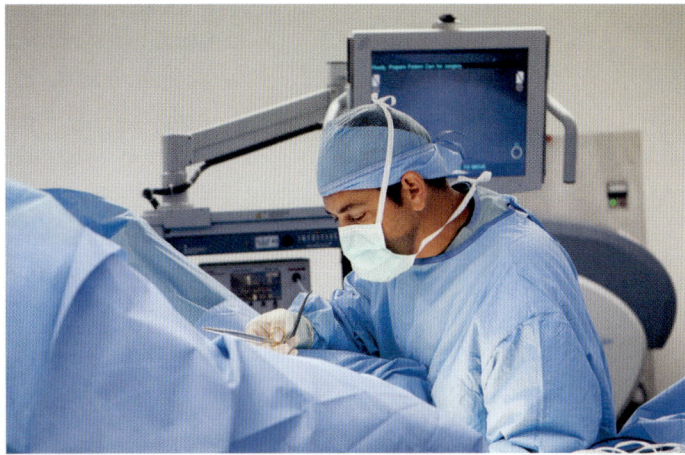

Introduction

1 Look at the photographs. Discuss these questions.

  a What talents or qualities do you think the people in the photos have which enable them to do these jobs or activities well?

  b Which of these jobs or activities could you do? Which couldn't you do? Explain why.

Reading and Use of English Part 7

Exam skills 1 In Reading and Use of English Part 7, it is useful to look for words and phrases in the text which have similar meanings to words and phrases in the questions. Match words a–f with two synonyms from the list below.

a accidentally   c currently   e participate
b ability   d cover (sth) up   f pressure

be involved   by chance   conceal   demands   hide   presently   take part
talent   these days   skill   stress   unintentionally

2 Look at the underlined words in questions 1 and 7 in the Exam practice task below. How could you paraphrase them?

Exam practice

Multiple matching 3 You are going to read an article about four extraordinary people on page 23. For questions 1–10, choose from the people A–D. The people may be chosen more than once.

Tip

Underline key words and phrases in the questions before you read the text. Check you understand what they mean. Then think of other words which have a similar meaning, or alternatively, think about how the words could be paraphrased.

Which person

1 did not complete his education?
2 gets away with the odd mistake?
3 accepts the fact that his career is dangerous?
4 took a long time to develop his abilities?
5 has found success despite having a disability?
6 improves his skill by doing something else at the same time?
7 received tuition to help him improve his talent?
8 doesn't do anything to protect himself?
9 changed his goal in life?
10 passes his skills on to other people?

Phrasal verbs: *turn* 4 Match the phrasal verbs in *italics* in a–f with their meanings 1–6.

a Ron White has trained up to six hours a day to *turn* his brain *into* a supercomputer.
b The snow started to fall heavily so we decided to *turn back*.
c She was offered a post with more responsibility but she *turned* it *down*.
d Everyone thought she was innocent but she *turned out* to be the thief.
e Jack always *turns up* at parties when everyone is leaving.
f When I can't do my homework, I *turn to* my mother for help.

1 arrive
2 prove to be sth
3 not accept a proposal or offer
4 go to someone for advice, etc.
5 become sth
6 stop and return to the place you started from

unit 2 talents

EXTRAORDINARY PEOPLE

A Derek Paravicini

Derek Paravicini was born blind, with severe learning difficulties and autism. He has limited verbal skills, poor short-term memory and cannot read even Braille, but he has an amazing talent: he can play any piece of music after only one hearing. He could play a toy organ when he was two, and when he was five his musical genius was recognized by music teacher Adam Ockelford quite by chance when his parents went round the school for the blind, where Adam gave lessons. In the following years, Adam painstakingly taught Derek how to play properly and, at nine, Derek gave his first of many major public performances. Derek – whose nickname is 'The Human iPod' – is able to play any song in any key and in any genre. He does occasionally play the wrong note, but because he is able to improvise, he can cover it up without anyone even noticing.

B Dr Norman Gary

Norman Gary's interest in bees started when he was fifteen. His ambition was to become a professional bee-keeper but instead he ended up becoming an academic, doing research in the field of apiculture (bee keeping). Norman's unique ability is that he is able to cover his body with thousands of bees; he can also control the bees to make them do what he wants using food (a sugar solution) and scent. He acquired these skills after years of practice and is considered to be the leading expert on bees in the United States. As such, his skills were sought by the likes of Hollywood film producer Chris Carter for a scene in the movie *The X-Files*. Despite having been stung around 75,000 times, Norman does not consider what he does as especially dangerous, explaining that bees only become aggressive when they feel threatened.

C Ron White

Ron White calls himself a 'brain athlete', but he's not your average memory master, despite earning the title of USA Memory Champion. A high-school dropout, Ron discovered his amazing talent when he enrolled in a memory class and noticed that not only did he have a passion for this skill, but that he could also beat everyone in the class. Since then he has trained up to six hours a day to turn his brain into a supercomputer, enabling him to memorize and recall data at record speeds. Ron says the key to his training is to be distracted while memorizing things; this gives his brain incredible focus. For example, to become the USA Memory Champion he memorized cards while snorkelling. Ron currently teaches memory techniques to people all over the United States. During conferences, he manages to learn the names of everyone in the audience that he has shaken hands with – up to 200 people.

D Eskil Ronningsbakken

Norwegian Eskil Ronningsbakken is an extreme artist known for the super-human balancing acts he performs in locations around the world. Eskil, whose love for heights stems from a childhood passion for climbing trees in the Norwegian countryside, was fascinated at an early age by a TV programme which featured an Indian yogi doing balancing acts. He decided that this was what he wanted to do and joined the circus at the age of eighteen, where he perfected his skills. Yoga and meditation naturally play an important role in what he does, too. He practises them regularly in order to better his focus and concentration. Eskil's jaw-dropping acts include doing a handstand on a pile of chairs precariously balanced above a 300-metre drop. He performs all his feats without a safety net or harness. One slip and he would fall to his death. Eskil is well aware of the risks involved in what he does. 'I feel fear, of course I do. We are humans and we have a natural sense of self-preservation,' he admits.

Over to you 5 Which of the four people described in the text do you most admire? Why?

Grammar (1)

can, be able to
▶ *Grammar reference* page 160

1 *Can* and *be able to* are often interchangeable. Rewrite these sentences using the other form.
   a Derek Paravicini *cannot* read even Braille, but he has an amazing talent; he *can* play any piece of music after only one hearing.
   b He *could* play a toy organ when he was two.

2 Why is it impossible to use *can* in these sentences?
   a *To be able to* do what he does, you need a special talent.
   b Ron White *has been able to* turn his brain into a supercomputer.

3 Rewrite these sentences using *can* or *could*, making any other necessary changes.
   a He's *able to* run 100 metres in just over twelve seconds.
   b When I was younger, I *was able to* run up a hill without getting out of breath.
   c They had eaten such a big breakfast that they *weren't able to* finish their lunch.
   d He *would* probably *be able to* touch his toes if he lost weight.
   e Even if I'd been stronger, I *wouldn't have been able to* lift those heavy weights.

4 *Could* or *be able to* are both possible in sentences a and b. Why is *could* not possible in sentence c?
   a Before Dave started smoking, he *could / was able to* hold his breath for three minutes.
   b The doctors *couldn't / weren't able to* save the woman's life.
   c After five hours, the firefighters *could / were able to* put out the fire.

Other ability structures

5 Which sentences in 4 can be rephrased with *manage to / succeed in*?

6 Complete these sentences with the correct form of the verb in brackets and another verb. You may sometimes need to use the negative.
   Example: He *managed to win* the election despite strong opposition. (manage)
   a Although they searched for several hours, the rescue party _____ (succeed) the climbers.
   b He did his best but he _____ (be able to) all his work before the boss got back.
   c Daniel was thrilled when he _____ (succeed) his driving test first time.
   d Although I was at home, the burglar _____ (manage) and steal my laptop without being seen.
   e Melanie _____ (be able to) three lengths of the pool when she was William's age.
   f Paul's interview was this afternoon. I wonder if he _____ (manage) the job.
   g I was so tense that I _____ (be able to) asleep, despite being tired.
   h Although he didn't have a corkscrew, he _____ (succeed) the bottle.
   i _____ you _____ (manage) any weight since you started your diet?

7 Which sentences in 6 could be rewritten using *could* or *couldn't*?

Over to you

8 Discuss these questions.
   a What can you do now that you couldn't do when you were a child and vice versa?
   b What difficult things have you managed to do in your life? (e.g. pass your driving test; save up enough money for something expensive)
   c What abilities do you (or someone you know) have?
   d What would you like to be able to do that you can't?

Reading and Use of English Part 2

Exam skills

1 Quickly read the text in **2**. Choose the most suitable title for the text.
  a How to find out what kind of learner you are
  b How different learners learn best
  c What determines the kind of learner you are

2 Read the text again. Choose the correct word in each pair to fill the gaps. What clues in the text helped you to choose your answer?

but / however   for / because   have / has   many / lots   must / need
order / fact   the / an   they / there   to / from   what / how

Everyone **(1)** _____ a different learning style and knowing what style may help you to learn most effectively can, according to some experts, optimize your learning experience. Although there are many different views on the subject, there is general agreement that **(2)** _____ are three basic styles: auditory, visual and kinaesthetic. Apparently, if you are **(3)** _____ auditory learner you learn best by hearing and listening, so you will do well in formal lectures. Visual learners learn by seeing and looking. **(4)** _____ of this, they will react best **(5)** _____ images and written information. Kinaesthetic learners learn by touching and doing things. They **(6)** _____ to do hands-on activities in **(7)** _____ to learn most successfully. Most people, **(8)** _____ , tend to fall into more than one category though one style tends to be more prevalent than the others. If you are unsure **(9)** _____ kind of learner you are, there are **(10)** _____ online questionnaires you can do to find out.

Exam practice

Open cloze

3 For questions 1–8, read the text below and think of the word which best fits each gap. Use only one word in each gap. There is an example at the beginning (0).

> **Tip**
> Look at the words which come before and after the gap to decide what kind of word is missing.

Strategies for improving how you learn

As soon **(0)** _as_ you have found out what your learning style is, there are **(1)** _____ number of strategies you can put into practice to improve how you learn. If you are a visual learner, you should take notes in class or in lectures **(2)** _____ you are not provided with handouts. You will find it helpful to use a highlighter pen **(3)** _____ emphasize the most important information. Also, try to find sources of information **(4)** _____ are illustrated. Visual stimuli, whether in a book or a video, will help you understand and remember things. If you are an auditory learner, you might benefit from recording a lecture **(5)** _____ than taking notes. You will learn from discussing your ideas with others, too. Kinaesthetic learners find it hard to sit still for long so if you are studying **(6)** _____ an exam, you will benefit from frequent breaks. Moving around **(7)** _____ trying to memorize something or doing another activity at the same time will also **(8)** _____ beneficial.

Over to you

4 Discuss these questions.
  a What kind of learner do you think you are?
  b What strategies do you use to help you understand and memorize new things?

unit 2 talents

Grammar (2)

Comparatives and superlatives
▸ *Grammar reference* page 161

1 Read the text below. How similar or different are secondary schools in your country? What changes have there been in the last fifty years?

Classrooms have changed considerably in the last hundred years. In the early 1900s, the average class in England was twice as big as the average in the 1960s – sixty pupils per class compared with thirty. Nowadays, the average class size in a secondary school is twenty-three, which is still higher than in many other countries. A hundred years ago, teachers were stricter than today. Punishment was also more severe: pupils were often hit for bad behaviour – a practice not allowed in schools today. The curriculum in the past was also less extensive and concentrated on the three Rs – Reading, Writing and Arithmetic – whereas today's curriculum includes everything from business studies to philosophy. Some people think that the teaching methods used in schools today are not as effective as those used in the past but, given the wide range of interactive tools available today, the 21st century is definitely the most interesting time to be in the classroom for teachers and pupils alike.

2 Read the text again. Underline seven comparative and superlative structures.

3 What are the comparative and superlative forms of these adjectives and adverbs? Think of other examples of each type.

a long / short
b large / late
c flat / thin
d heavy / funny
e important / independent
f clever / narrow
g good / bad
h well / badly
i quickly / carefully

4 What form does the adjective and adverb take when used in the structure *as … as*?

5 Complete these sentences with the correct form of the adjective in brackets.

a The film was just as _____ (good) as I expected it to be.
b This product is a little _____ (cheap) than that one.
c I must admit that my _____ (young) brother is _____ (clever) than me.
d Helena is by far _____ (unlucky) person I've ever met.
e I'm feeling a bit _____ (good) today, thank you.
f The weather is much _____ (hot) today than anyone expected.
g Today's exam was no _____ (difficult) than yesterday's.
h Sara writes slightly _____ (legibly) than me.
i It's considerably _____ (easy) to contact people nowadays than it was twenty years ago.
j The _____ (fast) you work, the _____ (soon) you'll finish.

6 Look at this list of modifiers used in **5** and answer questions a–c below.

Modifiers: a bit   a little   a lot   considerably   far / by far   just (as … as)
much   no   not nearly (as … as)   slightly

Which modifiers show …

a no difference?   b a small difference?   c a big difference?

Over to you

7 Write a paragraph comparing yourself with someone you know well. Try to use a range of modifiers.

unit 2 talents

26

Speaking Part 2

Exam skills 1 🔊 1.05 Listen to the Speaking Part 2 task instructions. Answer these questions.
   a How many photographs is each candidate given?
   b What do the candidates have to do first?
   c What do the candidates have to do next?

2 Before you listen to the candidates' answer, look at the photographs and discuss with a partner what you would say.

3 🔊 1.06 Now, listen to the candidates' answers and complete the table below.

Contrasting words	but
Words which give more information	and
Words which express preference	I'd prefer to do ... than ...

4 Can you add any more examples to the table above?

Pronunciation 5 🔊 1.07 Using stress appropriately gives meaning to what we say and makes us sound more interested. Listen and underline the word which is stressed most in a–d.
   a The lecture hall is much bigger than the classroom.
   b Teachers aren't nearly as strict as they used to be.
   c It's just as hard to spell a word in English as to pronounce it.
   d Class sizes are considerably smaller these days.

6 Underline the word which would usually have the most stress in these sentences.
   a My sister's only a bit older than me. She's a lot cleverer than me though.
   b This car's not nearly as expensive as that one. And it's far cheaper to run.
   c This lecture is just as hard to follow as yesterday's. Physics is by far the most difficult subject I've studied. It's much harder than chemistry.
   d Italian is no more difficult to learn than Spanish.

7 🔊 1.08 Listen, check and repeat.

> **Tip**
> When you're comparing the photographs, look for similarities and differences between them.

Exam practice

Long turn 8 Work in pairs. Turn to page 153 and follow the instructions.

unit 2 talents

27

Writing Part 2 – Letter / email

Think ahead

1 Discuss these questions.

a How much of your correspondence is through email compared with letters?
b Do you approach emails differently from letters? Does it depend who you are writing to?

Exam skills

2 Read this Writing Part 2 task. What points need to be addressed in the reply?

> This is part of an email you have received from your English friend, Charlie Black.
>
> **From:** Charlie Black
> **Subject:** Last night
>
> What happened to you last night? We waited ages for you! I hope you have a good excuse!! (Just joking ;-)) Seriously though, hope nothing is wrong!
> Let me know when you'd like to meet up and we can reschedule – OK?
>
> Charlie
>
> Write your **email** in 140–190 words.

3 Read these two answers to the task above. Which one is more appropriate and why?

To: Charlie Black
Subject: Last night

Hi Charlie,

Sorry about last night. No, nothing's wrong! The thing is I was held up. My tutorial went over time and I didn't get in till half six. I got changed and had a bite to eat, then I tried to get you on your mobile, but it was switched off, so I texted you just to let you know I was going to be late. I know you didn't get it 'cos by the time I got there you'd obviously given up and gone home. Sorry!!! Hope you're not too mad at me?

I'm pretty free next weekend, except for Saturday night when I'm going to a party, so Friday night or any time on Sunday would be good for me. Let me know if either of those days suits you. If you fancy eating out we could go to 'Mario's'. The pizzas are supposed to be very good. I can book us a table 'cos it tends to be busy at the weekend.

Can't wait to hear all about your holiday.

Speak soon,

Andreas

To: Charlie Black
Subject: Last night

Dear Charlie Black,

I am writing to apologize for yesterday evening. Unfortunately, I was delayed as my tutorial overran and I did not arrive home until 6.30. I changed, had a snack and attempted to contact you on your mobile phone, but it was switched off. I therefore sent you a text message to inform you that I was going to be late.

I realize that you did not receive my message because, by the time I arrived, you had obviously decided I was not coming and had returned home. I do apologize.

Could we reschedule for next weekend? I have several commitments already but I have a window on Sunday evening. Would Sunday be convenient for you? I have heard they serve excellent pizzas at 'Mario's'. I could reserve a table for us unless you would prefer to go elsewhere.

I look forward to hearing from you.

Yours sincerely,
Andreas Lombardi

Formal and informal language

4 Say whether formal (F) or informal (INF) writing is more likely to …

a have short sentences. _____
b have an impersonal tone. _____
c use contractions (e.g. *didn't*). _____
d include polite phrases. _____
e use passive verbs. _____
f use phrasal verbs. _____
g leave out words (e.g. pronouns). _____
h use very simple words or slang. _____

5   How many of the informal features from the list above can you find in the first email?

6   Here are some typical ways of starting and ending an email or letter. Which phrases are informal (INF) and which are more formal (F)?

Best wishes   Cheers   Dear Sam   Dear Sir   Good to hear from you!   Hello
Hi!   Hiya!   How are things with you?   I'm writing to …   Jo   Jo Hunter (Ms)
Regards   Thanks for your email   Thank you for your email of 15/12.
You asked me about …   Yours faithfully   Yours sincerely

7   Which words or phrases are used in the second email on page 28 instead of these informal words and phrases in the first email?

a   a bite to eat
b   tried
c   so
d   I texted you
e   to let you know
f   'cos
g   gone home
h   Sorry!

8   Which words or phrases are used in the second email on page 28 instead of the phrasal verbs *held up* and *get in* in the first email? Why?

9   Replace the words and phrases in *italics* with the correct form of one of these phrasal verbs.

back down   bring up   bump into   call off   put (sb) down   put up with

a   My boyfriend refuses to *admit he's wrong* even when he knows I'm right.
b   I wish people wouldn't eat at their desks. I just can't *tolerate* it.
c   I wish you wouldn't *criticize* me in public – it's really embarrassing.
d   *Quite by chance I met* someone I was at school with yesterday.
e   Have you heard about Tim and Jan? They've *cancelled* their wedding!
f   My grandparents *raised* five children on a very low income.

Meanings of get   10   *Get* has many meanings in informal English. Underline the examples of *get* in the first email on page 28. Then, find the more formal equivalents in the second email.

Exam practice

Email

▶ Writing guide page 181

Tip
Note down some ideas for all the questions before you start writing your answer.

11   You are going to answer an email. First, read the task. Then, work through stages a–d below.

This is part of an email you have received from your English friend, Sam.

From: Sam

So, you've started studying English again! That's great news. But you didn't tell me anything about your classes!!! Are they interesting? What sort of things do you do in class? Are you learning a lot?

Sam

Write your **email** in 140–190 words.

a   Which points must you address in the answer?
b   Who is the target reader? Will your answer be written in a formal or informal style?
c   Plan your answer before you start writing. Remember to use informal language.
d   Finally, read through your email, checking grammar, spelling and punctuation.

Reading and Use of English Part 3

Exam skills

1 Choose from the list the correct part of speech needed to complete these sentences. What clues helped you to decide?

adjective   adverb   noun   verb

a At the _____ of their career, top professional footballers earn in a year more than most people earn in a lifetime. HIGH

b Some people _____ that top sports personalities are worth every penny they earn and think they are grossly overpaid. AGREE

c He can pass the ball very _____. SKILL

d If you want to get to the top in any sport you need to be _____. AMBITION

2 Now, complete the sentences above with the correct form of the word in capitals.

3 Use the suffixes in A to form nouns from the verbs in B, making any necessary spelling changes.

A: -al   -ance / -ence   -er / -or   -ion / -ation   -ity   -ment

B: arrive   complete   employ   expect   improve   inform   perform   predict   prosper   protect   refuse   reject   work

4 Quickly read the text below. Think of a suitable title for it.

Tip

First, read the text quickly to get a general idea of the topic.

Exam practice

Word formation

5 Use the word given in capitals at the end of some of the lines to form a word that fits in the gap in the same line. There is an example at the beginning (0).

Nowadays, prize money for women tennis (0) _players_, at	PLAY
least in the major (1) _____, is equal to men's. But some	COMPETE
male players do not think this is fair. Their (2) _____	ARGUE
is that as men spend more time on the court per match, they should get paid more. Probably, and not surprisingly, many women tennis players (3) _____, saying that they	AGREE
train just as hard as the men, are just as skilled and the (4) _____ they provide is the same. However, and like	ENTERTAIN
many athletes, most of their income does not come from official prize money. Instead, it comes from (5) _____ contracts	SPONSOR
with fashion and sportswear companies, turning some sports stars into millionaires at a very young and vulnerable age. It is (6) _____ surprising then that some sports stars are	HARD
(7) _____ to cope with the pressure that goes hand in	ABLE
hand with being (8) _____ and consequently become	FAME
victims of their own success.	

Over to you

6 Discuss these questions.

a Who are the highest-earning sportspeople in your country? Do they deserve the money they earn?

b Do you agree that women sports players should earn the same as men?

c Do you know any sportsmen or women who have become victims of their own success?

Listening Part 2

Think ahead

1 You are going to hear someone talking about 'hyper-parenting'. What do you think this is? Before you listen, discuss these questions.

  a When you were a child, did your parents encourage you to take part in any activities outside school, such as sport or music? Did you enjoy them?

  b Are there any other extra-curricular activities which you wish you had had the opportunity to do?

2 Look at questions 1–10 in the text below. What words could go in the spaces?

> **Tip**
>
> Read the sentences you have to complete before the recording starts. Decide what kind of information you need to listen for.

Exam practice

Sentence completion

3 🔊 1.09 You will hear a man talking about hyper-parenting. For questions 1–10, complete the sentences with a word or short phrase.

Hyper-parenting

Cathy Hagner's children have _____ **1**, soccer and piano practice after school.

Cathy admits that everyone in the family is suffering from _____ **2** because of their lifestyle.

Hyper-parenting affects _____ **3** parents in the United States and Britain.

Expectant mothers are told that they have to eat _____ **4**.

More and more children are getting _____ **5** because they are so stressed and tired.

Many children have to attend _____ **6** after school because both parents work.

Some of the children who do activities outside school are only _____ **7** years of age.

Parents worry that they are _____ **8** their children if they don't give them every opportunity.

Terri Apter has found that many teenagers can't cope with _____ **9** they have when they start college.

Apter advises that, along with organizing extra-curricular activities for their children, parents should give them enough time for _____ **10**.

Adjective prefixes: *extra, hyper, over, under*

4 Match the adjective prefixes *extra, hyper, over* and *under* with the adjectives below. More than one answer may be possible.

active   curricular   indulgent   optimistic   populated   priced   sensitive   staffed   terrestrial   used   valued

5 Complete these sentences with the correct prefix + adjective.

  a Some children are _____: they can't sit still for a minute.

  b Some parents are _____: they give their children everything they ask for.

  c One of my friends is _____: she bursts into tears at the smallest criticism.

  d Many people would agree that hospitals in the UK are _____: this is because there is a shortage of doctors and nurses.

  e A number of _____ activities are reported in the USA every year: there have been sightings of flying saucers and strange goings-on.

Unit 2 Review

1 For questions 1–8, read the text below. Use the word given in capitals at the end of some of the lines to form a word that fits in the gap in the same line. There is an example at the beginning (0).

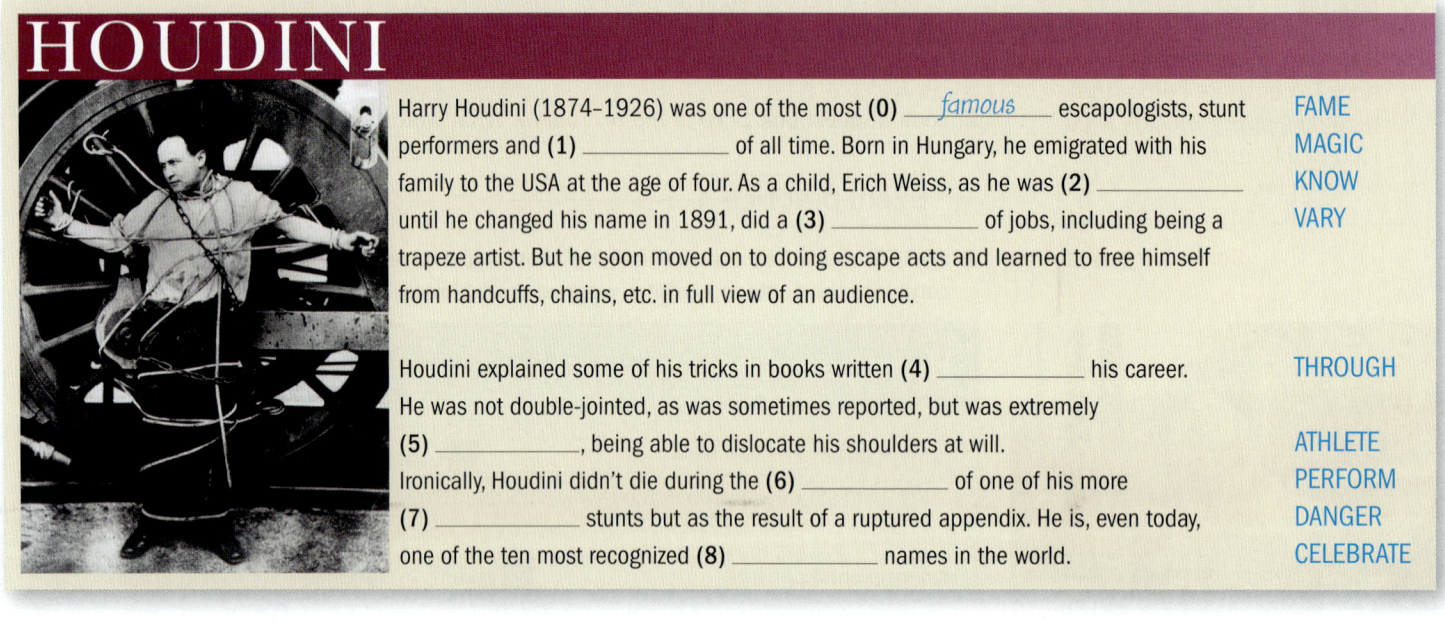

HOUDINI

Harry Houdini (1874-1926) was one of the most (0) _famous_ escapologists, stunt performers and (1) _____ of all time. Born in Hungary, he emigrated with his family to the USA at the age of four. As a child, Erich Weiss, as he was (2) _____ until he changed his name in 1891, did a (3) _____ of jobs, including being a trapeze artist. But he soon moved on to doing escape acts and learned to free himself from handcuffs, chains, etc. in full view of an audience.

FAME
MAGIC
KNOW
VARY

Houdini explained some of his tricks in books written (4) _____ his career. He was not double-jointed, as was sometimes reported, but was extremely (5) _____, being able to dislocate his shoulders at will. Ironically, Houdini didn't die during the (6) _____ of one of his more (7) _____ stunts but as the result of a ruptured appendix. He is, even today, one of the ten most recognized (8) _____ names in the world.

THROUGH

ATHLETE
PERFORM
DANGER
CELEBRATE

2 Complete these sentences with the correct forms of *can*, *be able to*, *manage* or *succeed*.

a _____ you speak Italian before you went to live in Italy?
b We _____ (not) to persuade Charlotte to come.
c After ten minutes of manoeuvring, I finally _____ in parking my car.
d I'm sorry but I _____ (not) to contact Gill yet. She isn't answering her phone.
e _____ you whistle? My brother taught me how to.
f They _____ (not) swim to the shore because of the strong currents.
g You _____ win the race if you really wanted to.
h Instead of calming the situation, he only _____ in making it worse.

3 Choose the correct word to complete the phrasal verbs in these sentences.

a Nobody thought he would be a success, but he turned *out / into* to be one of the most successful stars ever.
b They were on their way to the airport when Mary realized she had forgotten her passport, so they had to turn *up / back*.
c I was surprised to hear she had turned *up / down* his proposal of marriage.
d He always turns *to / into* his manager for advice on what to do.
e It started as a difference of opinion, but turned *to / into* a full-scale argument.
f Hundreds of people turned *up / over* to see the stars at the film premiere.

unit 2 talents

32

Unit 3   Compulsion

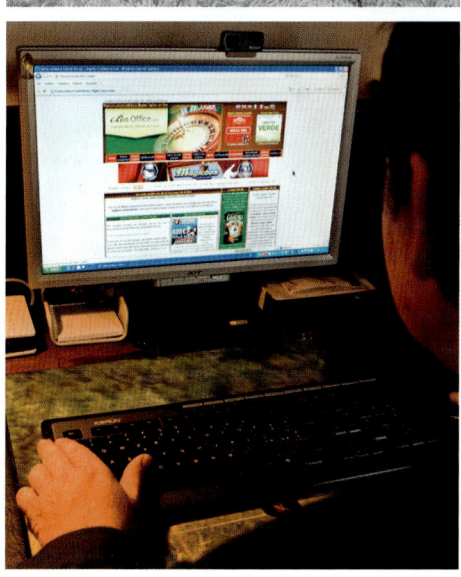

Introduction

1 **Look at the photographs. Discuss these questions.**

   a What is the connection between the unit title, 'Compulsion' and these photographs?

   b Which of the activities shown in the photographs do you do or have you done? Why do you do them?

   c Which things have you never done, or would you never do? Why not?

   d Which activities can cause serious problems for individuals who do them regularly? What problems can they cause?

2 **Now discuss these questions.**

   a Do you think some people have a tendency to become addicted to activities more quickly than others? If so, do you think it is something in a person's character that causes this tendency?

   b What can or should be done to help young people to avoid becoming addicted to substances or activities?

Listening Part 4

Think ahead 1 Discuss these questions with a partner.

   a How much time do you spend in an average day on the following activities?
   - talking to friends on your mobile phone
   - sending text messages
   - keeping in touch with friends on social networking sites
   - reading and replying to emails

   b Do you think you spend too much time on these activities? Are you a 'digital addict'?

   c How easy would it be for you to go without your computer and mobile for a week?

Exam practice

Multiple choice 2 🔊 1.10 You will hear part of a radio phone-in programme on the subject of people's use of digital technology. For questions 1–7, choose the best answer (A, B or C).

> **Tip**
> Before you listen for the first time, read the questions and the three options carefully, underlining key words.

   1 What are James' parents worried about?
      A that their son does not have many friends
      B that their son spends too much time with internet friends
      C that their son goes out with his friends too often

   2 When does James spend the most time talking to virtual friends?
      A when he is going to college
      B when he first wakes up
      C when he isn't at college

   3 What is James' own opinion of his behaviour?
      A He doesn't think it is unusual.
      B He realizes that it is antisocial.
      C He knows his behaviour will have to change.

   4 What generalization does James make about adults?
      A They don't understand young people.
      B They are too serious-minded.
      C They are always busy.

   5 What does Evan, the child psychologist, think about James' problem?
      A He supports James' parents' views.
      B He sympathizes with James.
      C He understands both points of view.

   6 What does Joanne Carter, the head teacher, suggest James should do?
      A get professional treatment for his addiction
      B take up new sports and other activities
      C gradually reduce the time he spends on virtual friends

   7 On what does Liz Winslett base her advice to James?
      A her professional experience
      B what happened in the case of one of her children
      C her observations of other teenagers she knows

Over to you 3 Discuss these questions.

   a Who are you more sympathetic to – James or his parents? Give reasons.
   b What advice would you give to parents who are worried about their children's use of digital technology?
   c What advice would you give to teenagers about how to deal with their parents' concerns?

unit 3 compulsion

34

Grammar (1)

Habits and typical behaviour
▸ *Grammar reference* page 162

1 Do these sentences describing habits or typical behaviour refer to the past, the future or any time?

a On a normal day, I'll update my status as soon as I wake up.
b It's what I'm used to doing.
c I used to play tennis with my dad most weekends.
d Sometimes we'd go fishing together.
e Try to spend more time with real people – you'll soon get used to it.
f I didn't use to drink coffee, but now I really like it.
g Where did you use to play when you were a child?

2 What is the difference in meaning between the sentences in each pair a–c?

a 1 I used to check my email every hour.
  2 I'm used to checking my email every hour.
b 1 On a normal day, I'll update my status as soon as I wake up.
  2 On a normal day, I'd update my status as soon as I woke up.
c 1 I'm used to spending time with real friends.
  2 I'm getting used to spending time with real friends.

used to* and *would

3 *Used to* and *would* are often interchangeable. However, sometimes we cannot use *would* and must use *used to*. Choose the correct option to complete a–e below. Sometimes both options are possible. Can you work out the rule?

a I *used to / would* play football on Saturday afternoons.
b When I was younger, I *used to / would* have long hair.
c My parents *used to / would* live in Italy.
d In the summer, we *used to / would* go for long walks.
e My grandfather *used to / would* drive an old Mercedes.

4 In which of these sentences can *used to* be replaced by *would*?

a When he was younger, George used to cycle to school.
b Where did you use to work?
c Both my parents used to smoke.
d When I was younger, I used to be very thin.

5 Compare aspects of your life ten years ago with your life now. Think about the following and write sentences using *used to* or *would*. Compare your answers with a partner.

food   getting around   holiday time   ideas and beliefs
musical tastes   spending money

6 Think about your life now and discuss these subjects with your partner.

a A change you are experiencing now – for example, at school or work.
b Changes you would like to make to your life. Which changes would you find easy to get used to? Which would you find difficult to get used to?

unit 3 compulsion

Grammar (2)

Countable and uncountable nouns
▸ Grammar reference page 163

1 Underline the countable and uncountable nouns in these extracts from 🔊 1.10.

'It's just a bit of fun. I think adults take these things too seriously.'

'I have to say I have great sympathy with your parents and completely understand their point of view… My advice to you would be to spend less time on your phone.'

2 Which of the following quantifiers can be used only with countable nouns? Which can only be used with uncountable nouns? Which can be used with both?

a few   a little   a lot of   all the   enough   few   little   many
most of the   no   none of the   not much   plenty of   several   some

3 To make uncountable nouns countable, use countable expressions. Match the expressions with the appropriate uncountable nouns. Some expressions can be used with more than one noun.

Example: *an item of news*

Countable expressions: a bit of   a box of   a glass of   a piece of   a sheet of
                      a stroke of   a word of   an item of

Uncountable nouns: advice   clothing   equipment   fruit   furniture
                      information   luck   milk   music   news   paper   research

4 Some nouns can be countable and uncountable. Put these nouns in sentences which show the different meanings.

Example: Would you like **some cheese**? / Cheddar is **an English cheese**.

~~cheese~~   chicken   chocolate   exercise   experience   language   light
noise   room   time

5 Read the text below about cupcakes without trying to fill the gaps. What does the writer say is the connection between cupcakes and children?

Exam practice

6 For questions 1–8, read the text below and think of the word which best fits each gap. Use only one word in each gap. There is an example at the beginning (0).

Cupcake addiction

It's well known that people can become addicted to (0) _almost_ anything. According to the writer of *The Fix*, people can even get hooked on cupcakes. Here's an extract.

'The modern cupcake is (1) _____ thing of wonder: a base of sponge under a layer of sugar and buttercream. It looks (2) _____ a miniature birthday cake – and indeed, birthdays are the perfect excuse (3) _____ hurry to your local supermarket to buy some. The old-fashioned charm of cupcakes helps us to forget about (4) _____ the sugar and fat. The advertising suggests that your mother (5) _____ to make them, but even if she didn't, the pastel-coloured icing implies that one bite will take you (6) _____ to your childhood.

Cupcakes are so innocent-looking you could leave one on your desk at work and no one (7) _____ comment. On the other hand, this everyday food item can get us (8) _____ trouble because it is an object of desire that can reinforce addictive behaviour.'

Over to you   7 Discuss these questions.
a Are you addicted to any kinds of food?
b Are there certain foods that remind you of your childhood?

Think ahead   1 Read this text. How does the writer of this text feel about their addiction?

Vocabulary

Think ahead 1 Read this text. How does the writer of this text feel about their addiction?

CONFESSIONS OF A CHOCOHOLIC

I'm a chocoholic. Don't laugh – it's serious. At the moment, my addiction isn't too bad. I've cut down my intake to one block a day, and some days I get by on a chocolate biscuit or two. But at its worst, it's a complete obsession – the sweeter, the stickier, the richer it is, the better. My eyes light up just thinking about it.

I can eat any kind, even the cheap cooking chocolate that turns most people off. And fortunately, I can eat as much sugar as I like without putting on weight. Like other addicts, most chocoholics deny they have a problem. I know I'm hooked on chocolate, but I don't intend to give it up.

2 Are you addicted to these or any other foods? Exchange ideas with a partner.

cheese   chillies   chips   chocolate   coffee   hamburgers   sugar   tea

Phrasal verbs 3 Find and underline six phrasal verbs in the text above. Replace the phrasal verbs with the correct form of a word or phrase from the list below.

Example: *I've reduced* cut down *my intake to one block a day.*

disgust   gain   reduce   shine   stop   survive (on)

Phrasal verbs with *give* 4 Match the phrasal verbs with *give* in a–e with their meanings 1–7. Some verbs have more than one meaning.

a give away
b give back
c give in
d give out
e give up on

1 surrender or admit you can't do something
2 distribute things to people
3 stop being involved with someone because they disappoint you
4 reveal secret information
5 return something to its owner
6 let someone have something without paying
7 hand (home)work to a teacher

5 Complete these sentences with the correct form of a phrasal verb with *give*.

a I've been watching this DVD ever since Rachel lent it to me. I really ought to _____ it _____ to her and buy it for myself.
b I feel like _____ James – he never does what he says he's going to do.
c One of the supermarkets in town is _____ free samples of a new kind of non-addictive chocolate. You should try it.
d I haven't had a cigarette for three days, and I'm not going to _____ now.
e All over town there are people _____ leaflets about how to stop smoking.

Pronunciation 6 🔊 1.11 Listen to some phrasal verbs. In the two-part phrasal verbs, is the main stress on the verb or the particle? Where is the main stress in the three-part phrasal verb?

7 🔊 1.12 Listen to two pairs of sentences with phrasal verbs. What general stress rules can you work out?

Over to you 8 Discuss these questions.

a Have you ever *given up on* someone because they disappointed you in some way?
b What do you do if someone doesn't *give back* something that belongs to you?
c Have you ever had to *give in* because you couldn't do something you tried to do?

unit 3 compulsion

Reading and Use of English Part 6

Exam skills

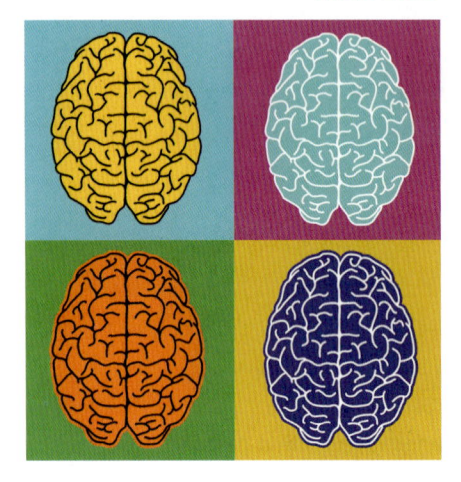

1 Read sentences a–f. Then, find the correct follow-on sentences in 1–6. Underline the words or phrases that helped you decide.

a People are always claiming they're addicted to things.
b I know there are people who sue fast food companies because they blame their health problems on the addictive nature of fast food and the refusal of restaurants to provide healthier alternatives.
c Would you be able to recognize someone who had a serious gambling habit? Would he look rich?
d The belief that addiction is a disease is becoming more accepted.
e Habitual behaviour is a natural part of our lives and includes everything from shutting down your computer to combing your hair. It isn't difficult to break these habits because we usually do them without thinking.
f We offer this eating plan to help food addicts.

1 Or would his eyes have a worried, slightly mad look?
2 Addictions, however, are conscious choices that can become very difficult to control.
3 A recent case involved a man who sued a restaurant for not telling customers that it used a certain kind of cooking fat.
4 It is not meant to be a diet, but a permanent change in eating habits.
5 I've heard them say, 'I'm addicted to coffee' or 'I'm hooked on that TV programme'.
6 This is not surprising as the loudest voices involved in defining conditions come from doctors and other health workers.

Exam practice

Gapped text

2 You are going to read an article about dealing with addiction. Six sentences have been removed from the article. Choose from the sentences A–G the one which fits each gap (1–6). There is one extra sentence which you do not need to use.

A Half an hour of intense aerobic exercise can produce five times the amount you'd have if you were sitting down.
B Low concentrations of these are closely linked to depression.
C It may be, though, that the thrill can never quite compare with that achieved by taking drugs.
D People become addicted to something because there's an underlying unhappiness.
E Steve, a personal trainer, used his work to mask his secondary addiction.
F The thrill from the exercise is the thing, the drug-like feelings brought about by the activity are what addicts want.
G With a negative addiction, on the other hand, exercise overrides everything.

> **Tip**
> Read the gapped text quickly. Then read the missing sentences and underline any reference words such as names, pronouns and times.

Over to you

3 Discuss these questions.

a Do you think addiction is mainly an individual or a social problem?
b Do you think that some addictions are harmless or are they all harmful?
c If you thought that you were becoming addicted to something, what would you do if you found it difficult to simply stop?

KICKING THE HABIT

The term 'exercise addiction' was coined in 1976 by Dr William Glasser when he was studying long-distance runners. He noticed that many of them experienced low moods when they couldn't train, and he came to differentiate between positive and negative addictions: a positive addiction involves a love of the activity, and the exercise is scheduled around other everyday activities. You run your running schedule, for example, rather than it running you, and an enforced day off isn't the end of the world. The results are increased feelings of physical and psychological wellbeing. [1] Relationships and work suffer, a day away from the gym causes distress, and health can decline as overtraining leads to injury and illness.

Two types of negative exercise addiction have since been defined. Secondary addiction is probably the most common, where the compulsion to exercise is driven by a need to control and change one's body shape, and is often accompanied by an eating disorder. [2] 'Whatever workout my client was doing, I'd do it, too, alongside them, supposedly to motivate them, but in fact it was to keep my weight down. In total, I was doing several hours of cardio every day, and I didn't actually enjoy the exercise. I hated the feeling of not having the perfect body even more, though.'

With primary addiction, body image isn't so central. [3] It works like this: when we exercise strenuously, we activate our sympathetic nervous system, causing a rise in the concentration of serotonin and other chemicals in the brain which make us feel happy.

At the same time, the body produces endorphins which shut down pain signals reaching the brain. [4] Add all these together, and you have a recipe for mild euphoria. Unfortunately, just as the body's tolerance of drugs increases, so it is with endorphins: more are required to produce the same thrill, so the exercise intensity has to be increased. [5]

Tony, who took drugs daily for almost a decade, then took to running half-marathons. He admits that getting the kick got harder. He said he'd lie awake at night thinking about the next day's session. It still wasn't as good as the drugs he was on before. Sports and exercise psychologist Paul Russell has encountered many people like Tony. 'Exercise addiction tends to be a more temporary addiction, marking time before the person returns to the basic ones, like drugs. [6] If they haven't sorted out the reasons for this state, via counselling for example, they'll have to direct that need to something else.'

unit 3 compulsion

Vocabulary

Adverbs

1 Read this short article. Have you heard of any of the superstitions mentioned in it?

Superstitions

When I was a boy, I clearly remember certain prohibitions in my grandmother's house. We were never allowed to open an umbrella inside because it was bad luck. If something good happened, we had to touch wood. When my grandfather accidentally broke a mirror once, he said dramatically, 'Seven years' bad luck'. Amazingly, he honestly believed this, but fortunately his prediction didn't come true. Superstitious beliefs like these are widespread. We even go through a childhood stage where we are guided by superstitions. Remember the old rhyme while walking along the pavement: 'Step on the line and break your mother's spine.' We not only walked with great care ourselves, we always made sure anyone with us avoided the lines, too. Most people would agree that superstitious thinking is based on the illusion that we can influence what happens in life. I know college students who will use only their 'lucky pen' to make sure they do really well in exams.

2 Compare ideas about superstitions in pairs.
   a How superstitious are you?
   b What superstitions are common in your family or your country?
   c What superstitions do you remember hearing about when you were a child?

3 Find examples of the following in the text, then think of two more examples of each type of adverb.
   - Four adverbs of manner (*Words which tell us how something happens.*)
   - Two comment adverbs (*Words which tell us someone's opinion.*)
   - Two focusing adverbs (*Words which draw attention to one part of a sentence.*)
   - Two frequency adverbs (*Words which tell us how often something happens.*)
   - An adverb of degree (*A word which tells us how much.*)

4 Rewrite these sentences by adding the adverbs or adverb phrases in brackets in the correct position. Some words and phrases can go in more than one position.
   a My sister failed her driving test last week. (sadly)
   b If someone sneezes, people say, 'Bless you!' (often)
   c I agree with you. (completely)
   d I checked my email before I left for work. (hurriedly)
   e I found out later that you'd been trying to phone me. (surprisingly)
   f I know his name and nothing else. (only)

5 Complete these sentences then compare what you have written with a partner.
   a When I have to go somewhere, I like to arrive _____.
   b In public I always try to behave _____.
   c Wherever I am I always try to eat _____.
   d Unfortunately, I'm not very good at _____.
   e I totally disagree with people who believe that _____.
   f I've always wanted to meet _____.

unit 3 compulsion

Speaking Part 3

1 🔊 **1.13** Speaking Part 3 consists of two phases. Listen to the examiner's instructions for the first phase and look at the task below.
  a How long do the candidates have to talk for?
  b What situation does the examiner ask the candidates to think about?
  c What does the examiner give the candidates to look at?
  d What do they have to do in relation to the prompts they are given?

Prompts around central question "How can we stop young people from smoking?": Increase prices, Raise the legal age, Medical alternatives, Health campaigns, Ban advertising

2 🔊 **1.14** Now listen to two candidates doing the first phase of the task.
  a Do the candidates talk about all the suggestions in the prompts?
  b Do they give examples?
  c How does the examiner end the discussion?

3 🔊 **1.15** Now listen to the examiner's instructions for the second phase of the task.
  a What do the candidates have to do?   b How long do they have to speak for?

4 🔊 **1.16** Now listen to the second phase of the task. What do the candidates decide?

5 In this part of the Speaking paper, you need to use a wide range of communicative language. Add these phrases to the 'Example' column in the table below.

for instance   How about …?   I think we should …   I'm absolutely sure that …
I'm not so sure.   What do you think?

Function	Example	From the recording
Making suggestions		
Giving opinions		
Asking for opinions		
Agreeing / Disagreeing		
Expressing certainty		
Giving examples		

Tip
Make sure you give your partner the opportunity to speak. If they don't say anything, ask them what they think.

6 🔊 **1.17** Listen again to the candidates doing both phases of the task. Add any other expressions they use to the table in **5** above.

Exam practice

Collaborative task

7 Work with a partner. Have your own discussion, using the same question for phase 1 and phase 2. Use expressions from the table in **5** to help you.

unit 3   compulsion

Writing Part 2 – Article

Think ahead

1 Discuss these questions.
   a In what situations do people read magazine articles?
   b Why do people choose to read or not to read a particular magazine article?
   c What sort of magazine articles interest you?

2 Read the Part 2 task below. Answer these questions.
   a What will you write about?
   b Who will read the article you are going to write?
   c What would be an appropriate style for this kind of article?

> You have seen the following announcement in an English language magazine.
>
> > We are looking for contributors to our series of articles: 'I'm just crazy about …'
> >
> > If you have got an interesting hobby, please send us **your** article.
> >
> > The best articles will be published in our magazine.
>
> Write your **article** in 140–190 words.

3 Read this article in response to the task above. Answer these questions.
   a How does the writer try to interest the reader?
   b How interesting do you find the article?
   c How would you describe the style? Formal or informal? Personal or impersonal? Serious or humorous? Is it suitable for the task?
   d In which paragraph does the writer describe a personal experience?
   e What descriptive language does the writer use?

I'm just crazy about rock climbing

You may be wondering how anyone can be crazy about something as dangerous as rock climbing. To be honest, I'm not sure myself why I'm so keen on it. It isn't because I'm good at it – I'm only a beginner.

I've come up with some reasons that non-climbers might understand. There are practical reasons. For example, climbing keeps you fit, and you meet lots of new people with the same interest as you.

In addition to this, there are reasons that only experienced climbers would understand. The main one is that climbing is scary – it gives you a fantastic thrill. I'll never forget my first climb – it was terrifying. Once you've got over the fear, you feel great because you've achieved something.

I must admit that sometimes I feel annoyed with myself because I can only do easy climbs. I feel terrible if I can't finish a climb and have to give up halfway. So, why do I carry on? I don't really know. It's just something I feel compelled to do.

Creating interest

4 Which of these are essential features of an article title? You can choose more than one answer.
   a It should attract your attention.
   b It should make you want to read the article.
   c It should tell you exactly what the text is about.
   d It should give you an idea of what the text is about.
   e It should be short.

5 Which of the titles a–d would make you want to read an article about sky-diving? Give reasons for your choice.

   a Sky-diving for beginners

   b No, I'm not completely mad

   c So you'd like to try sky-diving?

   d A complete history of sky-diving

6 Which of these opening sentences would make you want to continue reading? Give reasons for your choice.

   a Sky-diving is a relatively recent sport.

   b Have you ever wondered what it would be like to fall out of an aeroplane?

   c Sky-diving isn't for everyone.

   d The best thing about sky-diving is that anyone can do it.

Exam practice

Article
▶ *Writing guide* page 182

> **Tip**
> Think of an interesting title for your article. It could be a statement or a question, but it should tell the reader what the article is about.

7 Read the exam task below. Then, work through stages a–e.

> You have seen the following announcement in an English language magazine.
>
> > We are looking for contributors to our series of articles: '*I've always wanted to …*' in which people write about an activity they'd be keen to try.
> >
> > The best articles will be published in our magazine.
>
> Write your **article** in 140–190 words.

   a Decide on an activity to write about. Note down some key ideas. Choose an activity you would really like to try.

   b Plan your article. Make brief notes as you work through the following stages.

      • Think about who is going to read the article and how this will affect your writing style. Think about people of your own age: what interests them?

      • Work out a paragraph plan. Think particularly about what you will write in your first and last paragraphs.

      • How many other paragraphs will you need? Remember to plan a new paragraph for each main idea.

   c Think of a suitable title and an interesting first sentence.

   d Write an article based on the notes you have made. Include your own opinions and any personal anecdotes.

   e Finally, read through your article, checking your spelling, grammar and punctuation.

Unit 3 Review

1 For questions 1–8, read the text below and think of the word which best fits each gap. Use only one word in each gap. There is an example at the beginning (0).

WHAT IS A SHOPAHOLIC?

In recent years, shopaholics have come to the public attention (0) __on__ television and in newspaper articles. While the media sometimes use the word casually, shopaholics suffer **(1)** _____ a real, and sometimes frightening, lack **(2)** _____ self-control.

Without doubt, we live in a 'spend-happy' society. People live beyond their means and are **(3)** _____ debt. Many people, whatever their level of income, think of shopping as a hobby. They take weekend-long shopping excursions, spend money they do not have, and often regret their purchases later. But **(4)** _____ this mean that they have a problem? Not necessarily.

True shopaholics shop **(5)** _____ they can't help it. They go on buying things long **(6)** _____ they have huge debts. They shop when they feel depressed, and use spending as a way of coping **(7)** _____ life. They do not shop because they enjoy it, or because they need the things they buy. They buy things because they feel they have to. Shopaholics are **(8)** _____ of control.

2 Match a first sentence from a–e with a continuation (1–5).
   a I'm used to getting up early.
   b I didn't use to enjoy watching football.
   c I tend to reply to emails when I get them.
   d I am gradually getting used to not smoking.
   e When I first learnt to drive, I spent a fortune on petrol.

   1 I must admit, I feel a lot healthier than I used to.
   2 I do it every day, so it isn't hard for me.
   3 I used to drive all over the place going to see my friends.
   4 Otherwise, I completely forget.
   5 Now, I can't get enough of it.

3 Choose the correct alternative in these sentences.
   a We have *no / not* money left – we'll have to get some from the cash machine.
   b I'm so busy this week. I wish I had *little / a little* more time.
   c *None / None of* my friends likes the same music as me.
   d We had *enough / plenty* of time to finish our meal before the restaurant closed.
   e After winning the match the players had *a few / few* drinks to celebrate.
   f You seem to be tired *most / most of* the time. You must be working too hard.
   g Don't take the game so seriously, it was just *a bit / little* of fun.
   h My grandfather gave me *an item / a piece* of advice I shall never forget.

unit 3 compulsion

44

Unit 4   Roles

Introduction

1 Look at the photographs. Discuss these questions.
   a   What are the roles shown in each of the photographs?
   b   Are the roles equal or is one of the pair superior to the other?
   c   Do you think the roles shown in the pictures have changed in recent years?
   d   How do you think these roles may change in the future?

2 Now discuss these questions.
   a   Think about people you know well. What are their roles in relation to you? Are you an equal partner in these relationships?
   b   How many roles do you personally have?

45

Reading and Use of English Part 5

Think ahead 1 Read this extract from an article about space travel. Then, discuss the questions below.

> Women will set sail for the stars in less than fifty years, NASA scientists have predicted. Men will not be needed; the all-female crew will have children by artificial means. The spaceships will carry the first travellers to Alpha Centauri at a tenth of the speed of light. The journey will take forty-three years.

a How do you react to the idea of an all-female spaceship crew?

b What problems might a single-sex crew face on their journey? Why might a mixed-sex crew be a better alternative?

DISTANT SPACE TRAVEL BETTER AS FAMILY AFFAIR

'Forget the kind of macho astronauts you are used to seeing in science fiction films and television programmes – space travel to faraway solar systems will probably be a family affair conducted by married couples, their kids and generations to come,' according to US anthropologist, John Moore.

'The family has the kind of natural organization and motivation to deal with the tensions which are likely to characterize space trips of 200 years or longer to settle remote planets,' says John Moore. 'We are less likely to go crazy in space and more likely to accomplish our missions if we send crews into space that are organized along family lines. With clear lines of authority between parent and child as well as older and younger siblings, families provide a division of labour that can accomplish any kind of work,' says Moore. More importantly, they offer the rewards of getting married and having children.

'Whenever colonization is done on Earth, it is always by people looking for a better life. All of the colonizations that I know about have been done by families, especially young couples.' In the past, astronauts had to be specially trained and physically very fit to survive in very small space capsules, but spacecraft size is no longer the constraint it was, making it possible to take ordinary people such as midwives, electricians and cleaners. For a space crew that is going to colonize space and reproduce for many generations, these kinds of people will be just as important as space technologists.

Starting with a population of childless married couples also works best on board a spaceship because it will give the initial crew a few years to adjust to their new surroundings, without the distraction and responsibility of taking care of children. People may be horrified at the idea that children will be living and dying in space, with their only images of Earth coming from pictures and videos. But, says John Moore, parents have always made choices affecting the course of their children's lives. 'We change jobs, we move to another town, we go abroad to find work. If we educate our space kids properly, I think one day they might say, "Gosh, I'm sure glad I'm on this spaceship and not back on dirty old Earth."'

According to Moore, a starting population of 150 to 180 would best sustain itself at the same rate over six to eight generations. Every person would have the opportunity to be married – with a choice of at least ten possible spouses within three years of their age – and to be a parent. Ideally, the group should share social and cultural values. 'Having some people accustomed to monogamy and others to plural marriages would create some confusion when it becomes time for the sons and daughters of the first generation to marry,' says Moore. 'Designing morals for people on such a fantastic voyage is problematic because people on Earth would have little influence once the crew was on its own. If the space crew decided on a system of slavery for some and privilege for others, there is little the planners on Earth would be able to do to prevent it.'

Thinking about these issues is not as far-fetched as you might think. Experts predict that such a space mission will take place within the next hundred years.

Exam practice

Multiple choice

2 Read the article about space travel on page 46. For questions 1–6, choose the answer (A, B, C or D) which you think fits best according to the text.

1 What makes families especially suited to long-distance space travel?
  A They are good at organizing.
  B They are naturally better than other groups of people.
  C They will be able to cope with the stress of space travel.
  D They can settle down better in new situations.

2 Why will more ordinary people be able to go on space flights in the future?
  A Space travellers will be specially trained.
  B There will be a greater need for people with useful skills.
  C It will be easier for space travellers to keep fit.
  D Modern spacecraft will be much bigger than spacecraft in the past.

3 The writer's use of the word 'colonize' in line 23 suggests that he thinks one of the aims of future space travel will be to
  A find new places where humans can settle.
  B explore planets a very long way from Earth.
  C abandon the Earth as a place for humans to live.
  D establish a completely new way of living.

4 Why is it better for the first crews of space flights to be childless couples?
  A Childless couples are more responsible than couples with children.
  B Childless couples work harder than couples with children.
  C Crews need to get used to their environment before having children.
  D Couples with children would always put their children first.

5 Why is it difficult to design morals for space travellers?
  A People on Earth will be unable to affect the behaviour of space travellers.
  B No one knows what is the correct way for space travellers to behave.
  C Space travellers may have different ideas and values.
  D Travellers may be confused by their experience in space.

6 The article suggests that long-distance space travel
  A is a theoretical possibility.
  B will probably start within the next century.
  C could be a disaster.
  D will be a popular type of family holiday.

Tip

Read each question carefully and decide what information is required.

Collocations with *have* and *take*

3 Which verbs, *have* or *take*, are used in these collocations from the text?

  a _____ children
  b _____ care of children
  c _____ the opportunity to
  d _____ place

4 Complete these questions with an appropriate form of *have* or *take*. Sometimes both are possible. Then, ask and answer the questions with a partner.

  a What do you do to make sure you _____ a good time at the weekend?
  b Are there any college courses you'd like to _____ ?
  c In your opinion, what is the best age to _____ your first child?
  d Do you prefer to play it safe or _____ chances in life?
  e Are you someone who enjoys _____ arguments?
  f Have you ever had to _____ words with someone about their behaviour?
  g Do you _____ time to do all the things you want to do?

Over to you

5 Discuss these questions.

  a What kinds of people would be most suitable for the role of colonizing space? Suggest some of the personal qualities and skills they would need.
  b Would you be interested in helping to colonize space? Why? / Why not?

unit 4 roles

Grammar

The future
▸ Grammar reference page 164

1 There are many different ways of talking about the future in English. Match examples a–g with their meanings (1–7) below.

a The space rocket blasts off in precisely forty-eight hours.
b The crew is meeting to discuss final preparations on Friday evening.
c My sister is going to have a baby. It's due in three weeks.
d The astronauts are going to send regular reports back to Earth.
e The journey to Alpha Centauri will take forty-three years.
f That's the phone. I'll get it.
g Space travel to faraway solar systems will probably be a family affair.

1 an action or event that has been arranged
2 a prediction or expectation
3 an offer of help or an instant decision about the immediate future
4 a scheduled or timetabled event
5 a prediction based on evidence or prior knowledge
6 a future fact
7 an intention or plan to do something

2 Complete the email below using an appropriate form of the verbs in brackets. More than one answer may be possible.

New job!

To: Rav
Subject: New job!

Hi

Next Wednesday, **(1)** _____ (start) my new job as head of department – the first female department head in the company's history. To celebrate, my husband and I have got a great weekend planned. On Friday evening, we **(2)** _____ (have) a party. Then we **(3)** _____ (start) our mini adventure – on Saturday morning we **(4)** _____ (get up) early – that's the plan anyway – to drive to Dover to catch the ferry to France. The boat **(5)** _____ (leave) at 9.30.

When we get there, I expect we **(6)** _____ (stop) at a café for something to eat, and then we **(7)** _____ (drive) straight to Paris. We're not sure how long it **(8)** _____ (take). There's a jazz concert there that evening which we **(9)** _____ (probably / go) to.

We **(10)** _____ (catch) the Tuesday morning ferry back to Dover.
I **(11)** _____ (send) you a postcard if I have time.
Hope you have a good summer. **(12)** _____ (you / do) anything exciting?

I'll let you know how the new job goes.

Love Sue

---

3 How would you respond in situations a–c? Use appropriate future forms in your answers.

a You think that your boyfriend / girlfriend may be secretly going out with someone else. Tell a friend what you plan to do about it.
b A friend invites you to go on holiday with them. Apologize and tell them that you have already arranged to visit relatives.
c One of your friends is having a party this evening. They haven't got time to do everything themselves. Think about what needs doing, then offer to help.

Future continuous and future perfect

4 The *will* future can also be used in the continuous or perfect form. Match examples a–c with their meanings (1–3).

a People may be horrified at the idea that children will be living and dying in space.
b By the year 2100, people will have visited other planets.
c This time next year, we'll be living and working in the USA.

1 to refer to actions or events which will be in progress at a specific time in the future
2 to predict future trends, developments or possibilities
3 to refer to actions or events which will be completed by a particular time in the future

5 Think about your own future. Complete these sentences. Then, compare with a partner.

a This time next week I'll be …
b By this time next year I'll have …
c This time next year I'll be …
d In five years' time I'll have …

bound to / likely to

6 The phrases *to be (un)likely to* + verb and *to be bound to* + verb refer to the future. Think about the future of one of your friends or family members.

a What is likely / unlikely to happen to them in the future?
b What is bound to happen to them?

Example: Susie is (un)likely to get married. = It is (im)probable that Susie will get married.
Susie is bound to get married = It is certain that Susie will get married.

7 Quickly read the text below. Find out why there may be more women than men in the workforce in the near future.

Tip

Missing words are typically prepositions, pronouns, conjunctions, adverbs and verbs. They will not usually be nouns or adjectives.

Exam practice

Open cloze

8 Read the text below and think of the word which best fits each gap. Use only one word in each gap. There is an example at the beginning (0).

Women in the workforce

Some people think (0) ___*of*___ 'traditional' gender roles as being like a 1950s TV sitcom: Dad puts (1) _____ his suit and goes to the office, while Mum, in her apron, stays at home and (2) _____ the housework. But for most of human history, it (3) _____ taken the efforts of both men and women, whether working in an office (4) _____ in the fields, to look after the family. And that's the situation to which we now seem to be returning.

By 2050, women (5) _____ make up 47% of the workforce in the United States, up from 30% in 1950. But some experts are predicting that, at (6) _____ in the short term, the number of women in the workforce may actually overtake the number of men. What's the reason? During the economic recession that began in 2008, many jobs disappeared from industries traditionally dominated by male workers, (7) _____ as manufacturing. Unless many more manual manufacturing jobs appear, it may be that women, (8) _____ traditionally work in healthcare, education and other service industries, will take the lead in the labour market.

Over to you

9 Discuss these questions.

a What are the 'traditional' gender roles in your country? How have they changed in recent years?
b Why do you think many women work in 'healthcare, education and other service industries'?

Listening Part 3

Pronunciation 1 Mark the stressed syllables in these adjectives in this list as in the example.

ad**ven**turous   conservative   conventional   unconventional   extraordinary
fashionable   imaginative   normal   strange   surprising   traditional   unusual

2 🔊 1.18 Listen, check and repeat.

3 Describe each of the photographs below using adjectives from the list in **1** and other adjectives of your own. Then, compare your answers with a partner.

4 Which of these statements do you agree with? Discuss with a partner.
   a Mothers are better at bringing up children than fathers.
   b Mothers and fathers are equally good at bringing up children.
   c Children need mothers and fathers while they are growing up.

Exam practice

Multiple matching 5 🔊 1.19 You will hear five short extracts in which people are talking about bringing up children. For questions 1–5, choose from the list (A–H) what each speaker says. Use the letters only once. There are three extra letters which you do not need to use.

Tip

Before you listen for the first time, read statements A–H and underline any key words and phrases.

A Bringing up children is difficult and needs two people.
B Men are incapable of looking after children successfully.
C Fathers who looked after children were considered unusual.
D There is no difference between mothers and fathers.
E Women can't take on the role of fathers.
F Men get less practice than women at looking after children.
G People think men who look after children are strange.
H Mothers and children have a special emotional relationship.

Speaker 1 [1]
Speaker 2 [2]
Speaker 3 [3]
Speaker 4 [4]
Speaker 5 [5]

6 Discuss these questions which use expressions from the recording.
   a What do you understand by *a bond between children and their dads*? How might this be different from a bond between children and their mums?
   b What does the *day-to-day care of children* involve?
   c What is the role of *the main breadwinner* in a family? Can there be other breadwinners?
   d What do you understand by *an emotional tie*? What other ties are there between people?
   e What does the speaker mean by *he dedicated all his time to me and my sisters*?

unit 4 roles

Vocabulary

Phrasal verbs with bring

1 Replace the words or phrases in *italics* in a–i with the correct form of *bring* and one of the particles from the list below. Some of the particles can be used more than once.

about   back   down   forward   in   out   round   up

a *Raising* children is far too hard a job for one person to do.
b It took doctors an hour to *make her conscious again* after the accident.
c Most of the damage to the houses was *caused* by the recent storms.
d I hope she doesn't *mention* the embarrassing subject of money again.
e The government has *introduced* a new law banning smoking on public transport.
f Visiting Spain again *made me remember* lots of happy childhood memories.
g They'll have to *reduce* the price of cars. Nobody's buying them at the moment.
h They've *arranged* the meeting *for an earlier time*: 8.30 in the evening.
i My favourite crime writer, Henning Mankell, is *publishing* his latest novel next month.

2 Complete these sentences with your own ideas, adding appropriate particles.

a I find it very difficult to bring _____ the subject of _____ with my parents.
b If I had the power, I would bring _____ a law that would _____ .
c _____ always brings _____ memories of _____ .
d I think the hardest thing about bringing _____ children is _____ .

Words with several meanings

3 Look at the words in *italics* in a–e. What are their different meanings in each of the sentences (1–3)?

a WORK
  1 I know families where the father looks after the kids and it *works* perfectly well.
  2 This phone doesn't *work*.
  3 She spends much of her time *working* for the poor.
b KEY
  1 The *key* thing is to always put the interests of the children first.
  2 Press the return *key* to enter the information.
  3 There's a full *key* at the back of the book.
c INTEREST
  1 There are many places of *interest* in the city.
  2 The *interest* rates for borrowers have gone up by 2% since last year.
  3 As parents we always put the *interests* of the children first.
d EXPERIENCE
  1 Going on the London Eye was an unforgettable *experience*.
  2 They said that his lack of *experience* was the reason he did not get the job.
  3 I've always tried to learn from *experience*.
e MAKE UP
  1 My parents regularly have rows, but they always *make up* the next day.
  2 He always *makes up* excuses for being late. The truth is he always oversleeps.
  3 In many countries women *make up* the majority of the working population.

4 Now discuss these questions.

a What is the best excuse for lateness you, or someone you know, has made up?
b What cause would you work for if you had the opportunity?
c What have been the key events in your life?
d What are your main interests outside work?
e What is the most exciting experience of your life?

unit 4 roles

Reading and Use of English Part 4

Exam skills

1 Read these instructions for a Reading and Use of English Part 4 task. Then, answer the questions a–d below.

> For these questions, complete the second sentence so that it has a similar meaning to the first sentence, using the word given. **Do not change the word given.** You must use between **two** and **five** words, including the word given. Here is an example (0).
>
> Example:
>
> **0** Because of the fog at the airport, we took off three hours late.
>
> **DELAYED**
>
> Fog at the airport meant that _our take-off was delayed_ by three hours.

a How many words are given to help you complete the second sentence?
b How many words can you use to complete the second sentence?
c Does this number include the word you are given or not?
d Can you change the form of the word you are given?

2 Look at a student's answers to a Part 4 task. The key word is given in brackets. Find and correct the mistakes in the student's answers.

1 I think you should tell everyone exactly what happened. **(WERE)**
  If _I were you I'll_ tell everyone exactly what happened.

2 The last time I saw my sister was three years ago. **(SINCE)**
  It's _been ages since I last have seen_ my sister.

3 It has been reported that there are floods in the south. **(FLOODING)**
  There _have been reports of floods_ in the south.

4 'I don't share your political opinions,' she said. **(AGREE)**
  She told me _she didn't agree my_ political opinions.

Exam practice

Key word transformation

> **Tip**
>
> Think about what part of speech the key word is. This will help you to work out the correct grammar for the gapped sentence.

3 Complete the second sentences, following the instructions in **1**.

1 Some older people are finding it difficult to adjust to digital technology.
  USED
  Some older people can't _____ digital technology.

2 Many people think that Nick caused the accident.
  BELIEVED
  Nick _____ caused the accident.

3 In some places buying a flat is cheaper than renting one.
  MORE
  In some places it is _____ a flat than to buy one.

4 My brother looks much fitter. I think he's stopped smoking.
  GIVEN
  My brother must _____ smoking. He looks much fitter.

5 If it was my decision, I'd ban smoking in all public places.
  UP
  If _____, I'd ban smoking in all public places.

6 If you're worried about it, you should raise it at our next meeting.
  BRING
  Why _____ at our next meeting if you're worried about it?

Speaking Part 2

1 Look at the two photographs above. Discuss these questions.
   a Which of these places would you prefer to work in? Why?
   b What might be the problems associated with working in the other place?
   c How do you think the relationship between employees and their managers is different in these two workplaces?

2 🔊 1.20 Now listen to a Speaking Part 2 task in which a candidate is asked to talk about the same pictures. Does the speaker have similar ideas to yours?

3 🔊 1.20 Listen again. Complete these phrases with words or expressions which the candidates use to speculate about the photographs.
   a … sitting at their own computers, so they _____ can't see each other.
   b This _____ means that they don't talk to each other very often except in their breaks.
   c It _____ a very big office maybe with hundreds of employees, …
   d … so it _____ a call centre of some kind.
   e … the manager may work in a separate office so _____ he or she is quite remote from the staff.
   f _____ he or she knows the names of all the staff, …
   g In offices like these _____ it's possible to have regular meetings.
   h _____ the atmosphere in the other office might be very tense.

> **Tip**
> This part of the test assesses how well you can speak for longer periods. It is important that you keep talking for a minute.

Exam practice

Long turn   4 Work in pairs. Turn to page 154 and follow the instructions.

Writing Part 1

Think ahead 1 Discuss these questions.

a What kinds of people are often role models?

b Why do you think people need role models?

Exam skills 2 Read this short paragraph. Then, answer questions a and b below.

> [1] Children need role models in order to become mature adults. [2] The main reason for this is having a strong role model gives children a sense of security. [3] It has been shown that children need security to help them avoid risky behaviour when they are teenagers.

a In this example, the first sentence is the topic sentence. Which of these definitions describe a topic sentence? Tick all that apply.

has a clear topic ☐	contains an opinion ☐
interests the reader ☐	is quite short ☐
expresses the main idea(s) of the paragraph ☐	is a full sentence ☐

b What is the purpose of the second sentence? How about the third sentence? Choose from the list below.

gives an example   adds information
gives an explanation   gives a different point of view

3 Why are a and b not suitable as topic sentences? How could you improve them?

a Parents need to be sensitive.   b The end of the traditional family.

4 Write a topic sentence for each of these subjects.

celebrities   children   parents   teachers

Example: *Parents need to be involved in their children's education.*

5 Read sentences a–i from an essay about role models and put them in the correct order. Start by choosing the three topic sentences, which are in bold, and then find the two supporting sentences which relate to each topic sentence.

a Before becoming famous, many of them had to deal with failure and we can learn from this, too.

b However, our interest in celebrities has gone too far.

c To begin with, they can guide their children towards more positive role models.

d **In the end, parents still have a huge role to play in their children's lives.**

e For instance, they can show us the value of hard work.

f In addition, they should spend more time with their children, doing useful or interesting activities.

g Almost every day there is another celebrity scandal in the news.

h **Celebrities play an important part in our society.**

i The result of this media attention is that many young people copy their bad behaviour.

6 What words and phrases helped you decide the order of the supporting sentences?

Linking words

7 What words or phrases could be used to replace the words and phrases you identified in **6**?

8 Add two supporting sentences for each of these topic sentences. Use the phrases in brackets to help you.

  a Some children may be negatively influenced by television. (*For example / What is more*)

  b For some people, teachers make the best role models. (*To begin with / In addition / In the end*)

  c I believe that, generally speaking, celebrities make poor role models. (*For instance / However*)

> **Exam practice**

Essay
▸ *Writing guide* page 178

9 You are going to write an essay. First, read the task. Then, work through stages a–e below.

> **Tip**
>
> It is important that you plan how you are going to answer the question and organize the information before you start writing.

In your English class, you have been talking about role models.

Now, your English teacher has asked you to write an essay.

Write an essay using **all** the notes and give reasons for your point of view. Write your **essay** in 140–190 words.

> **Essay question**
>
> Is it better for young people to decide for themselves how to live, rather than following the example of a role model?
>
> **Notes**
>
> Things to write about:
>
> 1. the influence of role models
>
> 2. individuality
>
> 3. _____ (your own idea)

  a Think about the topic. Discuss the following in pairs and make brief notes.
  - What influence do role models have on young people?
  - Why do some young people have role models instead of expressing their own individuality?
  - Is it possible to have role models as well as expressing individuality?
  - Is individuality important? If so, why?

  b Think about what to include for 'your own idea'. It could relate to one of the following:
  - things that prevent people expressing individuality
  - ways of encouraging young people to express their individuality

  c Plan the content of each paragraph. Start by writing your topic sentences. Then, think about how to support these.

  d Write your answer in 140–190 words. Make sure you cover all the points and write in an appropriate style.

  e When you have finished, check your grammar, spelling and punctuation.

Unit 4 Review

1 For questions 1–6, complete the second sentence so that it has a similar meaning to the first sentence, using the word given. Do not change the word given. You must use between two and five words, including the word given.

  1 Everyone advised me to look for another job.
    SUGGESTED
    It _____ for another job.
  2 It has been reported that demonstrators and police have clashed.
    REPORTS
    There have _____ demonstrators and police.
  3 When I lived in Spain, I found it impossible to adjust to eating late.
    USED
    I _____ eating late when I lived in Spain.
  4 I'm sure she'll get the job.
    BOUND
    She _____ the job.
  5 Everyone thinks Molly is responsible for the mix-up.
    BELIEVED
    Molly _____ for the mix-up.
  6 I will probably be late for the meeting.
    UNLIKELY
    I _____ time for the meeting.

2 Complete these sentences with the correct future form of the verbs in brackets.
  a They're predicting that in future people _____ (retire) in their late sixties or early seventies.
  b I've decided I need to do more exercise, so from tomorrow I _____ (cycle) to work every day.
  c Don't worry about forgetting your credit card. I _____ (lend) you some money until tomorrow.
  d We'll have to get up very early tomorrow. Our train _____ (leave) at 6.45.
  e Next year, my father _____ (work) at the Central bank for forty years.
  f _____ you _____ (do) anything tomorrow evening? I've got tickets for the rock concert.
  g This time next week, we _____ (move) home and we _____ (live) on the other side of town.

3 Complete these sentences using the correct form of a phrasal verb with *bring*.
  a Jim was _____ by his parents to believe that stealing was wrong.
  b Hearing old pop songs often _____ memories of my younger days.
  c Paramedics sometimes use strong smells to help to _____ unconscious accident victims.
  d Giving up smoking can _____ a tremendous improvement in your health.
  e Sarah embarrassed her boyfriend when she _____ the subject of his driving difficulties.

Unit 5   Travel and culture

Introduction

1 Look at the photographs. Discuss these questions.
   a Where do you think these photos were taken?
   b What do the photos have in common?
   c In what ways has your culture been influenced by other cultures, both in the past and more recently? Think about fashion, language, music, etc.
   d Which of these changes have been positive and which have been negative?
   e What cultural influences has your country had on other countries?

Reading and Use of English Part 7

Exam skills 1 In Reading and Use of English Part 7, as well as looking for words and phrases which have similar meanings, it is useful to look for examples of the prompts. Look at prompts a and b below. For each one, find examples (1–4) which support each prompt.

a Tourism has beneficial effects on communities.
  1 Skyscraper hotels may spoil scenic places.
  2 There is increased demand for local arts and crafts.
  3 The host country can show off its land and culture.
  4 The money tourism brings into the country may not leave the hotel complex.

b Tourists are easily recognizable.
  1 They have a million cameras and camcorders hanging around their necks.
  2 They wear leisure clothes.
  3 They are often seen staring at maps, looking confused.
  4 They like to eat at McDonald's.

Exam practice

Multiple matching 2 You are going to read an article about tourism. For questions 1–10, choose from the paragraphs (A–F). The paragraphs may be chosen more than once.

> **Tip**
>
> Some people find it useful to read all the texts quickly for gist first. Other people might prefer to read each text quickly, trying to find at least one answer which matches the information in the text. Try both methods and see which you prefer.

Which paragraph

says that it is possible to be both a tourist and a traveller?	1
says that tourism has positive economic advantages?	2
mentions that some tourist spots were busy in the past?	3
puts forward the view that travellers are selfish?	4
observes that very few people have said anything positive about tourists?	5
gives the writer's definition of himself?	6
expresses the writer's anger at the assumed superiority of travellers?	7
describes the reaction of locals to the arrival of tourism?	8
explains how tourism begins?	9
mentions that many people will agree with the negative description of a tourist?	10

Over to you 3 Discuss these questions.

a Which places in your country are popular tourist destinations?
b What are the effects of tourism in your country?
c Do you consider yourself a tourist or a traveller? Why?
d What is the best holiday you have ever been on?

unit 5 travel and culture

58

Are you a tourist or a traveller?

Costa del sol

Machu Picchu

A As another holiday high season approaches, it's time to defend tourists. They need it. They've been under attack for generations. 'Of all noxious animals … the most noxious is the tourist,' wrote the diarist Francis Kilvert in the nineteenth century. Scarcely anyone has had a good word to say before or since. I sense heads nodding. This is the opinion of the cultivated.

B At dinner parties, no one admits to being a tourist. They are all travellers. They don't go to the Costa del Sol or even worse go on a coach tour. They are forever off the beaten track, seeking the authentic. Looking down on tourists is snobbery, a way of distancing oneself from the uncultured classes. And it infuriates me. To my way of thinking, there is no conflict between tourism and travelling. Just as one may eat one day at McDonald's and the next at a five-star Michelin restaurant, so one may both enjoy the beaches of the Costa del Sol and a trek through the Sarawak rainforest. These experiences are not mutually exclusive.

C Tourists are those who arrive in hordes, overrunning places and ruining them. Travellers are, by their definition, the people that get there first. But if they didn't wander off to unexplored spots, and write and talk about it on their return, the rest of us would be in ignorance. Some readers were inspired to follow. (What did the writers expect?) However, as long as numbers remain limited and they wore boots, they could be termed 'travellers'. But, at some stage, volume transforms travellers into tourists. Then people get very upset. (Hear them moaning about the crowds at Machu Picchu.) But if they don't like it, travellers have only themselves to blame: they were the trailblazers. Anyway, certain destinations positively benefit from crowds of visitors. I'm thinking of, say, the Colosseum in Rome. In its heyday, such places throbbed with people and commerce. That was their point. Today's abundance of tourists and traders is quite in line with original conditions.

D I've recently read Norman Lewis's book in which he recounts a stay in a remote Costa Brava village in the post-war years. It was on the hinge between a fishing past and tourism future. Lewis can't disguise his regret at this turn of events, at the loss of isolation, of ancient ways and village values. It has to be said, however, that before that the villagers were leading pretty miserable lives. No surprise then, that, with some initial reluctance, villagers embraced the tourism development – going to work in the new hotel, opening guest rooms of their own and running pleasure trips in their fishing boats.

E It is easy to romanticize herdsmen and fishermen when you're only passing through. Then you go home, and they're still collecting fresh water from five miles away. By wishing to leave the world untouched, travellers do absolutely nothing for economic development. By contrast, tourists – with all their varying needs – bring cash in buckets.

F Tourists like one another. Travellers apparently don't like anybody, unless they're wearing a loincloth or sari. They appreciate their genuine experiences so much that they resent sharing them. The presence of other visitors compromises the authenticity. Their own presence, curiously, does not. The writer Evelyn Waugh said, 'The tourist is the other fellow'. Then again, no. The tourist is me. I feel no shame.

unit 5 travel and culture

Grammar

Past time
▸ *Grammar reference* page 165

1 These sentences contain examples of the past simple, past continuous, present perfect simple and past perfect simple. Name the verb forms in *italics*.
   a I've recently *read* Norman Lewis's book.
   b In its heyday, such places *throbbed* with people and commerce.
   c … before that the villagers *were leading* pretty miserable lives.
   d When the villagers gave up their traditional jobs to work in the new tourist hotels, they realized *they had made* the right decision.

2 Which of the verb forms in **1** is used to describe past events or situations that …
   a happened before another past event or situation?
   b happened at an unspecified time in the past and are relevant to the present?
   c happened at a specific time in the past?
   d continued over a period of time?

3 Name the verb forms in the following pairs of sentences. What is the difference in meaning between the sentences in each pair?
   a When we arrived at the theatre, the play started.
      When we arrived at the theatre, the play had started.
   b I've bought some presents to take home.
      I've been buying some presents to take home.
   c I was crossing the road when I saw Adam.
      I crossed the road when I saw Adam.
   d She filled out the passport application last night.
      She was filling out the passport application last night.
   e He worked as a travel agent for two years.
      He's worked as a travel agent for two years.

4 Complete this text with the correct forms of the verbs in brackets, making any other necessary changes.

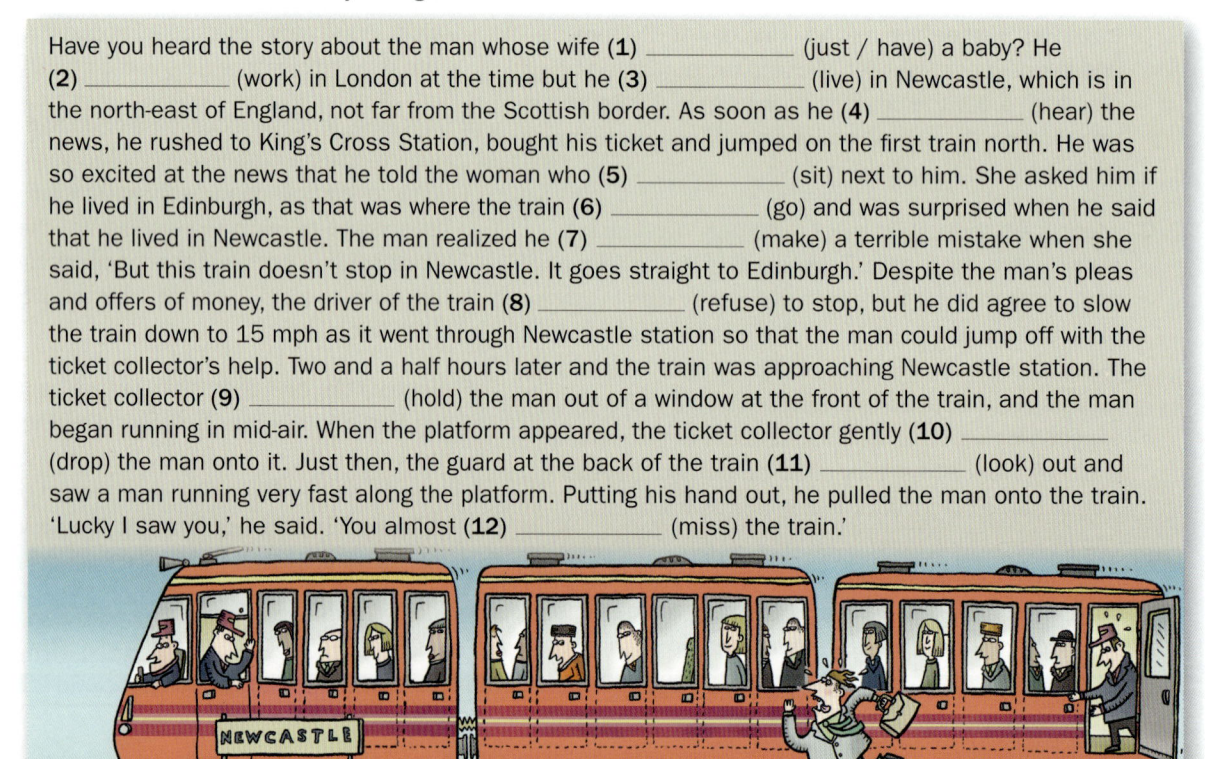

Have you heard the story about the man whose wife (**1**) _____ (just / have) a baby? He (**2**) _____ (work) in London at the time but he (**3**) _____ (live) in Newcastle, which is in the north-east of England, not far from the Scottish border. As soon as he (**4**) _____ (hear) the news, he rushed to King's Cross Station, bought his ticket and jumped on the first train north. He was so excited at the news that he told the woman who (**5**) _____ (sit) next to him. She asked him if he lived in Edinburgh, as that was where the train (**6**) _____ (go) and was surprised when he said that he lived in Newcastle. The man realized he (**7**) _____ (make) a terrible mistake when she said, 'But this train doesn't stop in Newcastle. It goes straight to Edinburgh.' Despite the man's pleas and offers of money, the driver of the train (**8**) _____ (refuse) to stop, but he did agree to slow the train down to 15 mph as it went through Newcastle station so that the man could jump off with the ticket collector's help. Two and a half hours later and the train was approaching Newcastle station. The ticket collector (**9**) _____ (hold) the man out of a window at the front of the train, and the man began running in mid-air. When the platform appeared, the ticket collector gently (**10**) _____ (drop) the man onto it. Just then, the guard at the back of the train (**11**) _____ (look) out and saw a man running very fast along the platform. Putting his hand out, he pulled the man onto the train. 'Lucky I saw you,' he said. 'You almost (**12**) _____ (miss) the train.'

Vocabulary

Travel phrasal verbs

1 Match the phrasal verbs in a–f with their meanings (1–6).

a We'll come to the airport to *see you off*.
b If they *set off* at seven o'clock, they should be here by eight.
c I can give you a lift to the station. I'll *pick you up* at six.
d The plane *took off* on time despite the bad weather.
e We had to *check in* two hours before the plane left.
f On our way to Australia we *stopped over* in Singapore for two days.

1 go somewhere to collect someone in a car
2 register as a passenger at an airport, or as a guest at a hotel
3 go to a railway station, airport, etc. to say goodbye to someone
4 break a journey to stay somewhere, especially when travelling by air
5 begin a journey
6 leave the ground and begin to fly

2 Complete these questions with an appropriate phrasal verb in an appropriate form. Then, answer the questions with a partner.

a If your flight was at 6 p.m., what time would you _____ for the airport?
b After you have _____ for a flight, what do you usually do?
c Do you like people to come to the airport to _____ you _____?
d Do you feel nervous when a plane _____ and lands?
e Would you _____ a friend _____ from the airport at 4 a.m.?
f Would you prefer to _____ somewhere or fly direct to your destination?

Exam practice

Key word transformation

> **Tip**
>
> Think carefully about the grammar of the gapped sentence. It may be active or passive and the key word may need a dependent preposition.

3 For questions 1–6, complete the second sentence so that it has a similar meaning to the first sentence. Do not change the word given. You must use between two and five words, including the word given.

1 My cousin lost his job two years ago.
   UNEMPLOYED
   My cousin _____ two years.

2 I last went abroad a year ago.
   LAST
   I have _____ year.

3 I haven't enjoyed myself so much for a long time.
   AGES
   It's _____ enjoyed myself so much.

4 As soon as we left the house, we realized we'd forgotten our passports.
   OFF
   We _____ when we realized we'd forgotten our passports.

5 After locking the door of the shop, she left.
   UNTIL
   She didn't _____ the door of the shop.

6 You really should take a few days' holiday.
   GET
   You really ought _____ a few days.

unit 5 travel and culture

61

Reading and Use of English Part 3

Think ahead 1 Read the text below. Is this true of the situation in your country? If so, what are the people and / or the government doing about it? Ignore the form of the words in *italics*.

In general, many young people around the world are *not satisfied* with their present situation, either because there is a shortage of work or because the type of work available *is not suitable* or *not regular*. Many graduates are becoming *not patient* and are emigrating to find work.

Another problem young people face is finding suitable accommodation. This is due to a *not adequate* supply of *not expensive* housing in the area they live in.

Exam skills 2 Read the text in **1** again and answer questions a–c.

a Make the phrases in *italics* in the text into negative adjectives.

b What are the negative forms of these adjectives?

appropriate   comfortable   correct   important   legal   moral
obedient   responsible   successful   suitable

c What rules are there for making adjectives negative?

> **Tip**
> When you read the text for a second time, use the words on either side of the gap to help you decide what kind of word is missing.

Exam practice

Word formation 3 For questions 1–8, read the text below. Use the word given in capitals at the end of some of the lines to form a word that fits in the gap in the same line. There is an example at the beginning (0).

> **Tip**
> Check the meaning of the sentence to see if a negative form is required.

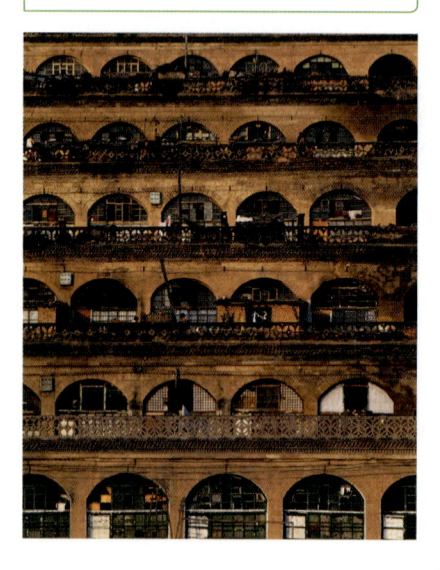

The Yaodong Cave Dwellings in China

With the huge numbers of high-rise modern buildings under
recent (0) _construction_ in China's main cities, it may seem   CONSTRUCT
(1) _____ that around 30 million Chinese still live underground.   BELIEVE
But this is the case. And it is through choice not (2) _____   NECESSARY
that they do so. In the Loess plateau region, 90% of the mostly
(3) _____ population live in caves. However, only 10% live in   FARM
the (4) _____ basic traditional type of yaodong, dug out of the   FAIR
mountainside. The remainder live in caves built into the mountainside,
or in free-standing concrete structures which use up (5) _____   VALUE
farmland and are energy (6) _____.   EFFICIENT
In the last fifteen years, however, a new housing project has built a
new kind of yaodong. Based on the traditional design, but costing
around half the price to buy as the 'more modern' western flats in
(7) _____ towns, and with solar energy reducing the cost of   NEAR
(8) _____ and ventilation, these new caves are proving very   HEAT
popular with the young people of the area.

Over to you 4 Discuss these questions.

a Many people around the world still live in caves. Would you want to live in a cave?

b How are modern dwellings in your country different from those built in the past? Are the changes positive or negative?

c What would your ideal home be like?

Listening Part 4

Think ahead

1 Look at the photographs below. How would you describe the texture of these foods? If you have never tried them, imagine how they would feel in your mouth. Choose from these adjectives.

chewy   creamy   crispy   crunchy   dry   gooey   hard   juicy
oily   slimy   slippery   smooth   soft   squishy   sticky

2 Discuss these questions.

a 'One man's meat is another man's poison.' What do you think this saying means? Do you have a similar expression in your country?

b What foods / dishes are typical in your country that foreigners might dislike? Why might they dislike them?

Exam practice

Multiple choice

Tip

As you listen for the first time, mark or make a note of the options which you think are possible.

3 🔊 1.21 You will hear a man talking about his experiences of eating in other countries. For questions 1–7, choose the best answer (A, B or C).

1 John chose the title of his book to reflect the fact that
  A every country has different rules of etiquette.
  B diplomats need to be able to eat anything.
  C he often suffered digestive problems.

2 What happened at his first official dinner?
  A He ate what he was given.
  B He asked for something different.
  C He embarrassed his hosts.

3 What is the worst food or drink he has been served?
  A dried bat
  B snake blood
  C sheep's eyeball

4 What makes a food or drink particularly repulsive to the writer?
  A its taste
  B its smell
  C its appearance

5 What advice does he give to people in a similar situation?
  A Eat the food as quickly as possible.
  B Never eat anything you don't want to.
  C Imagine you're eating something else.

6 Which word best describes his recent book?
  A entertaining
  B informative
  C factual

7 What would be the most appropriate title for his next book?
  A *A Businessman's Guide to China*
  B *Food Through the Ages*
  C *Diplomatic Disasters*

Over to you

4 Discuss these questions in pairs.

a What is the strangest food you have ever eaten?

b Is there any food you would never try?

Vocabulary

Think ahead 1 Read this short text. Answer these questions.
  a What is it not acceptable to do at mealtimes in China?
  b How is eating similar or different in your country?

Mealtimes in China

In China, the sorts of *plates / dishes* served at the three main meals are pretty much the same – soup, rice or noodles, and meat and vegetables. Each person has their own bowl of rice and a *couple / pair* of chopsticks, but helps themselves to the soup, meat and vegetables directly from the communal plates in the centre of the table. It is perfectly acceptable to reach across the table to take food. To eat the rice, the diner *raises / rises* the bowl to their lips and pushes the grains into their mouth with the chopsticks. The diner must finish all the rice. To leave even a tiny amount is considered bad manners.

Words often confused 2 Choose the correct word from each pair to complete the text above. Give an example of a sentence using the other word in each pair.

3 Here are some more words which are often confused. Choose the correct word in each pair.
  a That pudding was nice. Can I have the *receipt / recipe*?
  b In some religions, people *fast / diet* for periods of time.
  c Crisps and hamburgers are sometimes referred to as *junk / rubbish* food.
  d Most people prefer bottled water to *tap / running* water. Some people prefer sparkling water to *flat / still* water.
  e There are two main tastes: 'sweet', like cakes and biscuits, and '*savoury / salty*', like crisps and cheese.
  f Don't you think James is an excellent *cooker / cook*?
  g Waiter! Could we have another look at the *menu / list*, please? And could you bring us the wine *menu / list*, too?

Extreme adjectives 4 Which word in the text in 1 above means *very small*?

5 Here are some more extreme adjectives. What normal adjectives do they correspond to?

  amazed   boiling   delicious   delighted   exhausted   filthy   freezing   furious
  hilarious   huge   spotless   terrified

6 Complete these sentences with an ordinary or an extreme adjective.
  a I can't drink this coffee. I'll burn my mouth. It's absolutely _____.
  b The turkey was very _____. In actual fact, it was more like an ostrich than a turkey.
  c Her kitchen is so clean you could eat off the floor. It's absolutely _____.
  d Daniel was really _____ when the waiter spilt wine on his new shirt, but we all thought it was absolutely _____ and couldn't stop laughing.
  e Thank you for your invitation. We would be absolutely _____ to come for dinner next Friday.
  f This chocolate cake is absolutely _____. I think I'll have another piece if I may.

Over to you 7 Work in pairs or small groups. Plan a meal for one or more of the following people.
  - friends who are coming to your house to watch a film or sports match
  - a foreign visitor who would like to try something typical
  - members of your family who want to have a picnic on the beach

Speaking Parts 3 & 4

Think ahead

1 Imagine you could take six months off work or college. How would you spend the time?

2 🔊 1.22 You are going to hear an interview between two candidates discussing the Part 3 task below. As you listen for the first time, answer these questions.
  a On which of the experiences did they share the same opinion?
  b On which of the experiences did only one of them give an opinion?
  c On which of the experiences did one of them partially change their opinion?

What can you learn about a country and its culture from each of these experiences?
- Doing voluntary work
- Backpacking
- Sightseeing
- Working as an au pair
- Learning a language

3 🔊 1.22 Listen again. Complete the table below with words and phrases the candidates use for each of the functions.

Giving an opinion	(Personally) I think ...
Asking for an opinion	Do you agree?
Agreeing with an opinion	I guess so.
Disagreeing with an opinion	Not necessarily.

4 Now add these expressions for agreeing and disagreeing in 3 to the table.
  I don't know about that.   Absolutely!   I agree with you up to a point.
  Sorry, but I have to disagree with you there.   I'm not sure I agree with you there.
  I couldn't agree more.

5 Which of the expressions in 3 and 4 express ...
  a total agreement / disagreement?   b partial agreement / disagreement?

6 🔊 1.23 Now listen to the second phase of Part 3 and answer these questions.
  a Which two experiences did they decide on?   b Do you agree with their choices?

7 Add any new opinion language from the recording to the table above.

Pronunciation

8 🔊 1.24 Listen to the phrases in 4 above. Repeat after the speakers.

Exam practice

Collaborative task & discussion

9 Work in pairs. Turn to page 154 and follow the instructions.

10 In Part 4 the examiner will extend the Part 3 discussion with you. Discuss these questions with a partner.
  a Do you think it is better to travel alone or with other people?
  b What are the advantages of staying with a host family in the country you are visiting?
  c What are the benefits of studying English in an English-speaking country?

> **Tip**
> Remember to give reasons and explanations for your answers.

Writing Part 2 – Review

1 Read this Part 2 task. What do you have to do?

> Your English teacher has asked you to write a review of a hotel or guest house in your town. You should say why it is a good place to stay and any negative points about it, too.
>
> Write your **review** in 140–190 words.

2 Read this answer to the task in **1** above. Then, answer questions a–d below.

The Blue Mosque Guest House – Istanbul

It is easy to see why the Blue Mosque Guest House is a popular place for tourists to stay when they are in Istanbul. Situated in the historic district of Sultanahmet, it has the advantage of being just a short walk away from most of the important visitor attractions.

The four-storey, family-run guest house offers a variety of accommodation, but if you are travelling on your own you will need to book well in advance if you want a single room. All the rooms have central heating and air-conditioning – an essential if you are visiting Istanbul in summer.

Possibly the best thing about the Blue Mosque Guest House is the delicious typical Turkish breakfast of eggs, cold meats, tomatoes and olives, which is available between 8 and 10 a.m. in the kitchen on the top floor from which you have amazing views of the Bosphorus river.

If you are on a budget, this is the place for you. Luxurious it isn't and the steep stairs (and no lift) might not suit some, but the friendly welcome you will get there will more than make up for it.

    a What positive and negative points does the writer make?
    b What other factual information is given?
    c Have all the points in the question been answered?
    d Would you stay at the hotel? Give a reason for your answer.

3 Reviews are a mixture of factual information, description and evaluative comments. Underline all the adjectives in the answer above. What other adjectives could replace *amazing*?

Evaluative adjectives   **4** Divide these evaluative adjectives into two groups: positive and negative.

appalling awesome awful beautiful boring breathtaking brilliant
depressing disgusting dismal dreadful dreary excellent foul
gorgeous interesting poor sensational stunning tasteless tedious
terrible vile

5 Which of the adjectives in **4** could you use to describe …
    a a view?
    b a journey?
    c food?
    d the service in a restaurant?

Compound adjectives

6 Look back at the review in **2**. Find two compound adjectives.

7 Make compound adjectives from these sentences.
   a A meal which consists of three courses.
   b A walk which takes five minutes.
   c A restaurant where you can't smoke.
   d Food which you think costs more than it should.
   e Goods which are made by hand.
   f Rooms which have central heating.
   g Fish which is caught locally.
   h A boulevard which is lined with trees.
   i A price which includes everything.
   j A hotel which is situated in a convenient place for shops, transport, places of interest, etc.

Language of recommendation

8 Which sentence in the review in **2** is the recommendation?

9 Write recommendations for a–d using the language below and giving your own reasons.
   a a package holiday   b a city   c a car   d an airline

   I fully / wholeheartedly recommend … to … .
   I recommend … not only to / for … but also to / for … .
   I wouldn't recommend … if … but otherwise I would … .
   I definitely would not recommend … because … .

10 Say whether these words can be used to describe a hotel, a restaurant or both.

   à la carte menu   airport shuttle   amenities   book a table   buffet
   check-in / out   complimentary   dessert   en-suite   house speciality
   make a reservation   room service   self-service   set menu
   single / twin / double room   staff   wine list

11 Discuss these questions.
   a Which do you like best: an à la carte menu, a set menu or a buffet?
   b What amenities do you expect in a five-star hotel?
   c What's the best service you have experienced in a restaurant? And the worst?
   d What's the most breathtaking view you have ever seen?
   e Can you describe a house speciality you know?

Exam practice

Review
▶ *Writing guide* page 183

12 You are going to write a review. First, read the task below. Then, work through stages a–e.

> Your English teacher has asked you to write a review of a popular restaurant, bar or café you would recommend to visitors to your country. You should say why it is popular with locals and why foreign visitors would like it.
>
> Write your **review** in 140–190 words.

   a What points do you need to cover?
   b Decide which place you are going to review. It doesn't have to be a real place.
   c Make a note of your ideas about each point. Use these prompts to help you:
       • location   • description (decoration, etc.)   • food, service, staff
   d Use your notes to help you write your review. Write in an appropriate style. Try to express your ideas in different ways.
   e Check through your grammar, spelling and punctuation.

> **Tip**
>
> Once you have decided which place you are going to review, quickly note down your answers to both questions in the task. Do this before you start writing.

unit 5 travel and culture

67

Unit 5 Review

1 Read the text below and think of the word which best fits each gap **1–8**. Use only *one* word in each gap. There is an example at the beginning (0).

CHOPSTICKS

It is not known when chopsticks first began to be used. **(0)** _However_, it is fairly certain that they were invented in China, **(1)** _____ they have been traced back as far as the third century BC. There are those **(2)** _____ say that the philosopher Confucius, who lived over two hundred years earlier, influenced the development of chopsticks with his non-violent teachings. So, knives, which have associations with war and death, **(3)** _____ not brought to the dinner table **(4)** _____ they were in the West. Today, chopsticks are used in other countries such as Japan, Korea and Vietnam, as **(5)** _____ as China. Commonly made of bamboo, wood, ivory or, in modern times, plastic, **(6)** _____ are several differences. For example, Chinese and Korean chopsticks have a blunt end, **(7)** _____ in Japan the end is pointed. Chopsticks are the world's second most popular method **(8)** _____ conveying food to the mouth. The most popular method is using fingers.

2 Complete the texts using the correct forms of the verbs in brackets.

a I couldn't believe it! My alarm clock **(1)** _____ (not ring) and my plane was due to leave in two hours. Hastily, I **(2)** _____ (get) out of bed and **(3)** _____ (rush) downstairs. No time for a shower. Where was my passport? I was sure I **(4)** _____ (leave) it on the table, but it wasn't there. Eventually I **(5)** _____ (find) it. It **(6)** _____ (lie) on top of the clothes in my suitcase. I **(7)** _____ (pack) it by mistake.

b If you **(1)** _____ (ever ride) on an elephant, you will know how uncomfortable and scary it is. I was terrified the first and only time I **(2)** _____ (sit) on one's back. It **(3)** _____ (seem) a long way down, and it was frightening.

c The accident **(1)** _____ (happen) while I **(2)** _____ (travel) to Edinburgh for the weekend. It was foggy, and like everyone else I **(3)** _____ (drive) too fast, given the poor driving conditions. One minute I **(4)** _____ (listen) to the radio, the next I **(5)** _____ (lie) in a hospital bed. I **(6)** _____ (crash) into the car in front, but had a lucky escape.

3 Complete the phrasal verbs in these sentences with an appropriate word.

a On our way to Australia, we decided to *stop* _____ in Hong Kong for a few days.

b Could you *pick* me _____ from work tomorrow? My car is being serviced.

c After we had *checked* _____ at our hotel, we looked round the town.

d As soon as the plane *took* _____, I began to relax.

e If your class starts at nine o'clock, what time do you have to *set* _____ to get there on time?

f It upsets me to *see* people _____ at the airport.

unit 5 travel and culture

68

Unit 6 — The mind

Introduction

1 Read and answer these questions. Which questions do you think test IQ (Intelligence Quotient) and which test EQ (Emotional Intelligence Quotient)? When you have finished, compare answers in pairs.

a Look at these diagrams.

Which diagram is next in the sequence?
i)   ii)   iii)   iv)

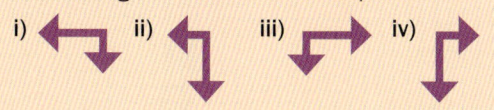

b Jack is poorer than Kate. Kate is richer than Mark. Mark is as rich as Ann. Ann is richer than Jack. Which person is the richest?

c You lent something to a friend. It isn't worth much money, but it means a lot to you. You've asked for the item back, but your friend has failed to give it back. What do you do?
  1 Tell your friend that the item has great sentimental value and that you would like to have it back.
  2 End the friendship. A real friend would have more consideration for you.
  3 Forget about it. Friends are more important than possessions.
  4 Don't speak to your friend until your item is returned.

d You are coming out of a shop when you suddenly trip and nearly fall over. What do you do?
  1 Feel angry and swear to yourself.
  2 See the funny side and carry on walking.
  3 Look around quickly to see if anyone was watching.
  4 Feel really embarrassed and walk on, pretending nothing has happened.

2 Discuss these questions.
  a How useful are IQ and EQ tests? How well do you perform on them?
  b To what extent can practising these tests help you get a better score?

Listening Part 2

Think ahead

1 These factors may determine whether a child will grow up a success or a failure. How could each factor be a positive or a negative influence?

character   education   intelligence   social class   upbringing   wealth

Exam practice

Sentence completion

2 🔊 1.25 You will hear part of a radio programme about factors which determine success. For questions 1–10, complete the sentences with a word or short phrase.

Tip

When you listen for the first time, complete as many sentences as you can. Don't worry if you can't complete all of them at this stage. The second time you listen, complete the rest of the sentences and check the ones you have already completed.

Many psychologists believe that EQ is _____ **1** IQ when calculating success.

The graduates who got high IQ scores at college weren't any more _____ **2** than those who got lower IQ scores.

One of the most significant factors for life success is _____ **3**

The children who didn't eat the sweet would receive _____ **4**

Approximately _____ **5** of the children couldn't resist temptation.

The children were retested when they were _____ **6**

On the IQ test, the group which had resisted temptation got _____ **7**

Another factor which determines success is _____ **8**

The _____ **9** of new salesmen is expensive.

Salesmen who are _____ **10** are more liable to leave during their first year.

Over to you

3 Discuss these questions.
   a Were you surprised by the results of the research? Why / Why not?
   b If you were in these situations, how much attention would you pay to IQ and to EQ? What other qualities would you look for?
      • a student choosing a private tutor
      • a university selecting new students
      • someone looking for a marriage partner
      • an estate agency looking for a manager
      • a hair salon looking for an apprentice hair stylist

Personal qualities

4 Which of these adjectives describe positive and which describe negative personal qualities? What are the nouns related to these adjectives?

confident   dependable   indecisive   pessimistic   self-reliant

5 Complete these sentences with an appropriate adjective or noun from 4.
   a Josie can never make up her mind. She's so _____.
   b It's important to believe in yourself and have _____ in your own abilities.
   c My grandmother lives alone and doesn't need any help from anyone. She's totally _____.
   d James isn't very _____. He doesn't always turn up when he says he will.
   e _____ always believe the worst will happen.

unit 6   the mind

Grammar

Gerunds
▸ Grammar reference page 166

1 Underline the gerunds in these sentences. Match each example in a–d with a description of its use in 1–4. Some will fit more than one use.
   a Thinking is somehow superior to feeling.
   b If the children could resist eating the sweet, he would give them two sweets.
   c Selling insurance is a difficult job.
   d Given the high costs of recruiting and training, the emotional state of new employees has become an economic issue for insurance companies.

   1 as the subject of a clause or sentence   3 after certain verbs
   2 as the object of a clause or sentence   4 after prepositions

2 Complete these sentences with a verb in the gerund form.
   a _____ a good memory is seen as an advantage by most people.
   b _____ people's names is an ability which can be developed.
   c _____ a person's name immediately after you have been introduced to them will help you remember it.
   d _____ things down in a diary will jog your memory.
   e _____ where you left your keys is an everyday occurrence for many people.

3 Complete each sentence with a preposition and a verb from each list, making any necessary changes.

   Prepositions: about   at   for   in   of
   Verbs: have   improve   memorize   remember   remind

   a Some people are better _____ new words for a test than others.
   b Some people have such good memories that they are capable _____ hundreds of facts.
   c If you are interested _____ your memory, there are lots of methods you can try which guarantee success.
   d Don't worry _____ a bad memory – it may be determined by your genes.
   e Secretaries are responsible _____ their bosses about meetings.

4 How many expressions do you know in English which express how much or how little we like something, e.g. *enjoy, can't stand*? Make a list. Then, put them in order from extreme liking to extreme disliking.

5 Work in pairs. Tell your partner about your likes and dislikes, using your list of verbs and expressions in **4**. Think about films, music, sports, travel, food and other people.

   Example: *I can't stand people interrupting me while I'm eating.*

Gerunds and infinitives
▸ Grammar reference page 166

6 Some verbs are followed by the gerund, others by the infinitive. Choose the correct verb in these sentences.
   a We just managed *to catch / catching* the bus.
   b We've arranged *to meet / meeting* outside the cinema.
   c Have you considered *to change / changing* jobs?
   d I expect *to be / being* home before nine o'clock.
   e You will risk *to lose / losing* your job if you tell your boss what you think of her.
   f He learned *to play / playing* golf when he was five.
   g I hope you didn't agree *to lend / lending* her any money!
   h The woman admitted *to drive / driving* over the speed limit.
   i I pretended *to understand / understanding* what he was saying.
   j We can't afford *to buy / buying* a new car.

unit 6 the mind

7 Some verbs can be followed by either the gerund or the infinitive. In some cases, there is a difference in meaning. In a–d match sentences A and B with the correct meanings, 1 or 2.

Example: **A** I've **tried taking** the pills but I still can't sleep.
B I've **tried to take** the pills but I just can't swallow them.
1 I've made an effort to do the action.
2 I've done the action as an experiment.

a **A** I *stopped to speak* to Richard to ask him about the weekend.
B I *stopped speaking* to Richard after he lied to me.
1 I finished an activity.
2 I interrupted one activity to do another.

b **A** I *regret to tell you* that I am unable to offer you the job.
B I *regret telling her* I was sacked from my last job.
1 I am sorry about something I did in the past.
2 I am sorry about something I am doing.

c **A** He *went on talking*, even after he'd been told to keep quiet.
B After he'd outlined the problems, he *went on to talk* about his solutions.
1 He continued to do the action.
2 He finished one activity and started another.

d **A** I *don't remember inviting* him. Are you sure you didn't?
B I *didn't remember to invite* him. Sorry, but I forgot.
1 I didn't do what I intended to do.
2 I have no recollection of doing this.

8 Complete these sentences with a gerund or infinitive.

a I hope he's remembered _____ the tickets.
b UK Air regrets _____ the late arrival of flight UA127.
c He's tried _____ the window, but it's stuck.
d Will you stop _____ while I'm talking?
e She doesn't remember _____ to babysit.
f He's tried _____ less but he hasn't lost weight.
g Do you regret _____ school at sixteen?

Exam practice

Key word transformation

Tip

You can use contractions but remember they count as the number of words they would be if they were not contracted. For example, *didn't* and *I'll* are counted as two words, *can't* is counted as one.

9 For questions 1–6, complete the second sentence so that it has a similar meaning to the first sentence, using the word given. Do not change the word given. You must use between two and five words, including the word given.

1 I hate it when people interrupt me when I'm talking.
STAND
I _____ me when I'm talking.

2 It worries me that I'll arrive late for the interview.
TIME
I am worried about not _____ for the interview.

3 At school I found it impossible to remember historical dates.
GOOD
At school I was _____ historical dates.

4 I've told John I'll meet him inside the restaurant.
ARRANGED
I've _____ inside the restaurant.

5 They didn't have enough money to go abroad on holiday last year.
AFFORD
They _____ abroad on holiday last year.

6 Joanne wishes she had stayed on at school.
REGRETS
Joanne _____ her education.

Speaking Parts 3 & 4

Exam practice

Collaborative task

1 🔊 1.26 Work with a partner. Listen and make a note of what you have to do in the first phase of the task. Then, do the task with your partner. You have two minutes to do this.

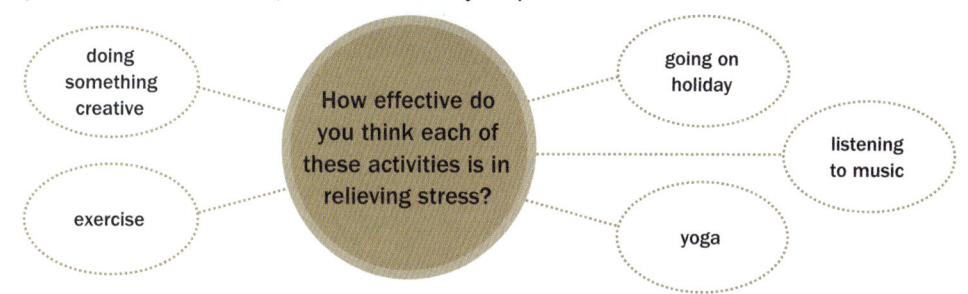

- doing something creative
- exercise
- going on holiday
- listening to music
- yoga

How effective do you think each of these activities is in relieving stress?

2 Now spend a minute deciding which two activities you think are most effective.

Exam skills

> **Tip**
>
> Listen carefully to what your partner says. The examiner may ask you the same question, so you should be prepared to agree or disagree with what your partner says.

3 🔊 1.27 Listen to two candidates answering these Part 4 questions. What reasons do they give to support their answers?
   a Do you agree that living in a city is more stressful than living in the country?
   b Do you think people today are more or less stressed than they were in the past?
   c Is it always a good thing to be relaxed?

4 🔊 1.28 Listen to these extracts from the interview. Complete the sentences.
   a Well, _____: first of all, _____ many cities nowadays …
   b This is stressful _____ they usually have to travel on crowded trains …
   c … _____ people live much closer together in cities, there is a …
   d Nowadays, they have to be all those things, _____ work as well.
   e I think _____ people feel more stressed today is because …
   f _____, I think technology has made life today more stressful.
   g _____, pilots need to be alert during take off and landing.
   h … surgeons, _____, and air traffic controllers.
   i _____ are people's lives in their hands, _____ …
   j And we mustn't _____ when people are driving.

5 Which of the words and phrases in **4** introduces …
   a a reason?   b an example?   c additional information?

Pronunciation

6 🔊 1.29 In English we sometimes link words together. Listen and repeat.

   but also   for example   forget about   not only   one of

7 Why are the words above linked together, but not these words?

   air traffic controllers   more stressful   people's lives

8 🔊 1.30 Which words would be linked in these sentences? Check your answers and repeat.
   a First of all, because many cities nowadays are huge, people spend a lot of time just getting to and from their workplace.
   b People work and sleep at different times so there is bound to be conflict here.

Exam practice

Discussion

9 🔊 1.31 Listen and make a note of these Part 4 questions. Then, discuss your answers with a partner. Try to use some of the language in **5** above.

unit 6 the mind

Reading and Use of English Part 6

Exam skills 1 Read this short text. What or who do the words in *italics* refer to?

Volker Sommer, Professor of Evolutionary Anthropology at University College, London, carried out research into how chimpanzees use sticks to avoid being bitten by the army ants they are trying to eat. In order to do *so*, *he* travelled to Nigeria's Gashaka Gumti national park. *There*, chimpanzees and army ants and sticks are plentiful – *the former* use *the latter* to dip into nests for the ants. *His* studies showed that the ants respond to predatory chimpanzees by streaming to the surface to defend *their* colony through painful bites. In response to *this*, chimpanzees typically harvest army ants with stick tools, thereby minimizing the bites *they* receive.

Exam practice

Gapped text 2 You are going to read an article about animal behaviour. Six sentences have been removed from the article. Choose from the sentences A–G the one which fits each gap (1–6). There is one extra sentence which you do not need to use.

A This use of a third individual to achieve a goal is only one of the many tricks commonly used by apes.

B When she looked and found nothing, she 'walked back, hit me over the head with her hand and ignored me for the rest of the day'.

C The ability of animals to deceive and cheat may be a better measure of their intelligence than their use of tools.

D So the psychologists talked to colleagues who studied apes and asked them if they had noticed this kind of deception.

E The psychologists who saw the incident are sure that he intended to get the potato.

F Of course, it's possible that he could have learned from humans that such behaviour works, without understanding why.

G Such behaviour, developed over hundreds of thousands of years, is instinctive and completely natural.

> **Tip**
> As you read all the missing sentences, underline any reference words, such as names, pronouns and times.

Over to you 3 Discuss these questions.

a Did you play tricks on your brothers and sisters when you were a child? Do you regret your behaviour now?

b Have you ever tried to deceive any of the following people? Why and how did you do it? What were the consequences?

a boss   a customs officer   a friend   a parent   a partner   a teacher

Nature's cheats

Anna is digging in the ground for a potato, when along comes Paul. Paul looks to see what Anna's doing and then, seeing that there is no one in sight, starts to scream as loud as he can. Paul's angry mother rushes over and chases Anna away. Once his mum has gone, Paul walks over and helps himself to Anna's potato.

Does this ring a bell? I'm sure it does. We've all experienced annoying tricks when we were young – the brother who stole your toys and then got you into trouble by telling your parents you had hit him. But Anna and Paul are not humans. They're African baboons, and playing tricks is as much a part of monkey behaviour as it is of human behaviour.

Throughout nature, tricks like this are common – they are part of daily survival. There are insects that hide from their enemies by looking like leaves or twigs, and harmless snakes that imitate poisonous ones. **1** Some animals, however, go further and use a more deliberate kind of deception – they use normal behaviour to trick other animals. In most cases the animal probably doesn't know it is deceiving, only that certain actions give it an advantage. But in apes and some monkeys, the behaviour seems much more like that of humans.

What about Paul the baboon? His scream and his mother's attack on Anna could have been a matter of chance, but Paul was later seen playing the same trick on others. **2** Another tactic is the 'Look behind you!' trick. When one young male baboon was attacked by several others, he stood on his back legs and looked into the distance, as if there was an enemy there. The attackers turned to look behind them and lost interest in their victim. In fact, there was no enemy.

Studying behaviour like this is complicated because it is difficult to do laboratory experiments to test whether behaviour is intentional. It would be easy to suggest that these cases mean the baboons were deliberately tricking other animals, but they might have learned the behaviour without understanding how it worked. **3** They discovered many liars and cheats, but the cleverest were apes who clearly showed that they intended to deceive and knew when they themselves had been deceived.

An amusing example of this comes from a psychologist working in Tanzania. A young chimp was annoying him, so he tricked her into going away by pretending he had seen something interesting in the distance. **4**

Another way to decide whether an animal's behaviour is deliberate is to look for actions that are not normal for that animal. A zoo worker describes how a gorilla dealt with an enemy. 'He slowly crept up behind the other gorilla, walking on tiptoe. When he got close to his enemy, he pushed him violently in the back, then ran indoors.' Wild gorillas do not normally walk on tiptoe. **5** But looking at the many cases of deliberate deception in apes, it is impossible to explain them all as simple imitation.

Taking all the evidence into account, it seems that deception does play an important part in ape societies where there are complex social rules and relationships and where problems are better solved by social pressure than by physical conflict. **6** Studying the intelligence of our closest relatives could be the way to understand the development of human intelligence.

Vocabulary

Think ahead

1 Work in pairs. Discuss these questions.
- How much sleep do you need each night? How much do you normally get?
- What happens if you don't get enough sleep?
- What is your favourite sleeping position?
- Do you ever have a nap during the day?

2 What advice would you give someone who suffers from insomnia?

3 Read this short text, ignoring the words in *italics*. Are any of your ideas in **2** mentioned?

It is difficult to sleep [1] *strongly / soundly* if you are stressed and worried. If your mind races as soon as your head hits the pillow, you need to [2] *meet / face* the problem before you go to sleep. It may help to actually write down what your [3] *deepest / hardest* anxieties are and try to think of solutions. Reading or watching a video can also help as it distracts you – not TV, as it indicates what time it is. The later it gets, the more anxious you may become.

Collocations

4 Choose the correct collocation from the words in *italics* in the text in **3**.

5 Choose the adjective which collocates with the noun in each of these sentences.
- a Susan is a *near / close / main* friend.
- b Armed robbery is a *significant / severe / serious* crime.
- c Digging is *hard / strong / heavy* work.
- d There will be *hard / strong / heavy* rain in the north.
- e Truancy is a(n) *important / serious / hard* problem.
- f Traffic is usually *heavy / strong / serious* during the rush hour.
- g We were almost blown over by the *hard / strong / heavy* wind.

6 The adverbs below all mean 'with intensity'. Match each adverb with an appropriate verb.

Adverbs: attentively   hard (2)   heavily   passionately   soundly
Verbs: argue   drink   listen   sleep   think   work

7 For each of these sentences, cross out the verb which does not collocate with the noun.
- a I'm *sitting / performing / taking* my exam in June.
- b We need to *reach / acquire / find* a solution.
- c Can I *say / give / express* an opinion?
- d The increase in traffic is *causing / creating / making* a problem.
- e Have you *made / chosen / reached* a decision yet?
- f We *set up / started / made* the business three years ago.

8 Use the verbs *catch*, *keep* and *put* to form collocations with the words and phrases in *italics* making any necessary changes. Then, discuss the questions in pairs.
- a Do you find it hard to _____ *a secret*?
- b On average, how many *colds* do you _____ a year? How do you treat them?
- c If you _____ *sight* of someone you didn't like, what would you do?
- d Have you ever _____ *your foot in it* really badly?
- e How do you _____ *costs down* when you're planning a holiday?
- f How good are you at _____ *a name* to a band you hear on the radio?

9 Which verb, *make* or *do*, is used with each of these phrases?

business with sb   the cooking   damage   a decision   an effort   exercises
fun of sb   a fuss   the housework   a job   a mistake   money   a noise
a profit   progress   research   sb an offer   a suggestion   trouble   your best

10 Complete these questions with *make* or *do* in the correct form. Then, discuss the questions with a partner.

a Who _____ the cooking in your house? Why?
b How good are you at _____ decisions?
c If your next door neighbours _____ too much noise, what would you do?
d If someone _____ fun of you, how do you respond?

11 Quickly read the text below, ignoring the gaps. How many hours of sleep do most people say they need?

Exam practice

Multiple-choice cloze **12** For questions 1–8, read the text below and decide which answer (A, B, C or D) best fits each gap. There is an example at the beginning (0).

Sleep

By the time we **(0)** *reach* old age, most of us have spent 20 years sleeping. **(1)** _____ nobody knows why we do it. Most scientists believe that when we sleep, we allow time for **(2)** _____ maintenance work to be done. Any **(3)** _____ there is can be put right more quickly if energy isn't being used up doing other things.

Sleep is controlled by certain chemicals, the effects of which we can alter to some extent: caffeine helps to **(4)** _____ us awake, while alcohol and some medicines make us sleepy.

Scientists have **(5)** _____ that when we first drop off everything slows down. Then, after about 90 minutes we go into what is **(6)** _____ REM* sleep, which is a **(7)** _____ that we've started to dream. You have dreams every night, even if you don't remember them.

Most people say they need eight hours' sleep every night, while others seem to **(8)** _____ on much less. One thing is certain; we all need some sleep.

*REM = Rapid Eye Movement

Tip

Look at the four options A, B, C and D and the words on either side of the gap. There may be a grammatical reason why some choices are not possible.

0	A arrive	B reach	C become	D get
1	A After all	B Generally	C Yet	D Therefore
2	A main	B elementary	C needed	D essential
3	A damage	B suffering	C harm	D hurt
4	A stay	B keep	C make	D maintain
5	A looked	B researched	C discovered	D watched
6	A named	B called	C known	D labelled
7	A message	B proof	C signal	D show
8	A need	B manage	C get	D deal

(B reach is circled)

Over to you **13** Discuss these questions.

a Do you remember your dreams when you wake up?
b Do you ever have recurring dreams or nightmares?

unit 6 the mind

77

Writing Part 1

Think ahead

1. What makes you happy? Rank these happiness factors from 1 (most important) to 5 (least important). Add any other factors to your list. Then, compare your views with a partner.

   a good family life   a good relationship with people   a good social life
   a lot of money   having a good job

2. Read this example of a Writing Part 1 task and the response that follows, ignoring the words in *italics*. Do you agree with the writer's views?

   In your English class you have been talking about what makes people happy.

   Now, your English teacher has asked you to write an essay.

   Write an **essay** using all the notes and give reasons for your point of view.

   Write your **essay** in 140–190 words.

   Essay question

   'Money doesn't bring you happiness. There are other more important happiness factors.' Do you agree?

   Notes

   Things to write about:

   1. people
   2. work
   3. _____ (your own idea)

It is probably true to (1) *mention / say / tell* that most people believe that if they were rich they would be happy. The question is whether money makes people happy or whether there are other factors which contribute more to happiness. There is no actual proof that being rich makes people happy. In fact, evidence seems to show the (2) *different / contrast / opposite*: some billionaires suffer from depression, and more than one lottery winner has regretted their win. There are (3) *several / few / more* other happiness factors we need to consider. People are important. Human beings are social beings and we feel happiest when we are not alone. A stable family life and a (4) *gang / circle / crowd* of good friends are also important. Work too can make us happy. If we have a job which gives us a sense of fulfilment, this can also give us a feeling of well-being. However, possibly it's the (5) *simplest / easiest / smallest* pleasures that bring us most happiness: things like reading a good book or walking in the sunshine. In summary, in my view, money may (6) *provide / contribute / bring* us short-lived happiness. Long-term happiness depends on a combination of other factors which will probably vary from person to person.

3. Read the text again and …
   - divide the essay into four paragraphs.
   - choose the correct options to complete the text.
   - underline the topic sentences.
   - decide if the supporting statements give examples, reasons or explanations.

Exam skills

4 Read these sentences. First, identify the punctuation marks in blue. Then, decide why each one has been used.

a John Paul Getty Jr, despite being a billionaire, suffered from depression.
b My next-door-neighbour won the lottery last Saturday.
c Not surprisingly, most people would be happy if they won a large sum of money.
d I would be happy if I had the following: a good job, a nice house and a new car.
e One of the most recent films about money is 'Slumdog Millionaire'. It tells the story of a young Indian man who wins a fortune on a quiz show. It's an excellent film and was awarded eight Oscars in 2009.
f Although he was extremely well off, his wealth did not bring him happiness.

5 Divide this text into three paragraphs. Then, add the appropriate punctuation where necessary.

The american rock legend Kurt Cobain was born on february 20th 1967 in the state of Washington He formed Nirvana in 1987 and the band broke into the mainstream with Smells like Teen Spirit in 1991. although he went on to achieve worldwide success Cobain remained a deeply troubled man. Cobains problems started from an early age His parents who had a stormy marriage finally divorced when he was nine. Cobain lived first with his father, until he remarried, and then with his mother. However he did not get on with his new step-father, who he couldnt stand. Having got into drugs when he was still a teenager Cobain was never able to kick the habit. Tragically he took his own life in 1994. He was just 27 years of age.

Over to you

6 Do you know of any other people who have or have had wealth and success, but have been deeply troubled?

Exam practice

Essay

▶ *Writing guide* page 178

Tip

First, decide if you agree or disagree with the statement. Then, think of one or two ideas for each of the points under 'Things to write about', remembering to add your own idea.

7 Read this Writing Part 1 task. Then, work through stages a–f.

In your English class you have been talking about stress.

Now, your English teacher has asked you to write an **essay**.

Write an essay using all the notes and give reasons for your point of view.

Write your **essay** in 140–190 words.

Essay question

'Life today is extremely stressful for most people.' Do you agree?

Notes

Things to write about:

1. work
2. family
3. _____ (your own idea)

a Think about whether you agree or disagree with the statement.
b Think of a couple of ideas for each of the prompts and make a note of these.
c Think about what to include as your own idea.
d Plan your introduction. Remember it shouldn't simply repeat the exam rubric.
e Plan what you will include in each of your paragraphs.
f When you have finished, read through your answer checking grammar, spelling and punctuation.

Unit 6 Review

1 For questions 1–8, read the text below. Use the word given in capitals at the end of some of the lines to form a word that fits in the gap in the same line. There is an example at the beginning (0).

TELEPATHY

Results of a recent survey show that one third of Americans believe in telepathy – that is (0) *communication* between two people without using any of the five senses. Twenty-five per cent claim to have (1) _____ had a telepathic experience. Knowing who's on the phone when it rings is probably the most common everyday experience of this kind. Yet (2) _____ guessing who is on the phone before you answer it should hardly be a matter of great surprise. Given the (3) _____ number of people who call any one of us in a year, and given our (4) _____ of how long it is since someone last called us, we could make a (5) _____ guess as to who will ring us next.

Laboratory results are also (6) _____ with anecdotal accounts. Even professional mind-readers fail to repeat what seem extraordinary results under (7) _____ conditions. No experiment has shown results higher than would be predicted by the laws of (8) _____.

COMMUNICATE
ACTUAL

CORRECT
LIMIT
KNOW
SENSE

CONSIST

SCIENCE
PROBABLE

2 Complete these sentences with the correct forms of the verbs in brackets.

a Don't forget _____ (post) this letter, will you? It's very important.
b When you've finished _____ (clear) the table, can you tidy your room?
c Job applicants should be good at _____ (deal) with people and should be prepared _____ (work) at weekends.
d The groom thanked everyone for coming and then went on _____ (say) how happy he was.
e Will you stop _____ (use) my pen and buy your own?
f I didn't expect _____ (get) such a good mark in the exam.
g You can't avoid _____ (meet) people you don't like if you live in a village.
h I don't know if I want the job. It will mean _____ (move) to London.

3 Choose the correct alternative in these sentences.

a He was sleeping so *soundly / hard* that he didn't hear the explosion.
b The opposite of *heavy / strong* tea is 'weak' tea, but the opposite of a *strong / severe* wind is a 'light' wind.
c The toothache was so *severe / strong* that I just wanted the tooth taken out.
d I've got a suggestion to *put / make*.
e I have such a *hard / heavy* work schedule at the moment that I don't have much free time.
f After several hours someone *came up with / carried out* a solution to the problem.
g I had a *strong / hard* suspicion that he was lying to me.

Unit 7　Free time

Introduction

1 **Discuss these questions.**
   a In your free time, do you do any activities similar to those shown in the photos?
   b Which of these activities do / would you particularly enjoy or not enjoy doing?
   c Approximately how much free time do you have in an average week?
   d Do you ever find that you have too much free time?

2 **Tick all the statements a–d that apply to you.**
   a I spend most of my time doing things I have to do.
   b If I'm not doing something creative, I feel that I'm wasting my time.
   c I think that free time and leisure activities are overrated.
   d At the end of a typical week I'm too tired to go out and have fun.

Reading and Use of English Part 5

Think ahead 1 Which of the activities below do you sometimes do while studying or working? Tick the activities that apply to you. Then, compare your answers with a partner.
- Contact friends or put messages on social networking sites. ☐
- Text, phone or email friends. ☐
- Play games on your computer or smartphone. ☐
- Listen to music. ☐
- Watch TV programmes. ☐
- Shop online. ☐

2 Discuss these questions.
   a Do you think it is becoming more common for people to mix leisure with their study or work? If so, why is this happening?
   b Do you think people should be allowed to mix leisure with study or work? If not, who should stop them? How could they be stopped?
   c How might mixing leisure with study or work affect the following groups?
   - students   • employees   • employers

Exam practice

Multiple choice 3 You are going to read an article about a phenomenon called 'weisure'. For questions 1–6, choose the answer (A, B, C or D) which you think fits best according to the text.

> **Tip**
> You only need to read the whole text once. Then, when you're answering each question, just read the part of the text where the information you want should be.

1 What does Dalton Conley expect to happen in the future?
   A More people will give up working regular hours.
   B More people will enjoy their jobs.
   C More people will combine work and enjoyment.
   D More people will work from home.

2 What does Dalton Conley say about the 1950s?
   A There were well-known codes of behaviour.
   B People were not certain about rules at work.
   C People did not enjoy their jobs.
   D It was acceptable for people to be friends with business partners.

3 How have working patterns changed in recent times?
   A More people are working at home.
   B People need to work more for economic reasons.
   C There are more rich people than there were.
   D Some people are having to work longer hours than in the past.

4 Who, according to Conley, belongs to the 'creative class'?
   A people whose job it is to make things
   B people who find their work satisfying
   C people who use computers at work
   D people who promote social networking sites

5 What is Conley referring to by using the word 'backlash' in line 49?
   A the fact that people are losing their private lives
   B social problems caused by politicians and bankers
   C the response to the mixing of work and leisure
   D the idea that weisure is changing the way people live

6 How does Conley see the future of weisure?
   A More people will turn against the idea.
   B He believes the situation will remain as it is now.
   C We will return to a more traditional approach to work.
   D More people will adopt this way of life.

Welcome to the 'weisure' lifestyle

The line dividing work and leisure time is blurring before our eyes, says one expert, and a phenomenon called 'weisure time' is being created. Many people who haven't already given up the nine-to-five working day for the twenty-four seven life of weisure will probably do so soon, according to sociologist Dalton Conley, who coined the term. According to Conley, it is no longer clear what is work and what is fun in an office, at home or out in the street, and it is becoming increasingly difficult to say whether activities and social spaces are more connected to work or play. These worlds that were once very distinct are now merging.

Conley uses the 1950s as a point of reference. 'Back then, there were certain rules,' he says, 'such as "don't do business with friends", and "keep work and leisure separate". That has completely changed.' However, there are limits: the merging of work and leisure does not mean, for example, that bankers are working on complex financial matters during their children's parties. But it does mean that more and more people are using smartphones and other new technology to contact business colleagues while they are with their families or to chat with Facebook friends during an office meeting.

So, what happened and why do people want to mix work and play? First of all, according to Conley, there's more work and less play than there was in the past. 'For the first time in history, the higher up the economic ladder you go, the more likely you are to have an extremely long working week,' he says. Busy people often want to save time by being involved in business and pleasure simultaneously. Obviously, many opportunities for that are offered by the internet.

At the same time, Conley says, people are more willing to let work invade their leisure time because, for many, work has become fun. Conley refers to professionals who get more enjoyment out of work as 'the creative class' because their work involves ideas, perhaps helping create a new software product or an advertising campaign. This makes their job interesting and fun; they enjoy their work and so choose to spend much of their time working. Conley points out that it is no coincidence that weisure has been growing with the popularity of personal computers. Many professionals have the more boring parts of their jobs done by computers, making many of their jobs more interesting.

Weisure has been fed by social networking sites, where 'friends' may actually be business partners or colleagues. 'Social networking is a strange activity,' Conley says. 'It's fun, but also an essential part of our knowledge-based society.' Networking sites give us many ways of doing business and having fun.

Although there are clear benefits, what is disturbing is the idea that we will be changed by weisure. 'We are losing our so-called private life,' Conley says. 'There's less time to relax if we're always mixing work and leisure.' But, if you're thinking that a backlash may be around the corner for the weisure concept, you're right. In fact, according to Conley, it has already begun. It is evident in the rise of alternative social movements involving people 'who live in a more environmentally conscious way,' he says. But, he believes that unless we are sent back to the Stone Age by a natural disaster of some kind, there's no turning back the clock on the spread of weisure.

4 Look at these extracts from the text. What do the words and phrases in *italics* mean?

a The line dividing work and leisure time is *blurring* before our eyes. (line 1)

b These worlds that were once very distinct are now *merging*. (line 10)

c … the higher up *the economic ladder* you go, the more likely you are to have an extremely long working week … (line 24)

d … unless we are sent back to the *Stone Age* by a natural disaster of some kind, *there's no turning back the clock* on the spread of weisure. (lines 54–57)

Grammar

Passive verbs
▶ *Grammar reference* page 167

1 Underline the main verbs in these sentences from the text. Which are passive and which are active? Name the tenses.

   a … a phenomenon called 'weisure time' is being created.
   b … many opportunities for that are offered by the internet.
   c … what is disturbing is the idea that we will be changed by weisure.
   d We are losing our so-called private life …
   e … anger against the bankers and politicians who have been blamed for our social and economic problems.
   f … unless we are sent back to the Stone Age by a natural disaster of some kind, …

2 How do we form the passive?

3 Rewrite the sentences in **1** above, changing passive into active verbs and active into passive verbs. How do the changes you have made affect the meaning?

4 Who performs the action in these passive sentences?
   a All the work is done by unpaid volunteers.
   b Some employees are being encouraged by their managers to work from home.

5 Look back at the sentences in **1**. Who or what performs the action in each case? Why is this information not always included in passive sentences?

6 Complete the text below using the correct active or passive form of these verbs.

   book   equip   furnish   guarantee   have   include   locate
   make   reserve   serve

Hotel Donatella

A friendly atmosphere (1) _____ at the Donatella, a small family hotel, which (2) _____ in the ancient centre of the city. All fifteen bedrooms (3) _____ to a high standard and (4) _____ en suite facilities. Rooms (5) _____ with satellite TV, a mini-bar and direct-dial telephones. Two rooms (6) _____ for smokers. We (7) _____ breakfast, which (8) _____ in the price, between 7 a.m. and 10 a.m. Dinner is available between 7 p.m. and 11 p.m. and can (9) _____ at our main reception. A small charge (10) _____ for use of the hotel's private car park.

7 Rewrite this text, changing the verbs in *italics* into the passive and making any other necessary changes. Only include the person who performs the action if it is important.

Congratulations!

You have won an all-expenses-paid weekend for two in London.
One of our chauffeurs *will meet you* at Heathrow Airport and *drive you* into central London. We *will put you up* in a five-star hotel close to Harrods, the world's most famous department store. We *have reserved* a luxury suite for you on the tenth floor. In addition to this, the competition organizers *will be giving you* £20,000 'pocket money'. You *can spend* this money as you like.

unit 7 free time

have / get something done
▸ *Grammar reference* page 168

8 What is the difference in meaning between these sentences? Who does the boring parts of the job?
  a Today, many professionals do the more boring parts of their job.
  b The more boring parts of many professionals' jobs are done by computers.
  c Many professionals have the more boring parts of their jobs done by computers.

9 What are the different meanings of *have something done* in these two sentences?
  a I had my tooth filled.
  b He had his leg broken in a climbing accident.

10 Rewrite these sentences using *have* or *get*.
  Example: *The mechanic changed the oil in my car.*
  I had the oil in my car changed.
  a The hairdresser cut my hair in a completely different style.
  b A decorator has repainted our apartment.
  c An electrician is going to repair my video next week.
  d My jacket is being cleaned at a specialist cleaner's.
  e The town hall has just been rebuilt by the council.

11 Think of as many answers to these questions as you can.
  a What can you have done at the dentist's?
  b Why do people go to the hairdresser's?
  c Why do people take their cars to a garage?
  d If you didn't want people to recognize you, which features of your appearance would you have changed?

12 What do you have done for you, rather than doing for yourself? Make a list and compare your answers with other students.

> **Tip**
> Don't leave any unfilled gaps. If you are not sure, make a sensible guess.

Exam practice

Open cloze **13** Read the text below and think of the word that best fits each gap. Use only one word in each gap. There is an example at the beginning (0).

Playing music should be fun

What is the first thing that comes **(0)** ___to___ mind when you think about playing your instrument? If it's 'Oh, not again,' it's time you ask **(1)** _____ why you are feeling this way. First and foremost, playing music should be **(2)** _____ enjoyable experience, but learning how to play should be fun, too. I know from experience that time and effort **(3)** _____ required to enjoy an instrument to the full, so it is essential to make learning an enjoyable process. So, if you think you've lost the initial joy that **(4)** _____ felt when you started, here are a couple of ideas. Listen to your favourite artists and get back to why you wanted to learn to play. Alternatively, simply take **(5)** _____ your saxophone, guitar or other instrument and start playing. Just play and have fun! Technique can **(6)** _____ practised later. Alternatively, get together **(7)** _____ a group of musical friends and have a jam. There's nothing better **(8)** _____ playing with friends.

unit 7 free time

85

Vocabulary

Think ahead 1 Read these newspaper headlines. Match each headline to one of the sports symbols and name each sport.

A **KEEPER GETS RED CARD 3 MINUTES AFTER KICK-OFF**

D **DISASTER AFTER PIT STOP FOR WHEEL CHANGE**

G **VITAL SECONDS LOST IN HANDLEBAR MIX-UP**

B **Finalist let down by unreliable serve**

E **GOLD FOR BRITISH SPRINTER**

H **Fans riot after heavyweight knocked out in first round**

C **Three holes to win The US Open**

F **Slam-dunk wins game**

Sports vocabulary 2 What is the name for the person who does each of the sports you have listed?

Example: Someone who does athletics is an athlete.

3 What equipment is associated with these sports? Think of two or three essential items for each sport.

Example: tennis: racket, ball, net

4 Which sporting activities take place … ?

on: a circuit   a course   a court   a pitch   a (race)track

in: a gym   a pool   a ring   a rink

5 Read this text and choose the best option (A, B, C or D) to fill each gap.

> To be good at whatever sport you (1) _____, you need to (2) _____ a lot of time and energy on it. Professional footballers, for example, need to develop particular (3) _____, like passing the ball and tackling, but they also need to improve their stamina and general (4) _____. They (5) _____ most days, which usually involves running round the (6) _____ and doing lots of exercises.

1	A do	B make	C practise	D take
2	A dedicate	B devote	C give	D spend
3	A talents	B qualities	C skills	D gifts
4	A state	B fitness	C shape	D format
5	A prepare	B train	C perform	D rehearse
6	A pitch	B route	C circuit	D course

Over to you 6 Discuss these questions.

a Which sports and activities have you actually taken part in yourself?

b Which are your favourite and least favourite sports? Give reasons for your choices.

c Which sports and activities do you enjoy watching live or on TV?

unit 7 free time

Speaking Part 3

Exam skills

1 Work in pairs. Read these Part 3 prompts. Talk to your partner about how popular these activities would be with students as after-school leisure activities.

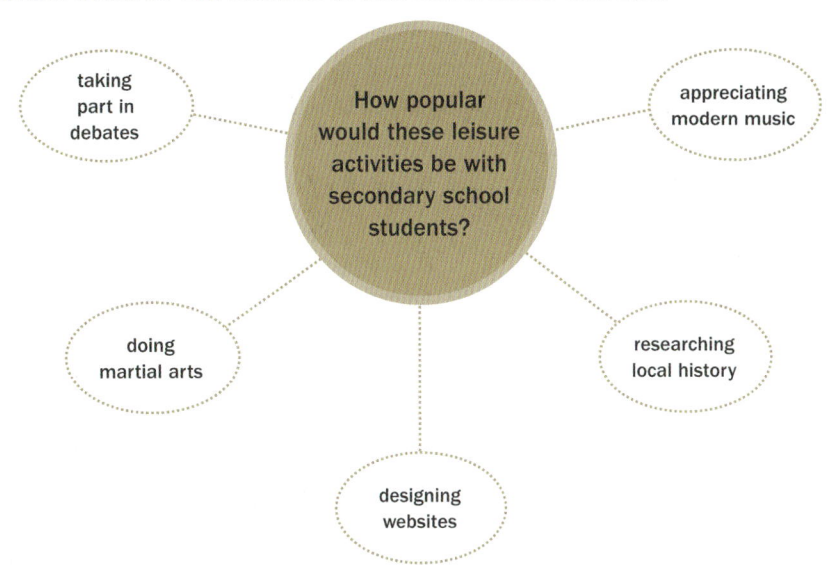

- taking part in debates
- appreciating modern music
- doing martial arts
- researching local history
- designing websites

How popular would these leisure activities be with secondary school students?

2 🔊 2.01 Listen to two candidates doing a Part 3 task. Answer these questions.
   a What arguments do the candidates put forward for and against martial arts?
   b Which two activities do they suggest would be most popular with students?

3 🔊 2.01 Listen again. How do the speakers express how certain or uncertain they are? Complete these extracts. Contractions count as one word, not two.
   a Yes, _____ (1 word) but only with a few people. Karate's like fighting…
   b It's also a way of keeping fit, so it _____ (1 word) be popular with more people than you think.
   c If you ask me, _____ (2 words) appreciating modern music would be really popular.
   d But if it was modern pop music, I _____ (1 word) it would attract a lot of interest.
   e But I _____ (3 words) how you would appreciate it.
   f I _____ (2 words) most people I know showing any interest in those kinds of subjects at all.
   g _____ (3 words) they'd find debates really boring.

Pronunciation

4 🔊 2.02 Listen to these sentences spoken by native speakers.
   a How many words do you hear in 1–5?
   b How are the words *a*, *an*, *but*, *could*, *to*, *be*, *was*, *and* and *of* pronounced?

Exam practice

Collaborative task

5 Work with a partner. Turn to page 157 and follow the instructions.

> **Tip**
>
> Listen carefully to what your partner says and agree or disagree with them in an appropriate way.

unit 7 free time

87

Reading and Use of English Part 1

Exam skills

1 In Reading and Use of English Part 1, a correct answer may depend on a preposition which follows the gap in the text. Answer questions a–d.

a Which verb comes before *with* in this sentence: *make*, *do*, *go* or *get*?
I'm really thirsty. I could _____ with a drink.

b Which verb comes before *of* in this sentence: *fright*, *worry*, *anxiety* or *fear*?
He's had a _____ of heights ever since he fell from a tree aged seven.

c Which adjective is followed by *of* in this sentence: *able*, *skilled*, *capable* or *fit*?
I'm sure you're quite _____ of passing. You just need to keep revising.

d The preposition may not come immediately after the gap. Which of these verbs comes before *somebody of + -ing* in this sentence: *blamed*, *accused*, *charged* or *criticized*?
They _____ the driver of the lorry of causing the accident.

"LET ME EXPLAIN SOMETHING ABOUT FLEXTIME. YOU STILL HAVE TO SHOW UP FOR WORK ONCE IN A WHILE."

Tip

First, try to eliminate the answers which are not possible grammatically. Then, if you are still not sure which is the correct answer, choose the one which sounds more likely.

2 Which prepositions are normally used with these words?

Verbs:	approve … sth	compare sth … sth	forgive sb … sth	pay … sth
Nouns:	an awareness … sth	amazement … sth	enthusiasm … sth	
	interest … sth			
Adjectives:	jealous … sb	keen … sth	late … sth	right … sth

Exam practice

Multiple-choice cloze

3 For questions 1–8, read the text below and decide which answer (A, B, C or D) best fits each gap. There is an example at the beginning (0).

Recharge your batteries

Working all year without a holiday is **(0)** _similar_ to driving a car for 12 months without changing the oil. You might keep going, but you are probably **(1)** _____ for a breakdown.

Holidays are an easy time to recharge your batteries and **(2)** _____ for the next challenge. But a recent study came up with an interesting finding – less than a third of Americans are planning to go on holiday this year. Maybe those people who aren't having a **(3)** _____ from work are employed by firms that are not holiday-friendly.

It is certainly **(4)** _____ considering holiday time when you are looking for work, even if it may not be at the **(5)** _____ of your list of items to ask about. While many job-seekers may feel very reluctant to **(6)** _____ about holiday plans at interviews or during salary negotiations, some younger workers don't **(7)** _____ to negotiate extra free time. **(8)** _____, many of them ask for additional weeks of holiday in exchange for a slightly lower salary.

0	A like	B similar	C compared	D identical
1	A going	B moving	C heading	D travelling
2	A prepare	B arrange	C practise	D organize
3	A gap	B pause	C stop	D break
4	A merit	B worth	C sensible	D reasonable
5	A peak	B first	C top	D height
6	A mention	B comment	C remark	D talk
7	A hesitate	B doubt	C wonder	D question
8	A However	B In fact	C Yet	D So

unit 7 free time

Listening Part 1

Tip

When you hear the recording for the second time, check your ideas and make your final choice. If you don't know the answer, make a guess.

Think ahead

1 Look at the photos on this page and discuss these questions.
   a What different kinds of music can you think of, e.g. classical, jazz?
   b In what situations do people listen to or hear music?
   c Other than enjoyment, what reasons do people have for listening to music?

Exam practice

Multiple choice

2 🔊 2.03 You will hear people talking in eight different situations. For questions 1–8, choose the best answer (A, B or C).

1 You hear someone being interviewed. What question are they answering?
   A What different kinds of music do you enjoy?
   B Where do you go to listen to music?
   C What is your favourite type of music?

2 You hear someone describing an event she went to. What kind of event was it?
   A an opera
   B the film version of a musical
   C a rock concert

3 You hear someone describing something she finds annoying. What is she describing?
   A the use of personal stereos in public
   B a particularly noisy type of music
   C increasing levels of noise pollution

4 You hear the presenter of a radio programme talking. What kind of programme does he present?
   A a phone-in programme
   B a request programme
   C a top-twenty hits programme

5 You hear someone talking about their favourite situation for listening to music. What situation is this?
   A when he's on a long train journey
   B when he's on a long walk
   C when he's driving his car

6 You will hear someone talking about a common human experience. What is this experience?
   A trying hard to remember a past event
   B remembering a past event without trying
   C remembering the first time you heard a song

7 You hear a man talking about somewhere he has just been. Where was this?
   A the doctor's
   B the dentist's
   C a concert

8 You hear someone talking about the beneficial effects of music. Who is the speaker?
   A a teacher
   B a musician
   C a doctor

Over to you

3 Discuss these questions.
   a One of the speakers talks about memories associated with a particular song. Are there any songs that have special associations for you? Can you remember the situation you were in when you first heard the song?
   b How important is music to you? Where and when do you listen to music?

unit 7 free time

89

Writing Part 2 – Email / letter

Think ahead 1 Discuss these questions with a partner.
  a On what occasions or for what reasons do people write formal letters these days?
  b When was the last time you wrote a formal letter? What was its purpose?
  c Why are people writing more or fewer formal letters than in the past?

Exam skills 2 Read this example of a Part 2 task and answer the questions.
  a What is the main purpose of the letter?
  b What information should be included?
  c How formal or informal should the style be?

> You see this advertisement on a college noticeboard.
>
> **Part-time staff needed**
>
> Do you enjoy computer work?
>
> Do you have a good range of computer skills?
>
> Do you have 10–20 hours a week free?
>
> If you answered yes to these questions, write to us asking for more information and giving details of your relevant experience and suitability for the job.
>
> Write your **letter** in 140–190 words.

3 Read this letter written in answer to the task. Is the relevant information included, and is the style appropriate?

> Dear Sir / Madam,
>
> I am writing to express my interest in the post which was advertised on the college noticeboard. I am particularly attracted to doing work which involves computers and I would welcome the opportunity to work for your organization.
>
> I am currently doing a Business Studies course at the college, but have no doubt that I could devote at least 15 hours a week to this work if I was fortunate enough to be selected. I have had a keen interest in computers since the age of ten and believe myself to be a highly efficient user in a range of different situations. I have developed a wide range of skills including word processing and website design as well as the creation of spreadsheets and databases. I would be very willing to demonstrate my skills if I were to be called for interview.
>
> Should you require this information, I will be happy to provide you with references from a previous employer and from people who have known me for some time.
>
> I would be most grateful if you could send me further details about the post. Thank you for your consideration.
>
> Yours faithfully,

unit 7 free time

Formal vocabulary 4 The writer uses some quite formal language to impress the reader. Find words and phrases in the letter which mean roughly the same as these.

am certain   chosen   give   job   like the chance   lot of different   lucky
need   show what I can do   tell sb about   think   very interested

Word building 5 Rewrite these sentences replacing the underlined words and phrases with more formal equivalents which have similar meanings.
a I would <u>like</u> the chance to tell you about my past experience.
b I <u>think</u> my written English is <u>very good</u>.
c I could <u>give you</u> the names of two referees.
d Please let me know if there's any other information you <u>need</u>.
e I have <u>a lot of</u> skills which are relevant to this work.
f I <u>am sure</u> I would be suitable for this <u>job</u>.
g If I'm lucky enough to be <u>chosen</u> for interview, I'll definitely go.
h I could come at any time which is <u>good</u> for you.

Exam practice

Letter 6 You are going to write a formal letter. First, read the task below. Then, work through
▸ *Writing guide* page 180   stages a–e.

> **Tip**
> Remember to begin your letter in an appropriate way and give your reason for writing in your first sentence.

You have seen the following notice in an international student magazine.

Holiday work suitable for students

Do you have 10–20 hours a week free?

Would you be interested in paid holiday work?

Do you have experience of working with young people?

If you answered yes to these questions, write to us asking for more information and giving details of your relevant experience and suitability for the post.

Write your **letter** in 140–190 words.

a Which key points should you include in your letter?
b Decide on an appropriate style for your letter.
c Make a paragraph plan, using the sample answer on page 90 as a model.
d Write your letter. Use formal words and phrases to make it sound convincing.
e Finally, read through your letter, checking grammar, spelling and punctuation.

unit 7 free time

Unit 7 Review

1 Complete the second sentence so that it has a similar meaning to the first sentence, using the word given. Do not change the word given. Use between two and five words, including the word given.

1 If I'm not doing something creative, I feel I'm wasting my time.
   UNLESS
   I feel I'm wasting my time _____ something creative.

2 You will be instructed on how to produce fresh cheese.
   GIVEN
   You _____ on how to produce fresh cheese.

3 We've arranged for our car to be serviced next week.
   HAVING
   We _____ next week.

4 There's no point worrying about jet lag.
   WORTH
   Jet lag is _____.

5 Most of the machines at my local gym were not working.
   ORDER
   Most of the machines at my local gym _____.

6 It was five minutes before I found someone who could help.
   TOOK
   It _____ find someone who could help.

2 Rewrite the following sentences using passive verbs. Do not include an agent.
   a The store detective caught a middle-aged woman stealing a bag of potatoes.
   b He informed the manager of the store and he called the police.
   c The police arrived and took the woman to the police station.
   d They will probably charge her with shoplifting.
   e This is not the first time police have arrested the woman.
   f On the last occasion the court fined her £200.

3 Complete each sentence with the word for a piece of equipment and a place.
   a Tennis is played on a tennis _____. Players hit the ball with a _____.
   b Football is played on a _____. Players try to kick the ball into the _____.
   c Boxers wear _____ and fight their opponents in a _____.
   d Golf is played on a (golf) _____. Players hit a ball with _____s.
   e Ice-skating takes place at an ice _____. You have to wear _____s.

Unit 8 Media

Introduction

1 **Look at the photographs which show different media. Discuss these questions.**
   a How effective is each medium in communicating information and ideas?
   b Do you read newspapers? If so, which ones? What is your definition of a 'good newspaper'?
   c What are your favourite radio and TV programmes?
   d How often do you use the internet?

2 **Read these quotes about the media. Do you agree or disagree with each one?**

> The media's the most powerful entity on earth. They have the power to make the innocent guilty and to make the guilty innocent, and that's power. Because they control the minds of the masses.
> *(Malcolm X)*

> Don't hate the media, become the media.
> *(Jello Biafra)*

> What the mass media offers is not popular art, but entertainment which is intended to be consumed like food, forgotten, and replaced by a new dish.
> *(W.H. Auden)*

3 **Discuss these questions.**
   a How do people regard the media in your country? How could it be improved?
   b How do you think new technological developments will change the media in the future?

Listening Part 3

Think ahead

1 What do you use the internet for? Use these words to help you.

blog   bookmark   download   online   search engine   social media
surf   website

Exam practice

Multiple matching

Tip

The first time you hear the recording, listen for general understanding. Note key words and make a first choice of answers.

2 🔊 2.04 You will hear five short extracts in which people are talking about how they use the internet. For questions 1–5, choose from the list (A–H) which main use each speaker describes. Use the letters only once. There are three extra letters which you do not need to use.

A as a source of free entertainment
B as a way of saving money
C for watching TV programmes they missed
D for downloading books
E for communicating with people
F for making online purchases
G to help with studies
H as a way of making new friends

Speaker 1 [1]
Speaker 2 [2]
Speaker 3 [3]
Speaker 4 [4]
Speaker 5 [5]

Over to you

3 How will the internet develop during the next fifty years in relation to these areas?

entertainment   money   personal communications   politics   work

4 What dangers or problems could be associated with these future developments?

Grammar

Reporting statements
▸ Grammar reference page 169

1 Read these reported statements from the recording in **2** on page 94. What words did the original speakers actually use in each case?
   a My dad said the information was almost always out of date.
   b One of my friends said she'd once spent five hours looking for information.
   c I said I'd show my brother how to do it tomorrow.
   d They say they're losing sales because people aren't buying CDs any more.

2 Answer these questions about the reported statements from **1**.
   a What often happens to verb tenses in reported speech – for example in sentences b and c?
   b How is sentence d grammatically different from the other three sentences? How does this affect the meaning?

3 Report the statements made by the people in a–c. More than one answer may be possible.
   a George: 'I've always found what I'm looking for.'
   b Tom: 'I'm messaging my older brother who's in Thailand.'
   c Lucy: 'It takes me half an hour to get there on the bus and the shops are always really crowded.'

Reporting questions

4 Read these examples of reported questions. What other changes, in addition to verb tense changes, do we need to make when we report questions?
   a 'Have you got the CD in stock?'
      Mick asked if they had the CD in stock.
   b 'When did you order the new CD?'
      My friend asked me when I had ordered the new CD.

5 When do we use *if* in reported questions? What other word could we use instead of *if* in **4a** above?

6 Report these questions.
   a 'Do you have an email address?' the girl asked him.
   b 'Do you use the internet?' Val asked Rob.
   c 'How long have you been interested in jazz?' Nick asked me.
   d 'Which of your old school friends did you contact, Sharon?' Rachel asked.
   e 'Would you like to contact people you were at primary school with?' Julie asked Tim.
   f 'Can you show me how to use the printer?' Juan asked Maria.
   g 'Will you take me to the station?' Ali asked his father.

Time references

7 The sentence below can be reported in two ways. What is the difference in meaning between sentence a and sentence b?

   'I'll see you tomorrow,' Lizzie told Ben.

   a Lizzie told Ben she would see him the next day.
   b Lizzie told Ben she would see him tomorrow.

8 How could we change the following time references in reported speech?

   last week   next month   now   three days ago   today   tomorrow
   tonight   yesterday

Other references

9 What other references may change when we report speech? Look at these examples.
   a 'Do you think this meat is all right?' Terry asked his wife.
      Terry asked his wife if she thought the meat was all right.
   b 'Shall we eat here?' Carol asked Denise.
      Carol asked Denise if they should eat there.

unit 8 media

95

10 Report these sentences, making all necessary changes.

a 'Does this work have to be finished today, Mr Hunt?' Marsha asked.
b 'Were there any phone calls for me yesterday?' asked Mr Gilbert.
c 'This car was stolen two weeks ago,' the police officer informed Ian.
d 'I wrote to her last week, and I phoned this morning,' Dorothy said.
e 'I've arranged to meet them after lunch tomorrow,' Matthew said.

Reporting functions

11 Read sentences a–h and answer questions 1–4.

a She told Bob she was leaving the next day.
b She told Bob to leave her alone.
c She asked Bob why he had done it.
d She asked Bob to leave his keys.
e She warned Bob not to try and get in touch.
f Alan advised Bob to try and forget her.
g She suggested talking it over.
h They suggested that we should leave.

1 How is the structure after *tell* different in sentences a and b? What is the difference in meaning?
2 How is the structure after *ask* different in sentences c and d? What is the difference in meaning?
3 What structure is used after *warn* and *advise* in sentences e and f?
4 What structures can be used after *suggest*?

12 Rewrite sentences a–h above in direct speech.

Exam practice

Key word transformation

13 Complete the second sentence so that it has a similar meaning to the first sentence, using the word given. Do not change the word given. You must use between two and five words, including the word given.

Tip
Check that you have not written more than five words in your answer.

1 'You'd better not swim there. It's dangerous!' the man told us.
   WARNED
   The man _____ there because it was dangerous.

2 'I wouldn't buy Dave a book if I were you, Pete,' said Laura.
   ADVISED
   Laura _____ Dave a book.

3 'Take that chewing gum out, Claire!' the teacher said.
   TOLD
   The teacher _____ the chewing gum out of her mouth.

4 'Can you speak Spanish, John?' asked Marie.
   ASKED
   Marie _____ speak Spanish.

5 'I'll pick you up from work if you like, Tracy,' said Jason.
   OFFERED
   Jason _____ from work.

6 'See you after class, Angie!' said Mike.
   SAID
   Mike _____ Angie after class.

Speaking Part 2

Think ahead 1 Discuss these questions.
- a How do you react to advertisements in the street, in magazines or on television? Do you take notice of them? Do you think they influence you?
- b Can you think of an advertisement which has particularly impressed you, perhaps because it is funny, shocking or unusual in some way?
- c Which of these two billboards do you think is most effective? Give at least one reason. Compare ideas with a partner.

2 🔊 2.05 Now listen to a Speaking Part 2 task in which a candidate is asked to talk about the same pictures. Do either of the speakers have similar ideas to you?

3 🔊 2.05 Listen to the recording again. What language do the two candidates use to …
- a give reasons or explanations?
- b express opinions?
- c talk about appearances?

Exam practice

Long turn 4 Work in pairs. Turn to page 155 and follow the instructions. Try to use expressions that the candidates in the recording used to give reasons, express opinions and talk about appearances.

Stage 1
Student A – you will answer the question about the first set of photographs on page 155. Student B will time you and answer a follow-up question.

Stage 2
Student B – you will answer the question about the second set of photographs on page 155. Student A will time you and answer a follow-up question.

> **Tip**
> When it is not your turn to speak, it is important to listen to what your partner is saying. This will help you to make your own 30-second comment when they have finished speaking.

Over to you 5 Look at the billboards again. Discuss these questions.
- a What kind of person do you think each advertisement is appealing to?
- b What technique does each advertisement use to sell its product?

Vocabulary

Compound nouns

1 Complete the following with the missing part of speech.

   a _____ + noun: *baby clothes*
   b _____ + noun: *cookbook*
   c _____ + noun: *greenhouse*
   d _____ + preposition: *fallout*
   e _____ + verb: *uptake*

2 Is the stress on the first or the second component of these compound nouns?

   blackboard   bookcase   breakdown   breakwater   checkout   credit card
   downfall   hard drive   input   music shop   search engine   software
   swimming pool   takeaway

3 Underline the compound nouns in this text. How many of each type in **1** are there?

No news is good news

An American news editor once said, 'If news is not really news unless it is bad news, it may be difficult to claim we are an informed nation.' The stories below are from The Good News Network, which does not publish bad news.

- Miami's crime rate has fallen dramatically. In the past eight years, homicides, break-ins and assaults have been cut in half. Tourist robberies have dropped 95%.
- 13.3 million teenage Americans donate time and effort to community service each week – a participation rate of almost 60%.
- Lake Tahoe is the clearest it's been in five years thanks to a $900 million clean-up organized by developers and environmentalists.

4 Use a word from each list to make compound nouns to describe jobs. More than one answer may be possible.

   A: care   computer   news   police   shop   television   university
   B: assistant   lecturer   officer   programmer   reader   reporter   taker

unit 8 media

5 Use a word from each list, A and B. Form compound nouns related to the media which match definitions a–j. Some compounds are written as one word, some as two. Check in a dictionary.

A: current   eye   foreign   head   mass   news   press   remote   soap   talk
B: affairs   agent's   conference   control   correspondent   line   media   opera   show   witness

a sources of information such as television, newspapers etc. which influence a lot of people
b a meeting at which someone gives information to a group of journalists
c a person who has seen a crime or an accident and who can describe it afterwards
d a shop where you can buy magazines and newspapers
e a story about the lives and problems of ordinary people which is broadcast frequently
f events of political or social importance that are happening now
g a television or radio programme in which famous people answer questions asked by an interviewer
h the title of a newspaper article printed in large letters, especially on the front page
i a device that allows you to operate a television, radio etc. from a distance
j a journalist who reports news from another country

Pronunciation

6 🔊 2.06 Listen and check your answers to **5**. Mark which component of the compound nouns in a–j is stressed more.

Exam practice

Word formation

7 Read the text below. Use the word given in capitals at the end of some of the lines to form a word that fits in the gap in the same line. There is an example at the beginning (0).

John Simpson – Still doing crazy things

Everyone I know takes risks, but rarely with their lives. Why should I, at an age when all (0) _sensible_ men and women are starting to think seriously about their (1) _____, want to go on doing crazy things? Why am I still standing on foreign pavements, arguing the toss with gunmen, (2) _____ and secret policemen? (3) _____ not because I have to. As the head of the BBC's foreign reporting, I can do more or less what I want. I have a (4) _____ office at Television Centre, filled with producers and correspondents who are (5) _____ friends. I could exist perfectly well on a professional diet of international summit meetings, conferences and (6) _____. I could stay at decent hotels, eat at reasonable hours, plan my social life properly and never again set foot in (7) _____ parts of the world. I could also go mad. That life – safe, (8) _____ and easy – would bore me to death.

SENSE
RETIRE
RIOT
CERTAIN
PLEASE
PERSON
ELECT
DANGER
PREDICT

Over to you

8 Discuss these questions.

a What do you think is a sensible age to retire?
b Are you a risk taker or do you prefer a safe, predictable and easy life?

Reading and Use of English Part 6

Think ahead
1 Before you read the article on page 101 about print media, discuss these questions.
   a If you wanted to catch up with the latest news, what would you do?
   b If you wanted to read literature of some kind – a novel, poetry or a play, what would you do?
   c If you wanted to find out the latest gossip about celebrities, what would you do?

2 Quickly read the article on page 101. How does the writer feel about the possibility that print will disappear?

Exam practice

Gapped text

> **Tip**
> Check that the sentence you've chosen fits the context and is grammatically correct.

3 Now read the article again. Choose from the sentences **A–G** the one which fits each gap (**1–6**). There is one extra sentence which you do not need to use.
   A This is because I can find all the news and information I need on the TV or the internet, which I can stream on my smartphone.
   B Until quite recently, everywhere you looked you could see books, newspapers and magazines on sale or being read by a majority of the population.
   C Even though digital media is increasing in popularity, print media still has its fans.
   D For some people, it is simply more convenient than buying physical products from shops or online.
   E Many people still prefer print for the very simple reason that they can touch it and hold it.
   F Like many others of my generation, I was brought up believing that the printed word was one of the cornerstones of our civilization.
   G This is because, with fewer copies sold, the money generated from advertisements has diminished.

so and such

▸ *Grammar reference page 170*

4 What do these extracts from the article show about the use of *so* and *such*?
   a Print has been with us for hundreds of years and has in that time been such an important feature of our everyday life.
   b Others seem to prefer the digital format, probably because so many books, magazines or newspapers can be stored on a computer.
   c … this was where so much of their income traditionally came from.
   d … even though music is so cheap and convenient to download.

5 Complete these sentences with *so* or *such*.
   a That concert was _____ exciting that I couldn't get to sleep afterwards.
   b I'd no idea that it was _____ an interesting film.
   c I've never seen _____ few people in town.
   d Why are you behaving _____ aggressively?
   e _____ a lot of daytime TV programmes are badly made.

6 Decide whether *so* or *such* would be used with these words and phrases, and then make sentences using each phrase with *so* or *such*.

   a lot of people   few cars   hot weather   little ears   little time   many people
   much money   tall buildings

100

Print: when will it disappear?

Print has been with us for hundreds of years and has, in that time, been such an important feature of our everyday life. [1] Now however, more and more people are predicting the disappearance of print, with speculation mounting that this could occur sometime soon.

Personally, I find this sad but not surprising. [2] When I was a child, my father would always bring a newspaper home from work with him. We'd all argue about who was going to look at it first. Mum was interested in the news, I'd want to look at the sports pages and my sister was desperate to know what was on television that night.

Ironically, now I'm an adult, I hardly ever buy a newspaper. [3] Everyone in my family has internet access, so we can all read anything whenever we like and wherever we are. Something similar is happening to books; although I love to read as much as ever, it's a while since I actually bought a book or took one anywhere with me. I now take my e-reader with me everywhere; incredibly, it can hold more books than I'll ever have time to read.

The plain fact is that, like me, fewer and fewer people are buying printed materials of any kind. Perhaps the underlying reason for this is laziness. [4] Others, however, actually seem to prefer the digital format, probably because so many books, magazines or newspapers can be stored on a computer or a small e-reader weighing less than a thin paperback book. Traditional print media cannot compete with this.

There are other factors to take into account, too. With sales of print in decline, commercial companies are spending less on publicizing their businesses in newspapers and magazines. [5] Even a small drop in revenue can be a massive blow to newspaper and magazine publishers, as this was where so much of their income traditionally came from. Many businesses have now moved into more profitable online advertising in digital publications as well as on social networking sites and in online games.

However, just because the statistics show that book sales have declined, and that less money is being made from newspaper advertisements, doesn't necessarily mean that physical publications will disappear completely in the near future. [6] It is similar in the case of recorded music: some people still buy CDs and even vinyl records, even though music is so cheap and convenient to download. In the end, as long as a proportion of the population continue to prefer printed books, newspapers and magazines, print will be with us for many years to come. It just remains to be seen for exactly how many years.

Over to you

7 Discuss these questions.

a How important are print materials in your country? Is their popularity declining?

b Are you one of those people who 'prefer print for the very simple reason that you can touch it and hold it'?

c Do you think print media will ever disappear completely? If so, when do you think this will happen? If not, why not?

Writing Part 1

Exam skills 1 Read this Part 1 essay task. Then, discuss questions a–c below.

In your English class you have read an article about press freedom and discussed the advantages and disadvantages of having a free press.

Now, your English teacher has asked you to write an essay.

Write an essay using all the notes and give reasons for your point of view.

Should newspapers be allowed to reveal secrets about the private lives of celebrities?

Notes

Things to write about:

1. why do newspapers want to write about the private lives of celebrities?

2. what effect can the revealing of secrets have on celebrities?

3. _____ (your own idea)

Write your **essay** in 140–190 words.

a How should an essay like this start and finish?
b What do you think is the best way of answering this kind of question – by agreeing, by disagreeing or by giving both sides of the argument?
c What is an appropriate style for this essay?

2 Read this essay, ignoring the gaps and the underlined words. Then, answer these questions.

a What is the purpose of each of the four paragraphs?
b What are the main points made in the second and third paragraphs?
c Where are the writer's opinions expressed?
d Is the style appropriate?

Famous people often complain that newspapers print too much about (a) <u>their</u> private lives, **(1)** _____ newspapers say that (b) <u>they</u> are simply responding to public curiosity and interest. I will consider (c) <u>these different points of view</u> in this essay.

 (2) _____, newspapers say that the public has a right to know about how celebrities spend (d) <u>their</u> money and who they are in love with. (e) <u>They</u> claim that it is particularly important for the public to know when famous people do something wrong.

 (3) _____, it seems that famous people want as much media attention as possible at the beginning of their careers. Once they are famous, **(4)** _____, they object if newspapers reveal personal information that (f) <u>they</u> would prefer to keep secret. **(5)** _____, they feel they have a right to a private life, like everyone else.

 (6) _____, I believe that the public should be told how stars live (g) <u>their</u> lives, **(7)** _____ stars should have some privacy, especially to protect members of their families. (h) <u>This</u> means that we need clear rules about what the media should be allowed to publish.

---

unit 8 media

Connecting ideas

3 Complete the essay using appropriate words and phrases from this list. More than one answer may be possible.

although   however   in fact   on balance   on the one / other hand   whereas

4 Match each phrase in the list below with its purpose a, b or c.

as well as (that)   besides (this)   by contrast   in conclusion   in short
nevertheless   on the contrary   on the whole   to summarize   what is more

a to introduce additional information
b to introduce information which contrasts with what has gone before
c to summarize or conclude an argument

Avoiding repetition

5 What do the underlined words and phrases in the essay refer to?

6 How has the writer avoided repetition in the second sentence in each of these pairs?

a I would like to give two examples of techniques the media use to obtain secret information about celebrities. The first is the widespread use of paparazzi.
b Some famous people take newspapers to court. I believe that such actions may do celebrities more harm than good.
c The photographers were waiting for the princess outside the nightclub on Friday night. They knew she would be there then.
d Celebrities frequently object to the presence of reporters outside their home. They know, however, that their objections will almost certainly be ignored.

7 Why is it important to avoid repetition in an essay? Discuss your ideas with a partner.

Exam practice

Essay
▶ Writing guide page 178

Tip

You can write about the points under 'Things to write about' in any order, but you must include all three points in your answer.

8 You are going to write an essay. First, read the task below. Then, work through stages a–d.

In your English class you have been talking about advertising.

Now, your English teacher has asked you to write an essay.

Write an essay using **all** the notes and give reasons for your point of view. Write your **essay** in 140–190 words.

Essay question
Should there be a complete ban on the advertising of dangerous products like cigarettes?

Notes
Things to write about:

1. what effect does advertising have on people?
2. would a ban have the right effect?
3. _____ (your own idea)

a Think about the topic. Discuss the following in pairs and make brief notes.
  • What are your first thoughts about 1 and 2 in Notes?
  • Where are cigarettes currently advertised? Who is influenced by these adverts?
  • Why do some people want a 'complete ban'?
  • Would a complete ban stop or discourage people from smoking or drinking?
b Plan your essay. Use the sample answer on page 102 as a model.
c Write your essay. Use connecting words and expressions to link ideas between sentences and paragraphs.
d Finally, read through your essay, checking grammar, spelling and punctuation.

Unit 8 Review

1 Read the text below and decide which answer (A, B, C or D) best fits each gap. There is an example at the beginning (0).

PAPARAZZI

Paparazzi are (0) __freelance__ photographers who take photographs of celebrities. Their actions are sometimes (1) _____ because they often go to extreme (2) _____ to get unusual shots. At times, their actions may actually be (3) _____, and in some countries they may be prosecuted. Wherever celebrities and stars are found, paparazzi are not usually far behind.

The term paparazzi (4) _____ from the name of the character in the Italian film *La Dolce Vita*. Signor Paparazzo is a photographer who is (5) _____ looking for his next photo opportunity and, at one point, photographs a woman who has recently (6) _____ a personal tragedy. His (7) _____ are remarkably similar to those used by real-life celebrity photographers today, which is why they came to be known as paparazzi. A single representative of this intriguing (8) _____ is known as a paparazzo, although it is rare to see a paparazzo alone, since these photographers often follow each other as well as famous people.

0	A free	B spare	C freelance	D temporary
1	A complained	B criticized	C disapproved	D scorned
2	A lengths	B measures	C methods	D extents
3	A wrong	B wicked	C illegal	D dishonest
4	A arises	B starts	C springs	D comes
5	A consistently	B constantly	C generally	D repetitively
6	A suffered	B underwent	C felt	D tolerated
7	A devices	B gimmicks	C plans	D tactics
8	A profession	B living	C work	D business

2 Rewrite this conversation in reported speech. Use the reporting verbs in brackets.

Jayne: I'm going on holiday tomorrow. (say)
Ben: Are you going anywhere special? (ask)
Jayne: Yes, Australia. We'll be staying in Perth for a week and then going on to Sydney. (reply)
Ben: Who are you going with? (ask)
Jayne: With two of my friends from work. (reply)

3 Rewrite these sentences in direct speech.
a Ben said he'd always wanted to go to Australia.
b Jayne asked him if he'd like to go with them.
c Ben replied that he certainly would.
d Jayne said she'd see if there were any places left on the flight.
e Ben said he wasn't sure if he could afford it.
f Jayne offered to lend him the money.

4 Complete these sentences with *so* or *such*.
a There's _____ little time left – we'll really have to hurry.
b I don't know how people can drive _____ fast in the rain.
c I can't remember when we last had _____ cold weather.
d That was _____ a difficult exam. I'm sure I haven't passed.
e But you've worked _____ hard – I'm sure you'll be OK.

unit 8 media

104

Unit 9 Around us

Introduction

1. Two of the photos above show kinds of extreme weather – extreme heat and extreme cold. How can extreme weather conditions like these affect people's lives?

2. Two of the photos above show types of natural disasters – flooding and a forest fire.
   a. How do these affect people's lives?
   b. What safety measures could be taken to prevent them happening?

3. Have you ever experienced either kind of extreme weather or natural disaster?

Reading and Use of English Part 5

Think ahead 1 Before you read the text below about volcanoes, try to answer questions a–c.

a Approximately how many active volcanoes are there in the world?
   1 457   2 1,350   3 16,000

b How many people live in the vicinity of an active volcano?
   1 1 million   2 10 million   3 1 billion

c Where is the world's largest active volcano?
   1 Italy   2 Hawaii   3 Mexico

2 Quickly read the text to check your answers.

They died where they stood. Violently, with almost no warning. Wealthy women in their jewels. Armed soldiers. Babies. Almost 2,000 years ago, two towns in southern Italy had the misfortune to be in the shadow of Mount Vesuvius – one of Europe's active volcanoes – at the wrong time. The 16,000 inhabitants of the Roman towns of Herculaneum and neighbouring Pompeii who were buried beneath thirty metres of dust on an August night in AD 79 bore silent witness to the destructive force of volcanoes.

Objects of terror and fascination since the beginning of human time, volcanoes take their name from Vulcan, the Roman god of fire. Today there are some 1,350 active volcanoes in the world. At any given moment, somewhere between one dozen and two dozen are throwing out ash and molten rock from the earth's core.

Approximately one billion people live in their dangerous shadows. Experts expect the number to rise. The rapid growth of population, greater competition for land and an increase in urban migration are driving more and more people to settle around volcanoes, significantly increasing the potential loss of life and property in the event of eruptions.

Despite major advances in technology, the ability to predict when a volcano might erupt remains imprecise. But meeting the challenge is vital because volcanoes are 'people magnets'. A recent study identified 457 volcanoes where there are one million or more people living within 100 kilometres. Many of these volcanoes – several in Indonesia and Japan, for instance – have surrounding populations greatly exceeding one million. For example, today, 3.75 million people live within 30 kilometres of the summit of Mount Vesuvius in the southern Italian city of Naples. 'What do they do if it starts erupting? No one can imagine evacuating a city the size of Naples,' said Dan Miller, chief of the US Geological Survey's Volcano Disaster Assistance Program.

'Persuading people to move permanently out of hazard zones is not usually an option. Many of the land-use patterns are long established, and people just won't do it,' Miller went on. 'The only thing you can do is have systematic volcano monitoring to detect the earliest departure from normal activity.'

Nowadays, it is easier to predict volcanic activity, but evaluating the threat of eruption is frequently still difficult. Mexico City knows the problem well. The city, which has a population of more than 20 million, lies within 60 kilometres of the summit of Popocatepetl, a volcano which has erupted at least 15 times in the last 400 years. The flanks and valleys surrounding 'Popo' have been evacuated several times since 1994 in response to earthquakes and eruptions of volcanic ash and plumes of steam. Each time the mountain has settled down without a major eruption, although some activity has continued. Yet when, or if, a major eruption will occur next remains unknown.

'There could be weeks, months or years between the time a volcano shows some activity and the time of its eruption,' said Miller. 'It may never erupt. Most people are willing to be evacuated once. But if nothing happens, the loss of credibility could cause people to ignore future warnings.'

Volcanic eruptions, when they do come, are sometimes relatively slow and quiet. There was no loss of life when the world's largest active volcano erupted in 1984. The people who lived in the proximity of Hawaii's Mauna Loa volcano had plenty of time to get out of the way when it erupted in 1984. Its lava crept down the slope at about the speed of honey. At other times the eruption is sudden and violent, and evacuation unfortunately comes too late.

Exam practice

Multiple choice

Tip

Choose the option you think is correct. Then check your answer by trying to eliminate the other three options.

3 For questions 1–6, choose the answer (A, B, C or D) which you think fits best according to the text.

1 What happened when Mount Vesuvius erupted in AD 79?
   A The rich managed to escape.
   B It covered many towns with dust.
   C A few people were killed.
   D People were unprepared.

2 What do experts think will happen in the future?
   A More volcanoes will become active.
   B More people will farm in volcanic areas.
   C More people will set up home near volcanoes.
   D Around one billion people will die in volcanic eruptions.

3 According to the article, what is the present situation regarding volcanic eruptions?
   A Eruptions are most likely to happen in Indonesia and Japan.
   B Technological breakthroughs have led to accurate predictions.
   C Most large cities have no appropriate evacuation plans in place.
   D People will be less affected than before.

4 What does the article say about Popocatepetl?
   A There was a major eruption in 1994.
   B There have been no eruptions in the last 20 years.
   C Nobody can say whether there will be a major eruption in the future.
   D People who live nearby are fed up with being evacuated.

5 Why was the eruption of Mauna Loa less dangerous?
   A People had been evacuated from the area beforehand.
   B People were able to keep ahead of the lava.
   C Scientists had warned people well in advance.
   D It was not a major eruption.

6 What would be the most appropriate title for this article?
   A Volcanoes: Sleeping threat for millions
   B Volcanic eruptions and other natural disasters
   C Volcanoes: Advances in their prediction
   D Volcanic eruption: A study of volcanic behaviour

Word building

4 Underline all the nouns in the text related to these root verbs. How are they similar?

compete   erupt   evacuate   fascinate   migrate   populate

5 Underline all the adjectives in the text related to these root verbs and nouns.

act   danger   destroy   system   volcano

6 Complete these sentences with an appropriate form of a word from the list.

act   devastate   fascinate   migrate   science   system

a A great deal of _____ research is being carried out on volcanoes.
b The early nineteenth century was a period of mass _____ from Ireland.
c Not long after the tsunami struck, a _____ search for survivors began.
d I have never really understood the _____ some people have for tornadoes.
e The recent hurricanes caused widespread _____ in the areas affected.
f Nocturnal animals, like foxes, are _____ at night.

Over to you

7 Discuss these questions.

a Why do people choose to live near volcanoes? Would you?
b What are the problems with evacuating a large city? Can you think of any solutions?

unit 9 around us

Grammar

Relative clauses
▶ *Grammar reference* page 170

1 Complete these sentences from the article with the relative pronouns *who*, *which*, *that* or *whose*. Give as many alternatives for each answer as you can. Then, check your ideas with the article.

   a The city, _____ has a population of more than 20 million, lies within 60 kilometres of the summit of Popocatepetl, a volcano _____ has erupted at least 15 times in the last 400 years.

   b The people _____ lived in the proximity of Hawaii's Mauna Loa volcano had plenty of time to get out of the way when it erupted in 1984.

2 Look at these two sentences. In which sentence does the speaker have one sister? In which sentence does the speaker have more than one sister? In which sentence is the information in the relative clause essential?

   a My sister who lives in Mexico has two children.
   b My sister, who lives in Mexico, has two children.

3 Decide whether the relative clauses in the following sentences are defining (they contain essential information) or non-defining (they contain non-essential information). If the clause is non-defining, add commas.

   a Scientists who study volcanic activity are known as vulcanologists.
   b Vulcanologists who study volcanic activity are often able to warn of possible volcanic eruption.
   c Lava which is the hot molten rock emitted from a volcano when it erupts is not necessarily the most dangerous thing associated with a volcano.
   d One of the worst things is volcanic ash which can be carried on the wind for thousands of kilometres.
   e Dozens of planes which have flown through clouds of ash have crashed or suffered serious damage.
   f Not all countries whose inhabitants are at risk from volcanic eruption are able to carry out large-scale evacuation.

4 Which of the relative pronouns in 3 can be replaced by other relative pronouns?

5 Relative clauses can also be introduced by *why*, *where* and *when*. Complete these sentences with one of these words, adding commas where necessary. Can the relative pronoun be left out in any of these sentences?

   a Bushfires are natural phenomena particularly common in Australia, but which also occur in many places around the world _____ there are plenty of forests that can burn.
   b The Northern Territory is most at risk of bushfires at the end of the dry season in September and October _____ temperatures have risen but monsoon rains have not yet arrived.
   c The reason _____ most bushfires start is because people are negligent or start them deliberately.

6 Look at the following pairs of sentences. What are the differences between the two sentences in each pair? What rules can you work out?

   a That's the man to whom I spoke.
      That's the man (who) I spoke to.
   b The speaker, about whom I'd heard so much, gave an extremely interesting talk.
      The speaker, who I'd heard so much about, gave an extremely interesting talk.

unit 9 around us

7 Complete the following sentences with relative pronouns. Indicate where there is more than one possibility and add commas if necessary. In which two sentences can the relative pronoun be omitted?

a Tornadoes _____ are commonly known as 'twisters' in the USA are a common phenomenon in the American Midwest.

b Scientists and amateur tornado chasers alike flock to Oklahoma, Texas and Kansas in the months of May and June _____ tornadoes are most likely to occur.

c Eric Rasmussen _____ is a world authority on tornadoes does most of his work here _____ 78% of the world's tornadoes occur.

d The scientists _____ mission it is to find out more about tornadoes can only predict where they might form.

e The people _____ go in search of the tornadoes often have a wasted journey.

f The damage _____ a tornado causes can be immense.

g One of the worst recorded events was in March 1925, _____ nearly 700 people lost their lives.

h On that day the Midwest was hit by seven tornadoes, affecting an area _____ covered over 320 km.

i Rescue workers found buildings _____ people had lived and worked completely demolished.

j No one yet knows the reason _____ there has been such a big increase in the number of tornadoes in the last few years.

8 Read the text quickly and answer this question. Who or what was responsible for the devastation of The Great Plains – the farmers, the weather or both?

Exam practice

Open cloze

9 For questions 1–8, read the text below and think of the word which best fits each gap. Use only one word in each gap. There is an example at the beginning (0).

The Great Plains Blew Away

In 1930 **(0)** _much_ of the United States and Canada, but particularly the area of the Great Plains, was affected **(1)** _____ a long-term drought, which continued for a decade. Years of bad farming practices, including the removal of native grasses **(2)** _____ their replacement with seasonal crops, were disastrous **(3)** _____ the farmers of the area. When the drought caused the crops to fail, **(4)** _____ was nothing left to anchor the top soil, **(5)** _____ had turned to dust. The winds that often blow across the plains picked up the fine dust, which formed into massive dark clouds that made breathing difficult and farm machinery useless. The ecological disaster known **(6)** _____ the Dust Bowl lasted through the 1930s, resulting **(7)** _____ useless farmland and homeless people in their hundreds of thousands. Many went to California in search **(8)** _____ work, but the situation was no better there. After the stock market crashed in 1929, millions of people were out of work across the whole of the USA.

unit 9 around us

109

Vocabulary

Think ahead 1 Discuss these questions.

a What is the weather like in different regions of your country at different times of the year?

b Has the climate of your country changed in the last five to ten years?

2 Read the text below. What does it say is to blame for climatic changes?

In recent years, the greenhouse effect has become the focus of large-scale scientific investigation. There is growing evidence that past emissions of greenhouse gases (carbon dioxide, chlorofluorocarbons and nitrous oxide) could already be altering the Earth's weather patterns and temperatures. Average global temperatures are steadily increasing, and if this trend continues the consequences for our planet could be disastrous. Carbon dioxide is believed to be responsible for approximately half of global warming. Tropical deforestation also leads to global warming by destroying one of the Earth's only ways of absorbing excess atmospheric carbon.

Dependent prepositions 3 Certain nouns, adjectives and verbs are followed by particular prepositions. Look again at the text in **2** and find out which preposition follows the words *consequences*, *responsible* and *leads*.

4 Match the nouns in A with the correct prepositions in B. Then, complete the sentences below with a noun and a preposition.

A: agreement   anger   ban   cure   damage   effect   respect   tax   threat

B: at   for   on   to

a Many of our medicines come from plants that grow in rainforests. Perhaps someday the _____ cancer will be found in a tropical rainforest.

b Deforestation poses a serious _____ indigenous peoples, as well as to the climate.

c Environmentalists warn that unless people show more _____ the environment, humankind will pay a heavy price.

d In many countries the government _____ leaded fuel is higher than that on unleaded fuel.

5 Choose the correct preposition which follows the underlined adjectives.

a Environmentalist groups in Britain are <u>opposed</u> *against / to* new road-building projects. They argue that they are <u>harmful</u> *for / to* the environment, often destroying plant and animal habitats.

b Environmentalists warn that unless governments become more <u>aware</u> *of / to* the effects of their actions, the world we leave our children will be very <u>different</u> *to / with* the world we know today.

c Everyone is <u>capable</u> *of / to* making lifestyle changes which would be <u>beneficial</u> *to / in* the environment. Walking or cycling to work is much <u>better</u> *for / to* you than taking the car.

d Although only comprising 7% of the global population, the USA is <u>responsible</u> *for / to* 22% of all greenhouse gas emissions.

unit 9 around us

110

6 Match the verbs in A with the correct prepositions in B.

A: appeal   believe   complain   contribute   depend   insist   invest   result   sympathize

B: about   in   on   to   with

7 Match these sentence beginnings a–e with their endings 1–5, adding an appropriate preposition.

a In all of nature, but particularly in rainforests, plants and animals depend
b Logging for tropical timber and gold mining have contributed
c Local councils need to invest more money
d It's no good complaining
e I sympathize

1 _____ recycling schemes.
2 _____ pollution. You have to be prepared to do something about it.
3 _____ each other for survival.
4 _____ people who live near big airports.
5 _____ the destruction of the tropical rainforest, though they are not the only factors involved.

Exam practice

Key word transformation

Tip

If you have written more than five words, your answer is wrong. You need to think of a different way of expressing the idea.

8 For questions 1–6, complete the second sentence so that it has a similar meaning to the first sentence, using the word given. Do not change the word given. You must use between two and five words, including the word given.

1 Cars are not allowed in the city centre.
   BAN
   There is _____ in the city centre.
2 We should invest in renewable energy sources like solar energy.
   MAKE
   We ought _____ renewable energy sources like solar energy.
3 Some people don't seem able to change their bad habits.
   INCAPABLE
   Some people seem to _____ their bad habits.
4 Switching off your television at night can save you 40% on your energy bill.
   RESULT
   Switching off your television at night can _____ 40% on your energy bill.
5 The environment can be negatively affected by modern farming methods.
   EFFECT
   Modern farming methods can _____ the environment.
6 They are planning to build a third runway, which is making people angry.
   ANGER
   There _____ to build a third runway.

Speaking Part 1

Think ahead   **1** Work with a partner and answer these questions.

     a What is the weather like where you live in different seasons?

     b Does the weather affect your mood? How?

2 Which of these adjectives describe (a) the weather (b) towns / cities? What other adjectives can you add?

     breezy   bustling   close   cosmopolitan   dull   freezing   historic   humid
     industrial   overcast   provincial   showery   sprawling   vibrant

3 🔊 **2.07** Listen to two candidates doing a Part 1 task. Work with a partner.

     a Student A: Write down the questions the examiner asks the candidates.
         Student B: Take notes on the answers the candidates give.

     b How would you answer the questions? Give as full answers as possible.

Pronunciation   **4** 🔊 **2.08** Listen to these sentences. Does the intonation go up or down on the words in *italics*? What rules can you work out?

     a I stay at home and maybe watch a *DVD*, play my *guitar* or listen to *music*.

     b You can find all sorts of small *shops*, *bars* and *restaurants* there.

5 🔊 **2.09** Listen and repeat.

     a After I got home, I made something to eat, watched TV and then did my homework.

     b Can you get me some milk, sugar and rice, please?

     c I'll have the prawns for starters, the duck for the main course and ice cream for dessert.

6 Work with a partner to answer these questions. Try to give 2 or 3 examples in each answer.

     a What languages can you say 'thank you' in?

     b How many countries (or cities in your country) have you visited?

     c What do you usually have for breakfast?

Exam practice

Short exchanges   **7** Work with a partner. Take turns to answer these Part 1 questions as fully as you can.

     a Is there any kind of weather you dislike? (Why?)

     b What did you do the last time the weather was good?

     c What do you dislike about your hometown?

     d Is your hometown interesting for tourists? (Why? / Why not?)

> **Tip**
> Answer the questions as fully as you can. Give explanations, examples or details as appropriate.

unit 9   around us

Listening Part 4

Think ahead

1 Discuss these questions in pairs.
   a How many flights do you take a year? Where was your last flight to?
   b What do you most like and most dislike about flying?
   c What are the negative effects of air travel on the environment? How can we reduce them?

Exam practice

Multiple choice

Tip

As you listen for the second time, make your final choice. If you are not sure of the answer, guess. Don't leave any questions unanswered.

2 ◆) 2.10 You will hear part of a radio programme about the effects of air travel on the environment. For questions 1–7, choose the best answer (A, B or C).

1 The presenter says you can find out what your primary carbon footprint is by
   A adding together your fuel and travel costs.
   B doing some simple mathematical calculations.
   C getting your computer to work it out based on information you provide.

2 The presenter says we can make our carbon footprint smaller by
   A buying from countries like China and India.
   B buying local produce and reducing automobile travel.
   C making our own wine and growing our own food.

3 What is Sue Hendry's attitude to global warming?
   A The government should do something about it.
   B It is her own personal responsibility.
   C There is nothing that can be done about it.

4 How much pollution might a domestic flight produce?
   A eight times as much as a train
   B the equivalent to eight cars over a year
   C the same as a train over the same distance

5 What are the most popular destinations for people flying from UK airports?
   A places in the UK and the continent
   B only other UK destinations
   C long-distance destinations outside of Europe

6 What is the attitude of the majority of frequent flyers?
   A They plan to cut down on short-haul flights.
   B They don't admit there is a problem.
   C They may feel guilty but do nothing.

7 What does Nigel Hammond think is the best solution to the problem?
   A encourage people to plant a tree for every flight they take
   B limit the number of flights that people can go on a year
   C increase the tax on aviation fuel

Travel collocations

3 Match each of the more formal verbs in A with its less formal equivalent in B.

   A: board   disembark   land   B: get off   get on   touch down

4 Complete the sentences with the most appropriate word, making any necessary changes
   a The plane _____ on time even though we took off 10 minutes late.
   b Due to engineering works between Colchester and London, passengers will need to _____ at Colchester and _____ one of the London-bound coaches.
   c You should _____ the bus outside the cinema and _____ at the park.

5 Match the verbs below with the modes of transport a–d. There may be more than one answer.

   board   disembark   land   touch down

   a plane   b bus   c ship   d train

Writing Part 2 - Report

Think ahead

UK Household Energy Use 2008

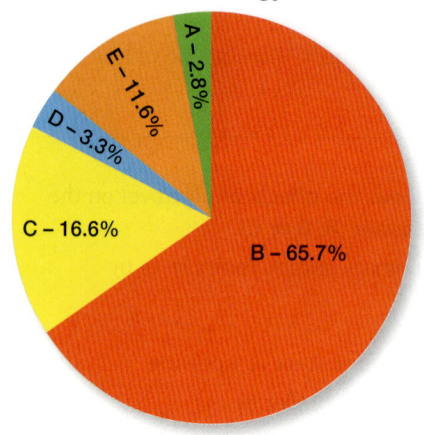

- A – 2.8%
- E – 11.6%
- D – 3.3%
- C – 16.6%
- B – 65.7%

Building Research Establishment Housing Model for Energy Studies [1970-2008]

1 Look at this pie chart. It shows how energy is used in an average British home.
  a Which piece of the pie chart (A–E) do you think matches each of the usages below?
    water heating ☐   cooking ☐   space heating ☐   lighting ☐   appliances ☐
  b How different do you think this usage is to your household and your country?

2 Do you think the following statements are True or False?
  a It uses up more energy to turn a light on than to leave it on. _____
  b Most of the energy used by a traditional light bulb is given off as heat, not light. _____
  c Newer energy-saving light bulbs cost the same as traditional bulbs. _____
  d Tumble driers use as much energy as washing machines. _____
  e Washing dishes in a dishwasher uses more water and more energy than washing them by hand. _____
  f Leaving appliances such as TVs on standby does not significantly increase their energy use. _____
  g Computer monitors use less energy when the screen saver is on. _____

Writing a report

3 One of the Part 2 writing options may be a report. Tick the features that are typical of reports.
  ☐ formal language   ☐ personal style   ☐ headings   ☐ bulleted lists
  ☐ suggestions   ☐ recommendations   ☐ anecdotes

4 Read this task and the example which follows. Then, choose the most appropriate missing headings a–f for the paragraphs (1–4). There are two extra headings which you do not need to use.
  a Recommendations
  b Ways in which families are increasing their carbon footprint
  c The present situation
  d Introduction
  e How easy is it to implement these changes?
  f Conclusion

> Your local council has asked you to write a report on what families could do to reduce their carbon footprint, and how easy it would be for households to implement these changes.
>
> Write your **report** in 140–190 words.

---

1 _____
The aim of this report is to recommend ways in which families could reduce their carbon footprint, and to comment on how easy it would be to put these into practice.

2 _____
1 Presently, cars are used to go everywhere, even short distances. Public transport is greatly under-used.
2 Most people do their shopping at an out-of-town supermarket. A great deal of the fruit and vegetables bought are imported from distant locations like Thailand and the United States.

3 _____
1 As an alternative to using their cars, people could use public transport more, or walk or cycle.
2 Instead of shopping at out-of-town supermarkets, people could buy their food from local shops and markets. Alternatively, they could order online and have the food delivered. Both these options would reduce petrol consumption. In addition, if people ate fruit and vegetables only when they were in season, these would not need to be flown in from faraway places.

4 _____
All of the above recommendations could be implemented quite easily. It simply depends on whether families are prepared to make a few lifestyle changes or not.

5 Answer these questions about the report in **4**.
  a Is it written in an appropriate style?
  b Does it contain everything that is asked for in the task?
  c What features of the layout make this report easy to follow?

Impersonal language

6 The passive may be used in reports to express ideas in an impersonal way.
  a Underline all the examples of the passive in the sample answer.
  b How could the following sentence from **4** be rewritten using the passive?
     Most people do their shopping at an out-of-town supermarket.
  c What modal verb is used to make suggestions?

7 Rewrite these sentences using the passive. The beginnings of the new sentences have been given.
  a If more people installed solar panels, they would use less electricity from non-renewable resources like coal, natural gas and oil.
     If more solar panels _____.
  b Much of the litter in the streets today is packaging from fast food outlets. Councils should make the fast food outlets clear up the packaging that people drop.
     Fast food outlets _____.
  c One way you can save money and help the environment is by turning down the thermostat on your heating.
     One way money _____.
  d We should use metal cutlery rather than disposable cutlery, which is usually plastic.
     Metal cutlery _____.
  e If you don't like the taste of your tap water, you could always filter it.
     Your tap water _____.
  f Don't throw away old computers. There are companies which recycle them.
     Your old computer _____. _____.

Exam practice

Report
▶ *Writing guide* page 184

Tip
Don't repeat the exact wording of the task in the Introduction to your report.

8 You are going to write a report. First, read the task below. Then, work through stages a–e.

> The director of your school has asked you to write a report on how to make your school more environmentally friendly. You should say what changes could be made and explain how these changes would help the environment.
>
> Write your **report** in 140–190 words.

  a Discuss with a partner what you could include in your report. Think about:
     • The classrooms. Do you have computers in the classrooms? Are they left switched on all the time? Are the windows open when the heating / air-conditioning is on? Is heating / air-conditioning on when it isn't necessary?
     • The cafeteria. What kind of eating utensils are used? How is the washing-up done? How are bottles, cans and food wrappers disposed of?
     • Other. Do the teachers do a lot of photocopying?
  b Select a few of your ideas. Make notes on what changes could be made and how these changes help the environment.
  c Plan your answer. Decide on an appropriate heading for each part of your report.
  d Write your report. Make sure you write in an appropriate style. Remember to include all the information required.
  e Finally, when you have finished, check your grammar, spelling and punctuation.

unit 9 around us

Unit 9 Review

1 For questions 1–8, read the text below and decide which answer (A, B, C or D) best fits each gap. There is an example at the beginning (0).

BUSHFIRES

Australia (0) _suffers_ more bushfires – wildfires which burn out of control – than any other country in the world. Most bushfires happen when temperatures are (1) _____ and conditions are dry and windy. One reason why Australia is so susceptible to bush fires is because the leaves of the native eucalyptus trees contain a highly-flammable oil which easily (2) _____ fire.

Approximately one quarter of all fires are started by lightning (3) _____, but the vast majority are caused by the (4) _____ of humans. Not all, however, are accidental; around 25 per cent are (5) _____.

The most obvious result of bushfires is the loss of plant, animal and human life and (6) _____ to property. But the effects of bushfires are not all negative as fire generates regrowth. Some species of eucalyptus, (7) _____, would be unable to reproduce otherwise as fire splits open the seed pods, (8) _____ them to germinate.

0	A bears	B suffers	C experiences	D tolerates
1	A big	B hot	C extreme	D high
2	A catches	B sets	C lights	D takes
3	A blows	B collisions	C strikes	D hits
4	A acts	B performances	C operations	D actions
5	A deliberate	B purpose	C intended	D calculated
6	A injury	B ruin	C damage	D harm
7	A actually	B also	C however	D for instance
8	A letting	B allowing	C making	D causing

2 Complete these paragraphs with the appropriate relative pronouns, adding any necessary commas.

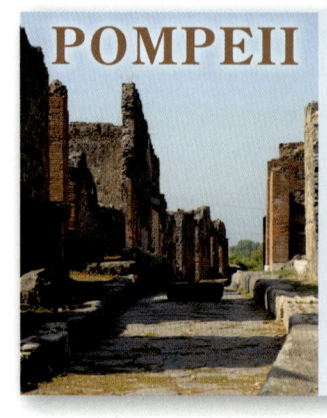

POMPEII

Mount Vesuvius (1) _____ is situated near the Bay of Naples is one of the world's most famous active volcanoes. The Romans (2) _____ believed it to be extinct built the city of Pompeii in its shadow. The violent eruption (3) _____ took place in AD 79 proved them wrong.

The eruption (4) _____ happened when no one was expecting it has gone down as one of the worst in recorded history. It happened during the daytime, (5) _____ people were going about their daily lives.

The remains of the 2,000 inhabitants of Pompeii (6) _____ did not escape lay forgotten for centuries. When excavation began in the eighteenth century, the remains were found of a much-loved family dog (7) _____ collar bore an inscription saying that he twice saved his owner's life.

3 Complete these sentences with an appropriate preposition.

a Do you believe _____ ghosts?
b Are you any good _____ maths? Could you help me with these problems?
c His flat is similar _____ mine.
d Some people are afraid _____ heights. Personally, I'm scared _____ the dark.
e That singer appeals _____ teenagers and over-fifties alike.
f Jamie insisted _____ helping me clear up after the party.

Unit 10 Innovation

Introduction

1 Look at the photographs. Discuss these questions.
   a What are the items in each photograph being used for? What was their original use?
   b Are there any items that you use for something other than their original use?
   c How many different uses can you think of for each of the items above?

Reading and Use of English Part 7

Think ahead 1 Look at the photos. Which of the materials below is each of the items made from? There may be more than one possible answer.

bamboo   cotton   linen   rattan   silk   steel   wood

2 What other items can you think of which can be made from these materials?

Exam skills 3 You are going to read an article about four pioneers of early flying machines. Look at the illustrations. Which machine would you most / least like to have tried out?

4 Read the texts quickly and match them to the illustrations on page 119. Are your ideas still the same?

Exam practice

Multiple matching 5 For questions 1–10, choose from the people (A–D). The people may be chosen more than once.

> **Tip**
> It may help to look at one text at a time and to go through all the questions to find the answers you want. There will be at least one answer for every text – often two or three.

Which person

was also an author?	1
got bored with his invention?	2
spent a long time on his invention?	3
almost lost a team member during his flight attempt?	4
accepted his death?	5
was not let down by his apparatus?	6
jumped from a building?	7
had more success with a different invention?	8
did trials before he flew in his invention?	9
flew with more than one other person?	10

unit 10 innovation

118

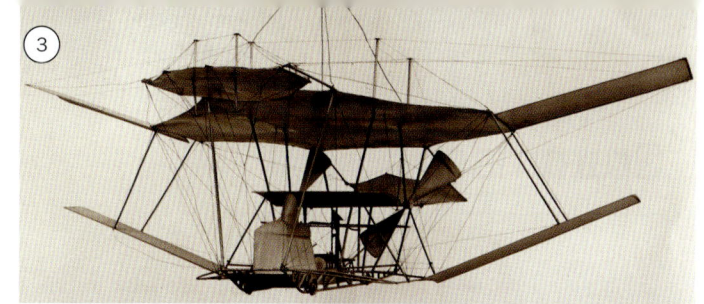

Pioneers of Flight

Since time immemorial people have wished they could fly. With hindsight, some may wish they hadn't tried.

A The Belgian de Groof worked for years on an apparatus intended to emulate the flight of birds. For this purpose, he constructed a device with bat-like wings. The framework was made of wood and rattan; the huge wings were covered with strong, waterproof silk, as was the long tail. The machine was controlled by levers. De Groof's first trial, which consisted of jumping from a great height to the Grand Place in Brussels, ended in failure, and he was lucky to escape unhurt. His second attempt was successful, but his third, on 9 July 1894, was not. Having planned to descend into the River Thames, de Groof was taken up by balloon and then released from a height of 1,000 feet. For some unknown reason the wing frame collapsed and he fell to his death. There was almost a second accident when the balloonist, having lost control of the balloon, landed in front of an approaching train, which just managed to stop in time.

B On 8 October 1883 Gaston Tissandier and his brother, Albert, became the first to fit an electric motor to an airship, thus creating the first electric-powered flight and enabling airships to be steered. In order to form some idea of the results which could be obtained, the brothers first performed tests on a small-scale model in their own laboratory near Paris. The airship they finally constructed was huge – ninety-two feet long with a diameter of thirty feet. The bamboo pannier, which was attached by twenty ropes to the envelope, contained the Siemens electric motor. The test was a relative success. The flight lasted just over an hour and the brothers landed safely. They had been able to steer the airship at will but said that they would have had problems had the weather not been fair.

C Otto Lilienthal studied the science of aviation and published two books on the subject. He constructed a machine in which he threw himself from a height, remained in the air for a time and then gradually descended to earth. His machine consisted of a framework of thin wooden rods covered with linen fixed securely to his shoulders. It took the shape of two slightly concave wings, with a raised tailpiece at the rear. A pair of rudders was fitted to help him steer. Mr Lilienthal first launched himself in his machine from a tower on a hilltop near Berlin. On 9 August 1896, Otto Lilienthal crashed to earth from a height of fifty feet while testing a new type of steering device. He died the following day. His last words were reported to be: 'Sacrifices must be made.'

D On 31 July 1894, for the first time in history, a flying machine actually left the ground, fully equipped with engines, boiler, fuel, water and a crew of three. Its inventor was Hiram Maxim, who had invested £20,000 in its construction. The machine was a large steam-driven structure formed of steel tubes and wires with five wings. Maxim began tests in 1894. On the third try the plane, which was powered up to forty miles per hour, left its track and continued on its way, cutting a path through the grass for some 200 yards. At times it reached an altitude of two to three feet above the ground before it finally crashed. After this Maxim lost interest in flying and went on to other inventions, making his fortune with the invention of the Maxim machine gun.

Over to you

6 Discuss these questions.

a How important has the invention of the aeroplane been?

b What do you think are the worst inventions ever?

Grammar

Wishes and regrets
▸ *Grammar reference page 172*

1 We use *wish* to talk about situations we would like to change but can't. Decide whether the following sentences refer to a present or future situation, or a past situation. What do you notice about the verb tenses after *wish*?

   a Since time immemorial people have wished they could fly.
   b With hindsight, some may wish they hadn't tried (to fly).
   c I wish I was / were more courageous.

2 We also use *wish* to refer to someone else's habits or intentions which we would like to change. These wishes can express impatience and irritation, or simply regret. What do you notice about the verb tenses after *wish* in these sentences?

   a I wish someone would invent a machine to make my bed in the mornings.
   b I wish you wouldn't keep interrupting me.

3 Which of these sentences expresses the stronger regret?

   a I wish I had invented the television.
   b If only I had invented the television.

4 Answer these questions using *wish*.

   a What things would you like to change about your appearance, your job, your home, etc.?
   b What regrets do you have about the past?
   c What things would you like to change about someone else's behaviour?

I'd rather and it's time …
▸ *Grammar reference page 172*

5 In these sentences, how is the verb tense different when the speaker is expressing a preference about their own action and when they are expressing a preference about somebody else's action?

   a I'd rather walk home.
   b I'd rather you walked home.

6 Which of these sentences suggests more urgency? Which form of the verb is used in each case?

   a It's time the children went to bed.
   b It's time for the children to go to bed.

7 Complete these sentences with a verb in an appropriate form.

   a It's 5.25 p.m. It's almost time _____ home.
   b I'd rather we _____ inside the cinema than outside, in case it's raining.
   c 'It's high time you _____ a haircut, Corporal,' the sergeant yelled.
   d 'Would you rather I _____ you what I've bought you for your birthday, or would you rather I did not?'
       'I'd rather you (not) _____ me. I like surprises.'
   e Isn't it about time you _____ that suit to the dry-cleaner's? When was the last time you had it cleaned?
   f 'Have you done the washing up yet?'
       'I'd rather _____ it till tomorrow.'
       'Sorry, but I'd rather you _____ it now.'
   g It's time you _____ your room. It's a terrible mess.

Reading and Use of English Parts 2 & 4

Key word transformation

> **Tip**
>
> Don't leave any questions unanswered. There are two marks for a correct sentence so, even if your answer isn't completely correct, you will still get some marks for it.

Exam practice

1 For questions 1–6, complete the second sentence so that it has a similar meaning to the first sentence, using the word given. Do not change the word given. You must use between two and five words, including the word given.

1 You never clean the bath when you've finished!

 I _____ the bath dirty when you've finished! **WISH**

2 Pete regrets forgetting to send Sally a Valentine card.

 Pete wishes _____ Sally a Valentine card. **REMEMBERED**

3 'It wasn't a good idea to stay so late,' said Justin, yawning.

 'I wish I _____,' said Justin, yawning. **EARLIER**

4 'I'd love to be the same height as my sister,' said Marie enviously.

 Marie wishes _____ her sister. **TALL**

5 I regret telling John.

 If _____ John. **TOLD**

6 I'd prefer you to wash up now.

 I _____ now. **RATHER**

Exam practice

Open cloze

2 For questions 1–8, read the text below and think of the word which best fits each gap. Use only one word in each gap. There is an example at the beginning (0).

An accidental invention: Post-it® notes

Did you know that Post-it notes, those small, sticky pieces of paper, were the result (0) __*of*__ a failed experiment? Apparently, Spencer Silver had been working in the 3M research laboratories trying to find a strong adhesive. He developed a new adhesive, but it was even weaker than (1) _____ 3M already manufactured. It stuck but (2) _____ easily be lifted off. No one knew what to do with it, (3) _____ Silver did not throw it away. Then four years later another 3M scientist called Arthur Fry was singing in the church choir. He used pieces of paper (4) _____ keep his place in the hymn book, but (5) _____ kept falling out. Remembering Silver's adhesive, Fry put some on the paper. With the weak adhesive, the paper stayed in place but came off (6) _____ damaging the book. In 1980 3M began selling Post-it notes worldwide. Today, they are (7) _____ of the most popular office products available. I wish I (8) _____ accidentally invented them.

unit 10 innovation

121

Speaking Part 2

Think ahead

1 How were people's lives different before these inventions? How have they changed people's lives?

the camera   the light bulb   the mobile phone   the motor car   the printing press

2 Look at the photographs. Do you know the names of items A–D? If you don't, how would you describe them?

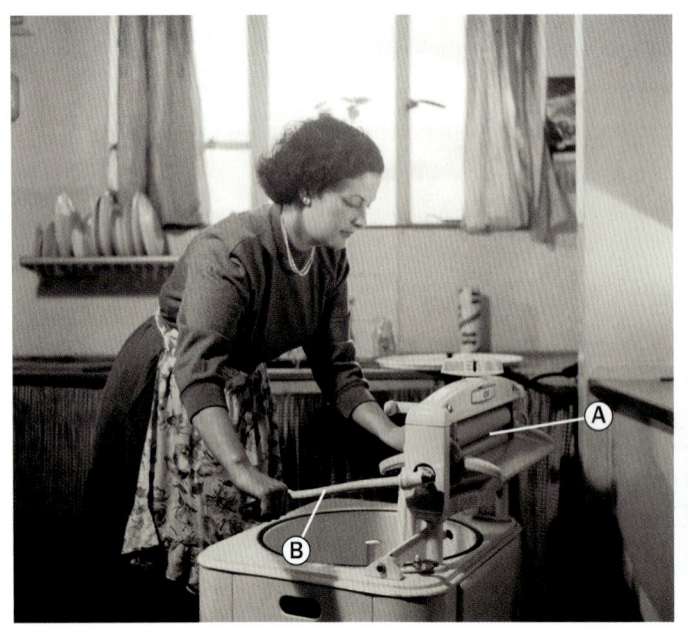

3 🔊 2.11 Listen to the interview. How many of the items in **2** does the first candidate know the exact word for?

Exam skills

4 🔊 2.11 Listen to the recording again. Complete these extracts. Which words did the candidates need but not know or remember?

   a In this photo a woman is _____.
   b There are a lot of _____.
   c In this picture, the woman is washing clothes _____.
   d She's using a kind of machine to _____ the clothes.
   e It _____ hard work.
   f The man looks _____.
   g You can be _____ and if you practise you can _____.
   h It's _____ than having a lot of clean clothes.

5 What strategy do the candidates use in **4** when they can't find the right word?

6 Work in pairs. Student A turn to page 155. Student B turn to page 156.

> **Tip**
> If you don't know the exact word, use an appropriate strategy to get round it.

Exam practice

Long turn

7 Work in pairs. Turn to page 156 and follow the instructions.

Over to you

8 Discuss these questions.

   a In your opinion, what have been the most important inventions or discoveries in your lifetime?
   b What inventions or discoveries would you like to see in the future?

Vocabulary

The name's the thing

1 According to the text, how are new products named? Can you think of more examples?

How do appliances, gadgets and products get their names? Sometimes they are named after their inventor, like the jacuzzi, named after Roy Jacuzzi. Sometimes the names are purely *descriptive*. They say what the invention does, like the can opener, or how it does it, like the *automatic* washing machine, or the *mechanical* digger. Some products are named by combining clever words or sounds together, like the mint sweet 'Tic Tacs'® or the chocolate bar 'Kit Kat'®. Nowadays, especially, a great deal of *careful* thought goes into naming any invention or new product, as a catchy name can guarantee the first few sales. Giving a product the wrong name can have a *disastrous* effect on sales. The Vauxhall Nova's name had to be changed for the Spanish car market. In Spanish 'no va' makes the car sound anything but *speedy* and *reliable*. It means 'it doesn't go'.

2 What are your favourite product names?

Adjective suffixes

3 Look at the adjectives in *italics* in the text above. What nouns or verbs are they related to? What suffixes have been added to the root words? What does the prefix *auto* mean?

4 Complete these sentences with an adjective related to the word in brackets.
  a Post-its® are small yellow pieces of _____ (stick) paper.
  b Some gadgets are _____ (use), but some are completely _____ (use).
  c The skirt is made from a _____ (fashion), _____ (stretch) material.
  d People who work in advertising need to be _____ (create) and come up with _____ (origin) ideas.
  e Wear _____ (protect) clothing when doing _____ (science) experiments which involve handling _____ (danger) chemicals.

Exam practice

Word formation

> **Tip**
>
> When you have chosen your answers, read through the whole text to check it makes sense.

5 For questions 1–8, read the text below. Use the word given in capitals at the end of some of the lines to form a word that fits in the gap in the same line. There is an example at the beginning (0).

If you invent something, it is always a (0) _sensible_ idea to	**SENSE**
patent it. A patent is simply an (1) _____ document which	**OFFICE**
protects your invention and stops other people stealing your	
ideas. Although it can be quite a (2) _____ process it is	**COST**
definitely (3) _____. However, don't assume that because	**WORTH**
your product is not for (4) _____ in a local store that	**SELL**
someone hasn't thought of the idea before. This,	
(5) _____, is often the case and then it's back to the	**FORTUNE**
drawing board again. Some inventors have been too slow to	
patent their inventions. In 1876 Alexander Graham Bell beat his	
rival Elisha Gray to the patent office by just two hours. Lack of	
funds is another reason why some have lost out while others	
have sold their ideas to (6) _____ before realizing their	**COMPETE**
true worth. After making some (7) _____ to the product,	**REFINE**
they claimed the glory. So learn from history and take my	
(8) _____ so the same thing doesn't happen to you.	**ADVISE**

unit 10 innovation

Listening Part 2

Think ahead

1 Which gadgets or appliances would you find it most difficult to live without for a month? Order them from 5 (most difficult) to 1 (least difficult).

2 What other gadgets do you have at home or at work which you couldn't live without?

Exam practice

Sentence completion

3 ◆) 2.12 You will hear someone giving a talk about gadgets. For questions 1–10 complete the sentences with a word or short phrase.

> **Tip**
>
> Make sure your answer fits the gap grammatically and your spelling is correct. You can write any numbers as either figures or words.

The gadget that British people spend the second most amount of time using is _____ **1** .

British people think the ability to speak _____ **2** is not at all important.

Despite the _____ **3** situation people are happy to pay for the latest gadget.

Some previously popular gadgets, such as _____ **4** , are rarely used any more.

In the fifties people showed as much _____ **5** as they do today when a new gadget comes on the market.

A historic televised event was sometimes shared with _____ **6** .

A 1950s housewife spent the majority of her day doing a variety of _____ **7** .

The introduction of household gadgets into many homes in the 1950s meant _____ **8** for women than they had previously had.

If a woman was given a household gadget as a present nowadays she would not be _____ **9** .

Many women prefer phones which have fewer _____ **10** .

Over to you

4 Discuss these questions.

a What was the last gadget or device you bought? Why did you buy it? Has it lived up to expectations?

b Have you ever bought a gadget or appliance which you rarely or never use?

c How important is it for you to have the latest electronic gadgets or games?

d Do you agree that people's attitudes to gadgets depend on their age and gender?

Vocabulary

Think ahead

1 These words have recently entered the English language. What do you think they mean?

agritourism   chatterboxing   cyberbullying   glocalization   jigsaw family

2 Read this short text. Then match the words below to their definitions.

Innovation in language

The English language is constantly changing. New words are being invented all the time, though not all of them are long-lasting. Lexicographers who work on revised editions of English dictionaries have to decide which new words to include and which not to include. In other words they have to decide which words will stand the test of time. To be included in a dictionary, words must have been used five times in five different sources over five years. Here are some words which have entered dictionaries in recent years.

jigsaw family	the adaptation of products to suit local and global markets
agritourism	the activity of using a platform such as Twitter to comment on what you are watching on TV
chatterboxing	a family in which two or more sets of children from previous relationships live together
cyberbullying	holidays where tourists visiting a country stay with local people who live in the countryside
glocalization	the use of electronic communication to intimidate someone

Compound adjectives

3 In the text above, words are described as *long-lasting*. What could be described using these compound adjectives?

labour-saving   mass-produced   home-made   user-friendly   cold-blooded
hard-wearing   last-minute

4 Which compound adjectives could be used to describe the following? You will need to use these words.

free   high   low   part   short

a a spread or yogurt which contains less fat than normal ones
b chewing gum which contains no sugar
c an investment with a lot of risk
d a shirt with sleeves which stop above the elbow
e a job where the employee only works for some of the day or week

Pronunciation

5 🔊 2.13 Listen to the compound adjectives in 3 and 4. Repeat after the speaker.

6 Match the words in A to the words in B to form compound adjectives which can be used to describe people's character.

A: well   open   self   hard   quick   level
B: working   headed   educated   motivated   tempered   minded

7 Look again at the words formed in 5. Which three of these qualities do you think it is most important for an inventor to have? Give reasons.

unit 10 innovation

Writing Part 2 – Review

Exam skills

1 Look at these stills from films which feature examples of innovative cinema techniques. Can you name the films? Do you know what innovative techniques they used?

2 What other innovations have there been in the movie industry?

3 Read this review and answer the questions.
   a Is the information you expected included?
   b What style is the review written in?
   c What star rating (★★★★★) do you think the writer would give the film?

Life of Pi

Directed by the acclaimed Taiwan-born director, Ang Lee, *Life of Pi* is the film version of the novel of the same name. In 2012 it won several Oscars, although it lost out to *Argo* on Best Picture.

The film, which uses state-of-the-art CGI, is a magical story of faith, friendship and perseverance. On one level *Life of Pi* is a fantastic epic adventure but on another it is an *allegorical tale about religion and faith. It tells the story, in flashback, of an Indian teenage boy called Pi who loses his entire family when the ship in which they are sailing to Canada sinks during a violent storm. The only survivors are four zoo animals, which were being transported to Canada for sale, and Pi himself. Eventually only Pi and a huge Bengali tiger called Richard Parker remain on the lifeboat, which drifts on the open ocean for over two hundred days before it reaches dry land.

Visually stunning – the digitally created tiger is so realistic you would swear it was real – and emotionally uplifting, *Life of Pi* is certainly one of the best films of recent years.

*allegorical tale – a story with characters or events that represent an idea or quality, e.g. truth, danger, etc.

Evaluative adjectives

4 Read the review on page 126 again. Underline any positive evaluative adjectives.

5 Divide these adjectives into two groups, positive and negative.

amateurish   clever   disappointing   dull   entertaining   exciting   fake
first rate   funny   hilarious   original   over-complicated   over-long
predictable   spectacular   unconvincing   witty   wonderful   wooden

6 Complete these sentences using an appropriate adjective from **5**. There may be more than one answer.

a The ending of the film was very _____. It was obvious that Meg and Drew would get married after the first five minutes.

b The photography was _____. The aerial shots of Niagara Falls in particular were out of this world.

c The acting was extremely _____. I have seen more convincing performances from children in a school play.

d The show was hugely _____. We enjoyed it from start to finish.

e I thought the plot was _____. It was hard to follow what was going on.

7 Reviews can be about many things, for example: books, concerts, films, music, musicals, plays and TV programmes. Write the words below in the correct place in the table. Some words can be used more than once.

~~act~~   acting   album   author   cast   chapter   choreography   commentary
conductor   costumes   design   director   episode   lighting   lyrics
orchestra   plot   published   released   scene   scenery   series   soundtrack
special effects   stunt   track

Books	Concerts	Films	Music	Musicals	Plays	TV
					act	

Exam practice

Review
▸ Writing guide page 183

Tip
It doesn't matter if the information you give in your review is true. You can make information up if you need to.

8 You are going to write a review. Read the task below. Then, work through stages a–e.

> You have seen the following announcement on an English-language website.
>
> **Can you recommend a film which you think people of all ages would enjoy?**
>
> Write a review of the film describing the plot in brief and saying why it would be appropriate for people of all ages.
>
> Write your **review** in 140–190 words.

a Which points do you need to cover in your review?

b Decide which film you are going to review.

c Make a note of your ideas. Use these prompts to help you.
  • name of film, type of film, main actors, setting
  • brief outline of the plot – but don't give away the ending
  • why the film would be suitable for viewing in your English class

d Write your review. Use your notes to help you. Try to use some of the language in **5** and **7**.

e Finally, when you have finished, check your grammar, spelling and punctuation.

unit 10 innovation

Unit 10 Review

1 For questions 1–8, read the text below. Use the word given in capitals at the end of some of the lines to form a word that fits in the space in the same line. There is an example at the beginning (0).

THE TURNER PRIZE

The Turner Prize, (0) _undoubtedly_ Britain's most well-known art award, is also its most (1) _____. The £25,000 prize is awarded annually to the British artist who has, in the opinion of a jury, made the greatest (2) _____ to art in the previous twelve months.

DOUBT
CONTROVERSY
CONTRIBUTE

The four short-listed candidates exhibit a work of their (3) _____ at Tate Britain, one of London's main galleries. The award ceremony, which is televised live, takes place in December, with the (4) _____ of the winner being made by a well-known celebrity.

CHOOSE
ANNOUNCE

The prize, which is a showcase for the (5) _____ in contemporary British art, has its critics. One of the main (6) _____ directed against it is that it appears to ignore more (7) _____ forms of art like painting. In recent years the prize has gone to a video artist, a sculptor and a photographer, which seems to support the critics' (8) _____.

LATE
CRITIC
TRADITION

ARGUE

2 Complete these sentences with the correct form of a verb.

a John regrets losing his temper.
   John wishes he _____ his temper.
b You are interrupting me. It's so annoying!
   I wish you _____ me. It's so annoying.
c Unfortunately I can't go to the party.
   I wish I _____ to the party.
d It's a pity I didn't meet her when I was single.
   I wish I _____ her when I was single.
e I'd love to have green eyes instead of brown eyes.
   I wish I _____ brown eyes. I wish I _____ green eyes.
f I really regret not applying for that job.
   I wish I _____ for that job.
g I really think we should leave now.
   It's time we _____.
h He's thirty-six. He should get a job.
   It's time he _____ a job.
i I'd prefer you not to bring Andrew.
   I'd rather you _____ Andrew.
j I'd like you to tell me your answer now, not later.
   I'd rather you _____ me your answer now, not later.

unit 10 innovation

128

Unit 11 Communication

Introduction

1 Which of these methods of communication do you use most frequently? Put them in order, starting with the most frequent.

email   face-to-face communication   internet webcam (Skype)
social networking (Facebook, Twitter etc.)   telephone (landline or mobile)
text messaging

2 For people in your country, how important are the means of non-verbal communication shown in these photographs?

3 Discuss these questions in pairs in relation to people in your country.

a Do people use frequent gestures when they are talking?

b Is eye contact important when people are talking to each other?

c Have you noticed people of other nationalities behaving differently with regard to gestures and eye contact?

Reading and Use of English Part 6

Think ahead 1 Look at the expressions on these faces and think of words which best describe the emotions expressed. Discuss your answers in pairs.

2 Try to copy each expression in the photographs. How easy do you find this? Are there any expressions you find difficult to make?

Exam practice

Tip

When you've finished the task, read through the whole text to check that it makes sense.

Gapped text 3 You are going to read an article about a project to classify human facial expressions. Six sentences have been removed from the article. Choose from the sentences A–G the one which fits each gap (1–6). There is one extra sentence which you do not need to use.

A Any other method of showing all 412 emotions, such as words, would have been far less effective.

B He said that the expression of these feelings was universal and recognizable by anyone, from any culture.

C Research has also been done to find out which areas of the brain read emotional expression.

D These are particularly difficult to control, and few people can do it by choice.

E These can be combined into more than 10,000 visible facial shapes.

F They decided that it was a mental state that could be preceded by 'I feel' or 'he looks' or 'she sounds'.

G It is as if they are programmed into the brains of 'normal humans' wherever they are and whatever their race.

I know just how you feel

Do you feel sad? Happy? Angry? You may think that the way you show these emotions is unique. Well, think again. Even the expression of the most personal feelings can be classified, according to Mind Reading, a DVD displaying every possible human emotion. It demonstrates 412 distinct ways in which we feel: the first visual dictionary of the human heart.

Attempts to classify expressions began in the mid-1800s, when Darwin divided the emotions into six types – anger, fear, sadness, disgust, surprise and enjoyment. 1 ☐

Every other feeling was thought to derive from Darwin's small group. More complex expressions of emotion were probably learned and therefore more specific to each culture. But now it is believed that many more facial expressions are shared worldwide. 2 ☐ The Mind Reading DVD is a systematic visual record of these expressions.

The project was conceived by a Cambridge professor as an aid for people with autism, who have difficulty both reading and expressing emotions. But it quickly became apparent that it had broader uses. Actors and teachers, for example, need to understand a wide range of expressions. The professor and his research team first had to define an 'emotion'. 3 ☐ Using this definition, 1,512 emotion terms were identified and discussed. This list was eventually reduced to 412, from 'afraid' to 'wanting'.

Once these emotions were defined and classified, a DVD seemed the clearest and most efficient way to display them. In Mind Reading, each expression is acted out by six different actors in three seconds.

4 ☐ The explanation for this is simple: we may find it difficult to describe emotions using words, but we instantly recognize one when we see it on someone's face. 'It was really clear when the actors had got it right,' says Cathy Collis, who directed the DVD. 'Although they were given some direction,' says Ms Collis, 'the actors were not told which facial muscles they should move. We thought of trying to describe each emotion, but it would have been almost impossible to make clear rules for this.' For example, when someone feels contempt, you can't say for certain that their eyebrows always go down.

Someone who has tried to establish such rules is the American, Professor Paul Ekman, who has built a database of how the face moves for every emotion. The face can make 43 distinct muscle movements called 'action units'. 5 ☐ Ekman has written out a pattern of facial muscular movements to represent each emotion. Fear, for example, uses six simultaneous 'action units' including stretching the lips and dropping the jaw.

Ekman has also found that although it is possible to classify and describe the natural expression of emotions, it may not be possible for people to reproduce them artificially. According to Ekman, we can't decide to be happy or sad; it simply happens to us. Apparently, the most difficult expression to reproduce is the smile. Ekman says a smile isn't only about stretching the lips, but tightening the tiny muscles around the eyes. 6 ☐ If we learned to recognize whether someone was using their eye muscles when they smiled, we would be able to distinguish true enjoyment from false.

This finding is of great interest to police authorities who are seeking Ekman's help in interpreting even the tiniest 'micro-expressions' – lasting only one twenty-fifth of a second – to detect whether or not someone is lying.

Over to you

4 Discuss these questions with a partner.
   a How easy or difficult do you find reading other people's emotions?
   b Do you find it easy to recognize when someone is 'really' smiling?
   c How useful do you think the results of this project are?

5 With a partner describe in detail how one of the expressions shown in the photographs is being made.

Grammar

Conditionals 0, 1 and 2
▸ *Grammar reference* page 173

1 These three conditional sentences are grammatically different. Which verb tenses are used in the two parts of each sentence?

   Type 0   If you *smile* genuinely, the muscles around your eyes *move*.
   Type 1   If you *communicate* effectively in the interview, you *will* probably *get* the job.
   Type 2   Even if I *told* you the truth, you *wouldn't believe* me.

2 The three sentences above are also different in meaning. Which sentences refer to …
   a an unlikely event or situation?   c a likely event or situation?
   b something that actually happens?

3 Which of these two conditional sentences refers to a future possibility? Which refers to something imaginary or impossible?
   a If he applied for that job, I'm sure he'd get it.
   b If he was a few years younger, I'm sure he'd get the job.

4 What is the difference in meaning between each of these pairs of sentences?
   a 1 If I get the chance, I'll work abroad.   b 1 If I got the chance, I'd work abroad.
      2 If I get the chance, I may work abroad.   2 If I got the chance, I might work abroad.

5 Complete these sentences with your own ideas to form Type 0 conditional sentences. There is an example at the beginning.
   a If I have bad news to pass on, I *usually send an email or a text message*.
   b If I have good news to pass on, I _____.
   c If someone has upset me, I _____.
   d If I need a friend's advice, I _____.
   e If I want to apologize for something I've done, I _____.

6 Conditional sentences are often used to persuade, to warn, to threaten and to promise. Complete these sentences with your own ideas.
   a If you play computer games for too long, _____.
   b If you don't go to bed earlier, _____.
   c If you lend me your car for the evening, _____.
   d I'd spend more time at home if _____.

Conditional 3
▸ *Grammar reference* page 173

7 Which verb tenses are used in this Type 3 conditional sentence?

   If you had given me your number, I would have sent you a text message.

8 What is the main difference in meaning between Type 3 conditional sentences and Types 0, 1 and 2?

9 Type 3 conditional sentences are often used for making excuses. Complete these sentences with an excuse of your own. There is an example at the beginning.
   a I would have answered the phone if *I had known it was you calling*.
   b Sorry, but I would have contacted you if _____.
   c Sorry, I wouldn't have been late if _____.
   d If I'd known when your birthday was, I _____.
   e If we hadn't got home so late, we _____.

10 What would you have done if you had been in this situation?

   When Jill Frame broke down on the motorway at 9 p.m. last Tuesday night, she got out of her car and went to find a telephone. The nearest one was on the opposite side of the six-lane motorway.

Mixed conditionals 11 What is the difference in meaning between these two sentences?
  a If I hadn't broken my leg, I would have gone on holiday with you.
  b If I hadn't broken my leg, I would go on holiday with you.

12 Complete these sentences with present or future results.
  a If I hadn't learned to read, _____.
  b If I'd won the lottery at the weekend, _____.
  c If I'd saved all my money for the last year, _____.
  d If I hadn't had a good education, _____.
  e If I'd been born into a very rich family, _____.
  f If my mother hadn't met my father, _____.

unless, as long as, provided that 13 Rewrite these sentences replacing *if* with the words in brackets.
  a If you don't work harder, you'll fail your exams. (unless)
  b You'll pass your driving test if you practise enough. (as long as)
  c You can borrow my car if you buy your own petrol. (provided that)
  d You can only phone me if you have some important news. (unless)

14 Now finish these sentences in several different ways. Two possible answers are given for the first one.
  a I'll come on holiday with you provided that *you don't drive too fast / you do your share of the cooking /* _____.
  b I'll never speak to you again unless _____.
  c I'll lend you the money you need as long as _____.

── **Exam practice** ──

Key word transformation 15 For questions 1–6, complete the second sentence so that it has a similar meaning to the first sentence, using the word given. Do not change the word given. You must use between two and five words, including the word given.

Tip

Most answers are likely to require you to add between three and four words plus the key word.

1 Although the weather was dreadful, we finished our game of tennis.
   SPITE
   We finished our game of tennis _____ weather.

2 The alarm woke the children up.
   OFF
   If the alarm _____, the children would have stayed asleep.

3 You can borrow my phone if you give it back to me as soon as you've made the call.
   PROVIDED
   I'll only _____ that you give it back to me as soon as you've made the call.

4 Students must cook their own meals.
   RESPONSIBLE
   Students _____ their own meals.

5 My T-shirt and hat stopped me from getting sunburned.
   WORN
   I would have got sunburned _____ my T-shirt and hat.

6 If you don't start revising soon, you won't get the marks you need.
   ENOUGH
   You won't get high _____ revising soon.

Speaking Parts 3 & 4

Collocations with *say*, *speak*, *talk* and *tell*

1 *Say*, *speak*, *talk* and *tell* have similar meanings, but are used in different ways. Complete these sentences with the correct form of the appropriate verb.
   a Can you _____ a second language?
   b Sorry, I can't _____ you the time – I haven't got my watch on.
   c If you've got such strong opinions, you should _____ your mind.
   d Some people _____ a short prayer before a meal.
   e Have I _____ you my favourite joke?
   f I swear to _____ the truth, the whole truth and nothing but the truth.
   g You know nothing about the subject. You're _____ rubbish.
   h My mother used to _____ me stories about when she was a child.

Confusing verbs: *hope*, *wait*, *expect*, *look forward to*

2 Match the verbs in *italics* in sentences a–d with their meanings in sentences 1–4.
   a I *hope* you feel better soon.
   b I'm *looking forward* to seeing you again.
   c He got off the train and *waited for* a taxi.
   d I *expect* it'll rain tomorrow.

   1 to believe that something will happen
   2 to stay somewhere until something happens
   3 to want something to happen or be true
   4 to want something to happen because you know you will enjoy it

3 Choose the correct verb in these sentences.
   a We've been *looking forward to / waiting for* the bus for half an hour.
   b We're *expecting / waiting for* good weather on our holidays.
   c I'm really *looking forward to getting / waiting to get* his letter.
   d I've bought you a little present. I *hope you'll like / expect you like* it.
   e Has the postman been yet? I'm *expecting / looking forward to* a letter.
   f I've worked hard this week. I'm really *looking forward to / hoping for* the weekend.

Showing you are listening

4 Work in pairs. Read these Part 3 prompts. Talk to your partner about how easy it is for people to make new friends in these situations. How might these actions help people to make new friends?

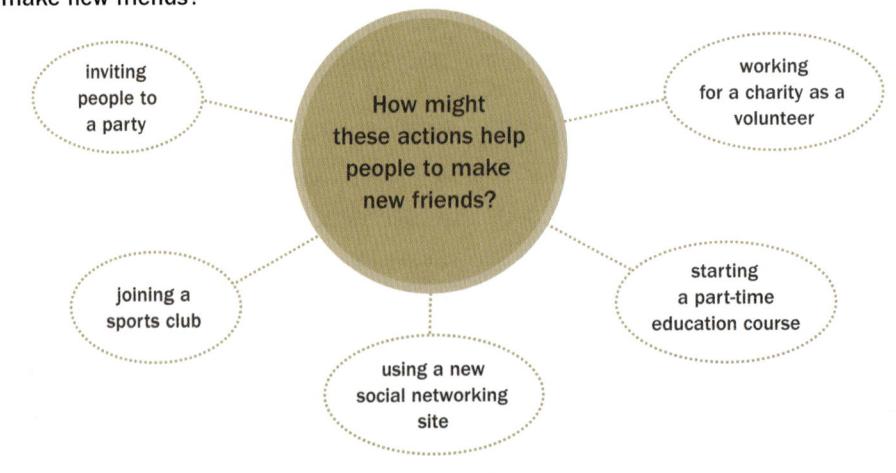

- inviting people to a party
- working for a charity as a volunteer
- joining a sports club
- starting a part-time education course
- using a new social networking site

How might these actions help people to make new friends?

5 🔊 2.14 Listen to two candidates doing a Part 3 task. Answer these questions.
   a What do the two candidates say about working as a volunteer for a charity?
   b Why don't they think that joining a new social networking site would be very helpful?

Question tags 6 🔊 2.14 One of the ways the two candidates keep each other involved in the conversation is to use question tags. Listen again and complete the tags in a–g.

a People are different, though, _____?
b Nobody actually does an education course to make new friends, _____?
c People do make new friends once they're there, _____?
d You must have made one or two friends while you were on a course, _____?
e You're working for other people, _____?
f People can seem to be good friends, _____?
g It shows how wrong you can be about a person when you haven't met them, _____?

Pronunciation 7 🔊 2.14 Listen again. Does the intonation go up or down on the question tags in 6?

8 🔊 2.15 Listen to sentences 1 and 2 below.

a Does the intonation go up (↗) or down (↘)?
  1 The theory part of the driving test isn't difficult, is it?
  2 The theory part of the driving test isn't difficult, is it?

b Underline the correct word in *italics* in A and B to complete the intonation rule for question tags.
  A *Rising / Falling* intonation = I am expecting you to agree with me.
  B *Rising / Falling* intonation = I don't know the answer and I want you to tell me.

c Match each rule A and B to sentence 1 or 2 above.

9 Add the appropriate question tags to sentences a–e. Then practise saying them with the intonation pattern given.

a It's harder to make friends when you're older, _____? (Falling)
b You will keep in touch when you move away, _____? (Falling)
c I don't suppose you're going to see Richard later, _____? (Rising)
d You haven't invited Mike to the party, _____? (Rising)
e It was such a good party, _____? (Falling)

Exam practice

Collaborative task & discussion 10 Work with a partner. Complete the second part of the Part 3 task below, using the prompts in 4 on page 134. Remember the examiner's instruction:

Now you have about a minute to decide which two actions would be most likely to help people to make new friends.

In your conversation, use question tags to keep your partner involved.

Tip
Remember to give reasons and explanations for your answers.

11 Work with a partner. Discuss these questions related to the Part 3 topic.
- Why do you think that some people find it easier than others to make new friends?
- Do you think it is easier or more difficult for people to make new friends than it was in the past? (Give reasons)
- Is there anything that schools, colleges and other organizations could do to help new students or members to make friends more easily?
- If people move to a new place, what can they do to make sure they do not lose touch with their old friends?
- Do you think it is more difficult to make friends as we get older? (Why? / Why not?)
- How important do you think friends are in today's world?

135

Listening Part 1

Think ahead 1 Think of an occasion when you told a deliberate lie. Discuss these questions.
   a Was it a serious lie, or just a bit of fun?
   b Did you lie for your own benefit or for someone else's?
   c Did anyone find out about the lie?

Exam practice

Multiple choice 2 🔊 2.16 You will hear people talking in eight different situations. For questions 1–8, choose the best answer (A, B or C).

Tip

Make sure you concentrate on the recording you are listening to. Don't continue to focus on the previous question.

1 You will hear a woman talking about an invitation she turned down. What excuse did she make?
   A She said she had arranged to go home.
   B She said she had already eaten.
   C She said she didn't like the food.

2 You hear a man being interviewed about his job. What is the job?
   A an economist
   B a TV interviewer
   C a politician

3 You hear a woman talking about meeting a neighbour in town. Why didn't the speaker say anything about her sister?
   A The rumour was not true.
   B The neighbour might tell other people.
   C She didn't know anything.

4 You hear a woman talking about a party she went to. Why did she lie to the man?
   A to see how he reacted
   B to make an impression on him
   C to keep the conversation going

5 You hear a man talking about an accident he was involved in. What was the cause of the accident?
   A The speaker had fallen asleep while driving.
   B There had been a lot of traffic on the road.
   C Something had gone wrong with the car.

6 You hear a woman talking about a phone call she answered. Why was her brother angry?
   A He had wanted to speak to Annie.
   B He had wanted to answer the phone himself.
   C He had wanted to speak to Barbara.

7 You hear two people talking about something which one of them has bought. What was wrong with this thing?
   A It was broken.
   B It wasn't genuine.
   C It wasn't very good.

8 You hear a woman talking about something she did for her sister. Why didn't she tell her sister her exam results?
   A She shouldn't have opened the letter.
   B It would have spoiled her sister's holiday.
   C She couldn't contact her sister.

Over to you 3 Have you ever known a compulsive liar or someone, like the fourth speaker, who lies for fun? How do you react to people like this?

Vocabulary

Think ahead 1 Read this extract from an email. Why do you think the writer objected to the word his friend used to describe him?

Re: Hi!

To: Matt
Date: 05 June
Subject: Re: Hi!

Hi Matt,

Thanks for the email. Glad you're enjoying your holiday. I'm fine. I've been trying to get fit for the marathon next month. I have to lose a couple of kilos by then, so I'm watching my diet.

While I was out running the other day I saw Eddie. He said he didn't recognize me because I looked so skinny. I'm sure he meant it as a compliment, but I wish he'd called me slim or even thin.

Do you still play tennis regularly? I remember the last time we played. It must have been three or four years ago – you beat me easily.

Positive or negative? 2 The story in the email shows that the words people choose can communicate positive or negative ideas. The two words in *italics* in sentences a–i have related meanings. Which of the words conveys a more negative idea?

a I've just bought a(n) *cheap / inexpensive* second car.
b To succeed in business you have to be *determined / ruthless*.
c My brother's a *well-built / fat* man in his mid-thirties.
d Is your coat made of *fake / imitation* leather?
e My neighbour spends all her time *chatting / gossiping* to friends.
f The football fans were *excited / hysterical* when their team scored.
g We had dinner at a(n) *expensive / pricey* restaurant last night.
h John *smiles / sneers* whenever he sees me.
i The *old / elderly* man next door takes his dog for a walk every day.

3 Which of these words would you prefer people used to describe you, for example in a reference for a job?

a cold / reserved
b easy-going / lazy
c curious / nosey
d cowardly / shy
e self-satisfied / self-confident
f serious / dull
g chatty / outgoing
h intelligent / clever

Over to you 4 There is a well-known English saying: 'Sticks and stones may break my bones, but words can never hurt me.' Can you remember an occasion when you have been hurt by words or when you have used words to hurt another person?

unit 11 communication

Writing Part 2 – Article

Think ahead 1 Read the two introductions, A and B, to each of the stories (1–3) below. Answer questions a–b.

a For each story, say which article you would choose to read and why.

b What makes a good opening to an article? Discuss your ideas with a partner.

Story 1

A

Motivation is the key to learning foreign languages

A recent survey has discovered that English children aged 12–15 are well behind their counterparts in other countries when it comes to foreign language learning.

B

Why are English teenagers so bad at learning foreign languages?

English teenagers are the worst in Europe at learning foreign languages. But perhaps this is not surprising, given how widely spoken English is.

Story 2

A

The day my silence ended

As the deaf son of hearing parents, Stuart was a lonely child. Then in his twenties, he had a device fitted which filled his world with sound for the first time.

B

New device can reverse deafness

A recently developed digital device is changing the lives of thousands of deaf people. The device, which has undergone rigorous testing, is now commercially available for the first time.

Story 3

A

Can Twitter open up a new space for learning, teaching and thinking?

Believe it or not, a few geeks have set up the Swedish Twitter University, which is bringing lectures as a series of tweets to a class of around 500 followers.

B

A famous social networking service opens its door to 'students'

Twitter, the social networking service used by millions of people around the world, is taking on a new role as a kind of online university.

Exam skills 2 Read this Writing Part 2 task. Then, discuss the questions below with a partner.

> You have seen the following notice in an online magazine for students learning English.
>
> > Calling all language learners!
> >
> > **Language learning activities that have helped me**
> >
> > What language learning activities have helped you?
> >
> > Where did you do these activities? How have they helped you?
> >
> > Write us an article answering these questions.
> >
> > We will publish the best articles on our website.
>
> Write your **article** in 140–190 words.

a What language learning activities have helped you to communicate with other people? (Think about activities you do outside as well as inside the classroom.)

b How are these activities different from less successful activities you have done?

c Who will read an article like this?

3 Now read the response on page 139 to the task in **2**. Then, discuss these questions.

a Has the writer answered all the questions?

b Does the writer mention any of the activities you discussed?

c Do you think the readers you described will find this article interesting?

d Is the style appropriate?

> **Language learning: what worked for me**
>
> Believe it or not, I have been studying English for almost five years, and what I want more than anything is to communicate successfully. For me this means being a fluent speaker. What I'll do now is describe two activities that have been especially effective for me.
>
> The first has to be role-play – making conversations with other students when we're playing the part of shopkeepers and customers or doctors and patients. It is because we're practising for possible future situations that this works for me.
>
> I'm not sure you can describe my second choice as an 'activity'. It was an experience I had when I stayed with an English family when I was 13. I found it frightening to start with. The thing is, I couldn't understand what anyone was saying. Gradually, of course, it became easier and I even managed to reply to questions. By the end of my stay, I felt quite comfortable and could say almost anything I needed to say.
>
> What has worked for me may not work for everyone, which is why I suppose language lessons consist of so many different activities.

4 The sample answer attempts to engage the reader by starting some sentences with a phrase which raises expectations. Read the article again and underline them.

5 Rewrite sentences a–f starting with one of these phrases.

Believe it or not   For me, …   It was because …   The thing is …
What I believe is that …

a I got a grade A in the Speaking exam. That's difficult to believe, isn't it?
b I didn't do very well in the Writing test because my spelling was so poor.
c I find that the most effective activities are group discussions.
d I believe we should pay more attention to correct pronunciation.
e I think the most important thing is not worrying about making mistakes.

Exam practice

Article
▸ Writing guide page 182

Tip
Before you start writing, make notes in answer to the questions in the task. Remember that articles should be both informative and interesting.

6 You are going to write an article. First, read the task below. Then, work through stages a–e.

> Calling all language learners!
>
> **The best thing about knowing another language?**
>
> What is the most useful thing that knowing another language enables you to do?
>
> When have you found or would you find this ability useful?
>
> How did / would it help you?
>
> Write an article answering these questions. We will publish the best articles on our website.
>
> Write your **article** in 140–190 words.

a Think about the topic. Discuss the following in pairs and make brief notes.
   • What would you most like to be able to do using a second language?
   • What problems can arise if people do not know a second language?
   • What problems have you had personally?
b Plan each paragraph of your article, using the sample answer in **3** as a model.
c Think about how to start your sentences in a way which will engage the reader.
d Write your article. Make sure the style is appropriate. Check that you have answered the question in full.
e Finally, when you have finished, check your grammar, spelling and punctuation.

unit 11 communication

Unit 11 Review

1 Read the text below and think of the word which best fits each gap. Use only one word in each gap. There is an example at the beginning (0).

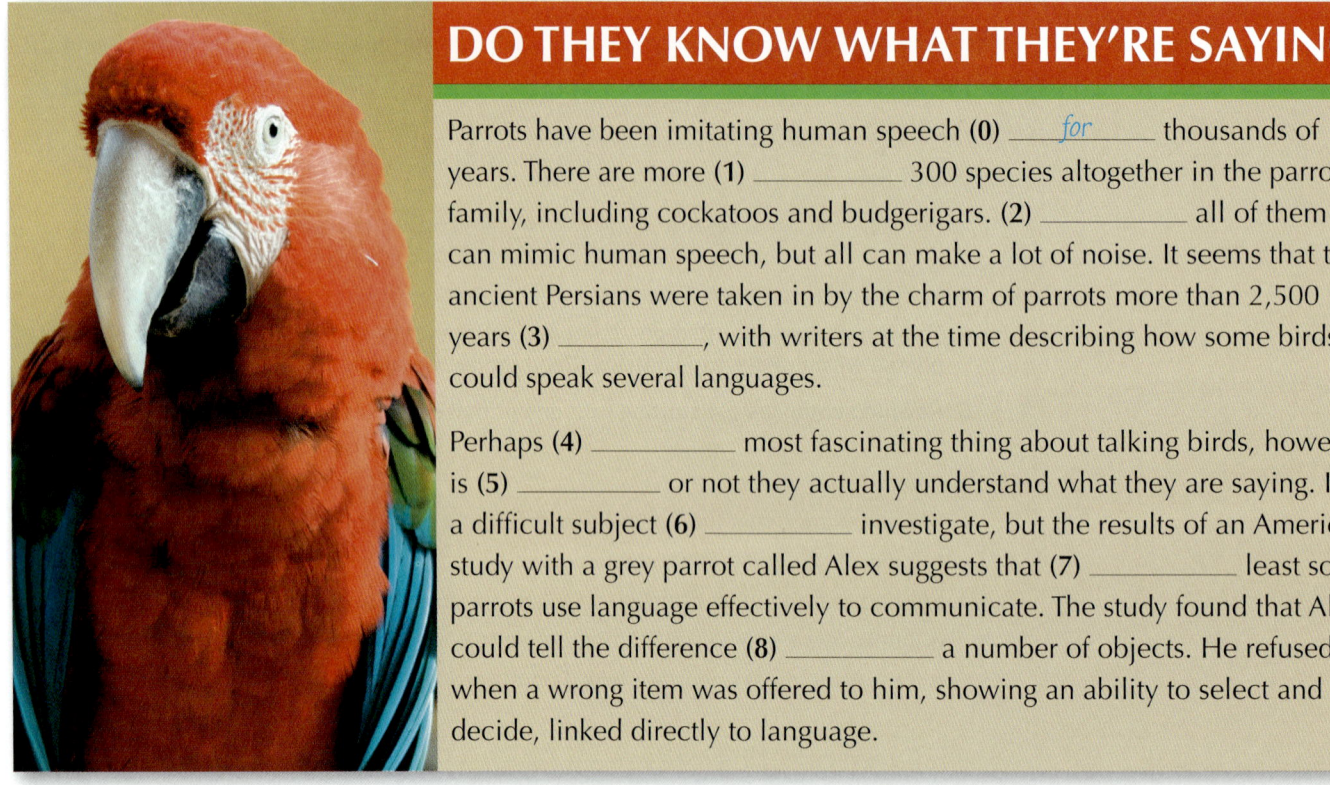

DO THEY KNOW WHAT THEY'RE SAYING?

Parrots have been imitating human speech (0) ___*for*___ thousands of years. There are more (1) _____ 300 species altogether in the parrot family, including cockatoos and budgerigars. (2) _____ all of them can mimic human speech, but all can make a lot of noise. It seems that the ancient Persians were taken in by the charm of parrots more than 2,500 years (3) _____, with writers at the time describing how some birds could speak several languages.

Perhaps (4) _____ most fascinating thing about talking birds, however, is (5) _____ or not they actually understand what they are saying. It is a difficult subject (6) _____ investigate, but the results of an American study with a grey parrot called Alex suggests that (7) _____ least some parrots use language effectively to communicate. The study found that Alex could tell the difference (8) _____ a number of objects. He refused when a wrong item was offered to him, showing an ability to select and decide, linked directly to language.

2 Choose the correct alternative to complete these sentences.

a If I have a headache, *I take / I'd take* some tablets and go to bed.
b If the classroom caught fire, *we'll go / we'd go* down the fire escape.
c We'd have won the match if our goalkeeper *hasn't / hadn't* been injured.
d You can come to the party, as long as *you bring / you'll bring* something to eat and drink.
e If I see Nick, *I tell / I'll tell* him you'd like to speak to him.
f I'd be a lot richer now, if I *accepted / had accepted* that job in America last year.
g I can't help you unless *you tell / you'll tell* me what the problem is.
h If I were you, *I'll text / I'd text* him back straightaway.

3 Complete these sentences with the correct form of one of the verbs in brackets.

a The trouble with you is that you never _____ what you think. (say / speak)
b You've got to learn to _____ your mind. (say / speak)
c I'm OK at writing in Russian, but I'm not very good at _____ it. (speak / tell)
d He hardly ever _____ the truth. In fact, I'd say he was a born liar. (say / tell)
e Good luck in the competition tomorrow. I really _____ you win. (expect / hope)
f Are you _____ starting your new job? (expect / look forward to)
g What a surprise! I didn't _____ to see you here this evening. (expect / hope)

140

Unit 12 Society

Introduction

1 Work in small groups. What negative aspects of society does each photograph illustrate?

2 Choose two or more of the photographs and discuss these questions.

   a What similarities or differences are there between the issues in the photographs and the situation in your country?

   b What is being done to solve these problems in your country? What would you do?

Reading and Use of English Part 7

Think ahead

1 Discuss these questions in pairs.
   a Are people born bad?
   b Is it possible for people to change their character? How?

2 You are going to read a text about five people who got into trouble with the authorities when they were young but went on to become respectable members of society. Read the text quickly and answer these questions.
   a What crimes did each person commit?
   b What event or person caused each of them to change?
   c What jobs did they go on to do?

Exam practice

Multiple matching

3 Read the text again. For questions 1–10, choose from the people (A–E). The people may be chosen more than once.

> **Tip**
> If you can't find an answer quickly, go on to the next question and come back to it.

Which person

feels he disappointed his family?	1
believes he was a danger to society?	2
says he was negatively influenced by others?	3
describes in detail the event which made him change?	4
says a family member set a bad example?	5
understands a family member's reaction?	6
states that his job helped change his life?	7
thinks one person's decision changed his life?	8
believes that young people can usually change?	9
regrets the pain he caused?	10

Crime vocabulary

4 Complete these sentences with the correct word from this list.

   burglary   drink-driving   hooliganism   mugging   shoplifting   vandalism

   a The youth admitted smashing the windows on purpose. Such acts of _____ are commonplace nowadays.
   b The man lost his licence for _____. He was well over the legal limit.
   c The _____ took place in the early hours when the woman was walking home. She was assaulted and her mobile phone and wallet stolen.
   d The store detective stopped the man at the exit and accused him of _____.
   e _____ in football is rife with so-called 'fans' more interested in fighting rival fans than actually watching the game.
   f The _____ took place in the five minutes I was out. They took my laptop.

5 Complete these sentences with the correct form of *rob* or *steal*.
   a That bank _____ twice this year. Each time over £500,000 _____.
   b More and more people are fitting their cars with anti-theft alarms in an attempt to stop them from _____.
   c 'Oh, no! I _____! They've taken everything. My credit cards, cash, the lot!'
   d The thieves were accused of _____ jewellery worth over £250,000.
   e The shoplifter _____ £500 worth of goods from the store.

They turned their lives around

A The Film Star

As a juvenile, Mark Hudson was arrested for various things including car theft, drink-driving and burglary. 'I was a bad boy,' Hudson recalls. 'The turning point came when I was arrested for robbing a store at the age of twenty-one. I remember a police officer pointing a gun at my head ready to shoot. I realized at that moment that it could have been over for me. Anyway, I served my time and when I got out I was lucky to get into acting and I was able to move into a different world.' Ironically, these days Hudson often plays a criminal on screen.

B The former US Senator

At 17, Edward Jackson served two years' probation for vandalizing property. 'It's difficult to understand how I ended up in prison when my father had been a US senator and I grew up in a loving, stable home. I remember the look my parents gave each other when the judge passed sentence. They must have thought: "Where have we failed?"' Jackson followed in his father's footsteps and became a US senator. He thanked his probation officer publicly during his first election campaign. 'He helped me make it to where I got to – he was a great influence in my life. It's so important to give kids a second chance as most children will and do turn out all right in the end – I am proof of that.'

C The Criminal Defence Lawyer

'I was always getting into fights when I was young,' recalls Ray Terry. 'I ended up in a juvenile detention centre for six months when I was ten because of it. Even my mother gave up on me. She said she'd had enough and kicked me out when I was sixteen. I can't blame her. I must have been a nightmare in those days.' Reflecting on this period of his life, Terry remarked, 'I had so much anger, so little respect for authority that I could easily have killed someone.' Today Terry is a successful criminal defence lawyer. He says he owes this to several individuals – teachers and counsellors – who helped him.

D The Corporate Tax Lawyer

Son of Chinese immigrants, Lawrence Hu, was an extremely bright child who was never in trouble with the law. 'Things went wrong after my dad left home when I was fourteen and we ended up having to move house,' Hu recalls. 'There was a big gang culture in the new neighbourhood and I ended up in one of them. I dropped out of school as that wasn't considered "cool" and my life revolved around the gang. Things might never have changed if I hadn't been arrested for attempted murder. That was my wake-up call. I left the gang, went back to school and turned my life around.' Hu now works as a corporate tax lawyer, but says, 'I still feel awful about what I must have put my mother through at that time'.

E The Olympic Athlete

Former long-jump Olympic athlete, Sam Smith, was already getting into trouble by the time he was nine. 'My mother died when I was three and my father wasn't the best role model. He was constantly in and out of prison. So a criminal life just seemed normal to me.' Smith vividly recalls the day when he stood in front of a judge accused of assault. 'The judge must have seen something in me. He said he was going to take a chance. Instead of sending me to jail, he sent me to an alternative school along with other juvenile delinquents. While I was there I had plenty of time to reflect. And that's when I also took up sport.'

Over to you

6 Discuss these questions.

a At what age do you think children should be held legally responsible for their actions?
b Should parents be held responsible for their children's actions?
c Should society punish criminals or try to re-educate them?

Grammar (1)

Probability and possibility

▶ *Grammar reference page 174*

1 Underline the modal verbs in these sentences.
   a Things might never have changed if I hadn't been arrested.
   b They must have thought: "Where have we failed?"
   c I could easily have killed someone.
   d It can't have been easy for these people to turn their lives around.

2 Match the meaning of each modal verb in **1** with these explanations.
   1 The speaker is almost certain that something is the case.
   2 The speaker is almost certain that something is not the case.
   3 The speaker is not certain that something is the case but thinks it is possible.

3 Read dialogues a–d and decide whether the second speaker is talking about a past, present or future situation.
   a 'Is that Pete driving that BMW?'
      'Yes. He must have sold his sports car.'
   b 'I haven't seen Jennifer for ages!'
      'She might be studying. She's got exams soon.'
   c 'Isn't Daniel coming?'
      'He might come later.'
   d 'I'm starving!'
      'So am I. It must be almost lunchtime.'

4 Which structure follows the modal verbs in each dialogue in **3**? What other structures or words do you know with similar meanings, for example, *maybe*?

5 Complete these sentences using an appropriate modal verb and the correct form of the verb in brackets. There may be more than one answer.
   a Joan loves chocolate cake, but she didn't want any when I offered her some. She _____ (be) on a diet, or she _____ (be) hungry.
   b Susan seems to be angry with me, but I don't know why. I _____ (say) something to annoy her because I haven't seen her for ages.
   c James didn't answer the door when I rang his doorbell last night. The doorbell has a very quiet ring, so he _____ (hear) me.
   d Have you seen Peter anywhere? He _____ (leave) the building because his jacket's right there. He never goes out without it.
   e Julie _____ (get) a shock when she received her exam results. She was expecting an A but she only got a C.
   f The missing teenager _____ (wear) a white T-shirt – no one's quite sure.
   g I don't know where Darren is. He _____ (forget). He never does. Something _____ (happen) to him. He's always so punctual. I suppose his car _____ (break down).
   h If it wasn't you, then Kathy _____ (take) the last chocolate. No one else could have.

6 Read the newspaper report and answer the questions.
   a Where was Raymond Miller murdered?
   b When was he murdered?
   c How was he murdered?
   d What do police believe was the motive?
   e How many suspects are they interviewing?

MILLIONAIRE MURDERED IN HIS HOME

Millionaire Raymond Miller was murdered in his own home late on Friday evening. He was shot once in the head. Police believe the crime was motivated by money. Miller's personal safe was discovered to be empty. It is believed that the millionaire usually kept at least twenty thousand pounds in cash in the house. Police are currently interviewing three suspects about the crime.

7 🔊 **2.17** Inspector Hurst is in charge of the murder case you read about in **6**. He is reporting his progress to his superior officer. Listen and complete the suspects' profiles.

Simon Prince

Relationship to Miller
_____

Marital status
_____

Possible motive
_____

Bad habits
_____

Margaret McKenzie

Relationship to Miller
_____

Marital status
_____

Possible motive
_____

Bad habits
_____

Timothy Carlyle

Relationship to Miller
_____

Marital status
_____

Possible motive
_____

Bad habits
_____

8 Look for clues in this photograph of the crime scene. In pairs, talk about who you think might have murdered the millionaire.

Example: *The murderer must have known the victim because there are no signs of forced entry.*

9 🔊 **2.18** Listen to another conversation between Inspector Hurst and his superior officer. Did you guess correctly?

Listening Part 3

Think ahead

1. Do you think money is more important or less important to people in today's society than it was in the past? How important is it to you?

2. What problems can it cause?

Exam practice

Multiple matching

3. 🔊 2.19 You will hear five short extracts in which people are talking about money. For questions 1–5, choose from the list (A–H) what each speaker says. Use the letters only once. There are three extra letters which you do not need to use.

> **Tip**
>
> The second time you hear the recording, make your final choice of answer. Remember you will not use three of the letters.

A I accept responsibility for my problems.
B I wouldn't want to earn less.
C I was motivated by money in the past.
D I don't intend to pay back what I owe.
E Lack of money ruined my relationship.
F I may have no moral conscience.
G I never had money for long.
H Money affected my health.

Speaker 1 [1]
Speaker 2 [2]
Speaker 3 [3]
Speaker 4 [4]
Speaker 5 [5]

Over to you

4. What is your attitude to money? Rewrite sentences a–g so that they are true for you. Then, compare ideas with a partner.

a I never buy anything I don't need.
b If I want something, I save up till I can afford it.
c I save about 10% of my income.
d I worry about what I will live on when I am old.
e I would only do a job if it was well paid.
f I always run out of money before the end of the month.
g I never lend people money.

Speaking Parts 1, 2, 3 & 4

Exam practice

Short exchanges 1 Work in pairs. Turn to page 157 and follow the instructions.

Long turn 2 Work in pairs. Turn to page 157 and follow the instructions.

Collaborative task 3 Work in pairs. Read these Part 3 prompts. Talk to your partner about which changes would attract more shoppers to a town.

Tip

If you don't know your partner, introduce yourself before the exam starts. This will make you feel more relaxed.

If you don't understand what the examiner wants you to do, you can ask them to repeat the instructions.

If you don't understand what your partner has said, ask them politely to repeat. You get marks for how well you interact with your partner.

Try to treat the exam as if it were a class speaking activity. If you are more relaxed, you will perform better.

What changes would attract more shoppers to a town?
- provide cheaper parking
- improve facilities for people with disabilities
- create a pedestrian zone
- provide free public transport
- reduce rents for independent shopkeepers

4 Decide which two changes would help to attract shoppers the most.

Discussion 5 Work in pairs. Take turns to answer each of the questions.
- Is public transport good in your town? (Why? / Why not?)
- Where do people do their shopping in your town? (Why?)
- How do you think shopping will change in the future? (Why?)
- Is it easy for people with disabilities in your country to lead a normal life? (Why? / Why not?)

Grammar (2)

Think ahead 1 Look at these birthday cards and match each card with the correct continuation a–c. What do they tell you about some people's attitude to age?

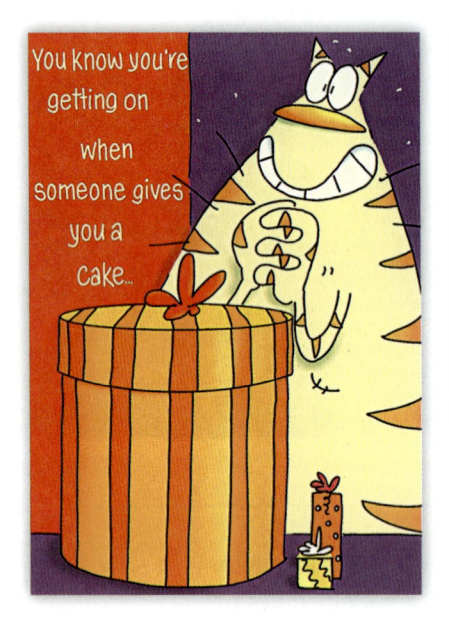

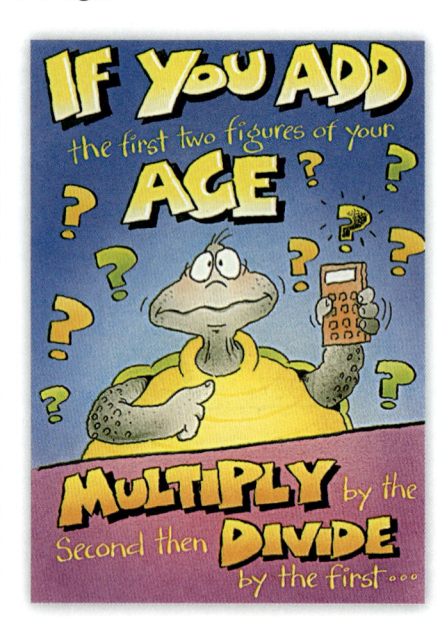

You know you're getting on when someone gives you a cake...

The SECRET of STAYING YOUNG is the careful use of MAKE UP...

IF YOU ADD the first two figures of your AGE MULTIPLY by the Second then DIVIDE by the first...

a ... it won't change a thing, you'll still be a year older.

b ... and you can't see it for the candles.

c ... just make up an age and stick to it.

Articles
▶ Grammar reference page 174

2 Complete this text with the articles *a*, *an*, *the*, or Ø where no article is needed.

At sixty-three, I was unexpectedly made redundant from my job of forty years. Not wanting to retire yet, I decided to look for **(1)** _____ new job to take me up to **(2)** _____ retirement age and to prevent me from just sitting at **(3)** _____ home all day. Finding one, however, turned out to be **(4)** _____ most difficult task I've ever faced, since **(5)** _____ elderly are often viewed negatively by **(6)** _____ employers. After a year and nearly **(7)** _____ hundred applications, I was invited to **(8)** _____ interview in **(9)** _____ Scotland. I was nervous but I needn't have been. **(10)** _____ interview was very relaxed, and **(11)** _____ interviewer was impressed by my experience and took me on. I couldn't believe my luck. It's **(12)** _____ brilliant job. I'm working as **(13)** _____ activity organizer on **(14)** _____ cruise ship for older people in **(15)** _____ West Indies. Sailing round **(16)** _____ Caribbean is not my idea of **(17)** _____ work at all!

3 Discuss these questions in pairs or small groups.

a How are elderly people treated in your country?

b Is unemployment a big problem in your country? Does it affect one particular age group more than others?

c What, if anything, worries you about getting old?

unit 12 society

Vocabulary

Think ahead

1 Do you give money to charity? Which charities do you support?

2 What fund-raising events are there in your country? How do charities raise money?

3 Read the text below about a charity event which takes place in the UK. Answer these questions.
   a How often does it take place?
   b How much money has been raised so far?
   c Who takes part in it?

Exam practice

Multiple-choice cloze

4 Read the text again. For questions 1–8, decide which answer (A, B, C or D) best fits each gap. There is an example at the beginning (0).

Comic Relief

Comic Relief is a charitable organization (0) __based__ in London. It was set (1) _____ by comedians in 1985 in response to the famine in Ethiopia, and uses comedy to (2) _____ serious messages across. Over the years thousands of celebrities have helped to raise over £600 million to date.

Every two years, usually on a Friday in March, Comic Relief organizes a nationwide fund-raising event (3) _____ 'Red Nose Day'. On Red Nose Day everyone in the country is encouraged to put on a red nose and do something silly to raise money (4) _____ charity.

Every contribution is important, whether it is standing in the street (5) _____ money from passers-by, or taking (6) _____ in a sponsored event like not talking for a(n) (7) _____ day.

The event is televised in the evening, when the combination of comedy and hard-hitting documentaries persuades (8) _____ to make donations on their credit cards – over the phone or via the internet – to those less fortunate than themselves.

0	A established	B based	C constructed	D stationed
1	A on	B off	C out	D up
2	A have	B do	C get	D make
3	A known	B named	C called	D described
4	A to	B for	C towards	D on
5	A collecting	B earning	C asking	D gathering
6	A involvement	B place	C participation	D part
7	A whole	B all	C total	D complete
8	A spectators	B viewers	C audience	D observers

unit 12 society

149

Writing Part 2 – Report

Think ahead

1 How many ways of raising money for a charitable cause can you think of? Use the photos to give you some ideas.
   a Which would raise the most money?
   b Which would be the easiest to organize?

Exam skills

2 Read the Part 2 task and answer questions a–c.
   a What style would you write the report in?
   b What information would you include in your answer?
   c Would you make a recommendation?

> Your teacher has asked you to write a report on ways of raising money to buy books for your school. You should suggest some ideas for raising money and explain which way you think would work best. Write your **report** in 140–190 words.

3 Read this report and answer the questions.
   a How many suggestions has the writer made?
   b Do you agree with her recommendation?

Introduction

In this report I will look at ideas to raise money to buy books for our school and recommend one of these ideas.

Fund-raising activities

1 One thing we could do is organize a sponsored race with a prize for the winner. The prize could be a meal for two at a local restaurant. I am sure one of the restaurants in town could be persuaded to give the prize as it would be good publicity for them.

2 Another thing we could do concerns the end-of-year show, which is usually free. At the next show we could charge people. People who sit at the front could pay more than people who sit at the back. **All the money we raise would go towards the purchase of books. I am certain our families and friends would be happy to contribute.**

Recommendation

I personally think the show would be the best idea as it does not need much organization. Students who are not actually taking part could help by printing and selling the tickets as well as showing people to their seats on the night. That way everyone would be involved.

Complex sentences

4 You can make your writing more interesting by combining your ideas in more complex sentences like the underlined sentences in **3**. How could the **bold** sentences be written as one sentence?

5 Join these sentences together using the word or phrase in brackets.

a You could collect money in the town centre on a Saturday. This is the busiest day. (which)

b We collected a lot of money. The school was able to buy the books it needed. (so)

c They were able to buy books. They were also able to buy a new computer. (in addition to)

d The weather was very bad. People still collected a lot of money. (despite)

e The show was a huge success. We're going to organize another one next year. (as)

f Students donated games they don't play with any more. They also donated books they don't read any more. (both … and)

g The sponsored bike ride was very enjoyable. It raised a lot of money, too. (not only … but also)

h A local restaurant offered a prize of dinner for two. The restaurant also made a donation to the school. (as well as)

i The school raised £500. It wasn't enough to buy everything they wanted. (Although)

j The director thanked all the students. They had helped to make the event a success. (who)

Exam practice

Report
▸ *Writing guide* page 184

> **Tip**
>
> Remember to use headings in your report. You can also make recommendations in your final paragraph even if the task does not require you to do so.

6 You are going to write a report. First, read the task below. Then, work through stages a–e.

> Your local council has asked you to write a report on leisure-time activities for young people in your area. You should explain what activities young people enjoy and say what activities are needed the most in your area. Write your **report** in 140–190 words.

a Before you write, make a list of possible activities you could include. Think of some examples for each of these categories:
- social activities
- sports activities

b Choose two activities for each category and write some factual information about them. The information does not need to be true. Use these prompts to help you:
- How much does it cost to do them?
- How popular are they? Why are they popular?
- Where and when do they take place?

c Choose one or two activities which are needed most and make notes on why you think the council should provide them.

d Write your essay. Use the sample answer in **3** to help you. Try to use some complex sentences.

e Finally, when you have finished, check your grammar, spelling and punctuation.

unit 12 society

Unit 12 Review

1 For questions 1–8, complete the second sentence so that it has a similar meaning to the first sentence, using the word given. Do not change the word given. You must use between two and five words, including the word given.

1 They arrested the boy because he had vandalized property.
   VANDALIZING
   The boy _____ property.

2 Ray Terry said he was successful because of his teachers.
   OWED
   Ray Terry said _____ his teachers.

3 Ray wouldn't allow his mother to hit him any more.
   LET
   Ray refused _____ him any more.

4 The judge wanted to help kids.
   INTERESTED
   The judge _____ kids.

5 I'm almost positive Susan heard what I said.
   HAVE
   Susan _____ what I said.

6 Maybe John didn't want to come.
   NOT
   John _____ to come.

7 Elderly people need to keep active.
   THE
   It's important _____ active.

8 The concert was very popular so they're going to put on a repeat performance.
   SUCH
   The concert _____ that they're going to put on a repeat performance.

2 Complete the text with *a / an*, *the* or Ø. There may be more than one possible answer.

A (1) _____ police arrested Smith for (2) _____ attempted theft. He was caught breaking into (3) _____ store on (4) _____ Main Street which sells (5) _____ electrical appliances. (6) _____ shop alarm had gone off when (7) _____ front door was forced open, and (8) _____ passer-by had telephoned (9) _____ police station to advise them of (10) _____ incident.

B Promoting (1) _____ good causes can be good for business, too. Businesses have been making (2) _____ charitable donations for (3) _____ long time. The term 'cause-related marketing' was first used by American Express to describe its efforts to raise money to restore (4) _____ Statue of Liberty. Every time (5) _____ cardholder used their charge card, American Express donated some money towards refurbishing (6) _____ monument, eventually raising nearly $2 million. (7) _____ number of new cardholders went up 45% and card usage increased. This type of marketing suits everyone. The customers feel good when they buy (8) _____ product concerned, and the companies appear thoughtful and caring.

Extra material

Unit 1 page 16 exercise 4

The feeling that a painting is watching you can be both impressive and worrying. But this illusion is not that hard to explain. Find a photo of someone looking directly into the camera. From any angle, the eyes still look into the camera, and still seem to stare at you. The image is two-dimensional. This means that if it appears to look at you from one angle, it will appear that way from every angle. The effect is achieved in the same way by painters. If an artist chooses to depict a person looking out at viewers, he or she will paint the eyes as if they were 'gazing into the camera'. The success of the illusion depends on the artist's skill in portraying eyes that stare straight out.

Unit 2 page 27 exercise 8

Student A   Compare the two photographs below, and say what you think are the advantages of these methods of learning a language. Remember you have to speak for about a minute.

Student B   When your partner has finished speaking, answer this question:
Which of these methods of learning a language would you prefer to use? Why?
Talk for approximately 30 seconds.

What are the advantages of these methods of learning a language?

Student B   Compare the two photographs below, and say what talents you think the people need to do these activities. Remember you have to speak for about a minute.

Student A   When your partner has finished speaking, answer this question:
Which of these activities would you find easier? Why?
Talk for approximately 30 seconds.

What talents do the people need to do these activities?

153

Unit 4 page 53 exercise 4

Student A Compare the two photographs below, and say how you think family relationships are different in the two situations. Remember you have to speak for about a minute.

Student B When your partner has finished speaking, answer this question:
Which type of family would you fit into most comfortably? Why?
Talk for approximately 30 seconds.

How are the family relationships different in the two situations?

Student B Compare the two photographs below, and say how you think husband and wife roles have changed in recent times. Remember you have to speak for about a minute.

Student A When your partner has finished speaking, answer this question:
Do you think the changes to family roles have benefited men or women more?
Talk for approximately 30 seconds.

How have husband and wife roles changed in recent times?

Unit 5 page 65 exercise 9 Part 3

Imagine that you are visiting a foreign country for the first time and you want to experience as much of the country as possible. Here are some of the ways of travelling around the country and a question for you to discuss. Talk to each other about the advantages and disadvantages of travelling around a foreign country using these means of transport.

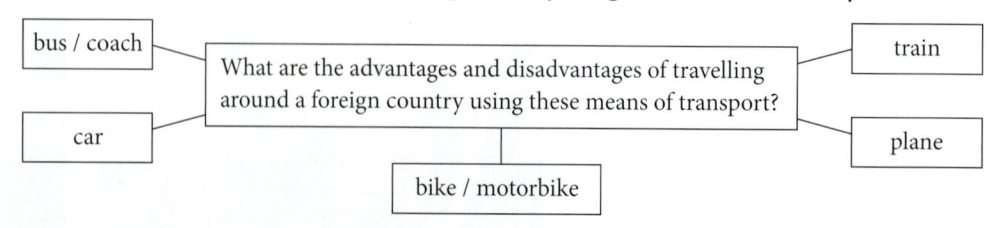

- bus / coach
- car
- train
- plane
- bike / motorbike

What are the advantages and disadvantages of travelling around a foreign country using these means of transport?

Now you have about a minute to decide which two means of transport would be the best if you wanted to experience as much of the country as possible.

Unit 8 page 97 exercise 4

Student A Compare the two photographs below, and say why you think companies advertise in places like these. Remember you have to speak for about a minute.

Student B Time Student A. If they stop talking before one minute, ask them to continue. At the end of a minute, stop them and answer this question:
Which of the two advertisements do you find more interesting? Why?
Talk for approximately 30 seconds.

Why do you think companies advertise in places like these?

Student B Compare the two photographs below, and say why you think advertisements like these are worth the money companies spend on them. Remember you have to speak for about a minute.

Student A Time Student B. If they stop talking before one minute, ask them to continue. At the end of a minute, stop them and answer this question:
Which advertisement do you find more effective? Why?
Talk for approximately 30 seconds.

Why are advertisements like these worth the money companies spend on them?

Unit 10 page 122 exercise 6

Student A Take turns with Student B to describe one of the objects (1–12). Do not use the name of the object in your description. Student B will listen to your description without interrupting and when you have finished talking will write down the number of the object he / she thinks you are describing.

Example: *I'm going to describe my number 1. It's a gadget used for …*
When you have finished, compare your answers.

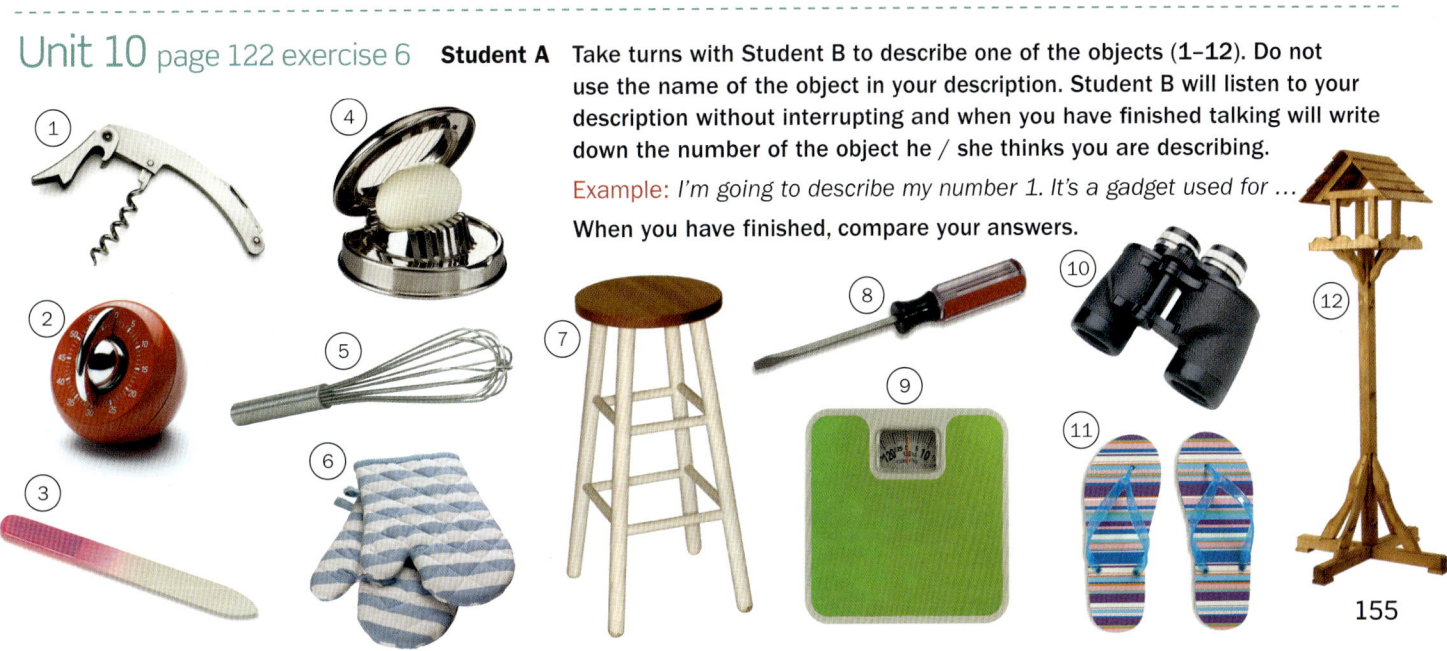

extra material

155

Unit 10 page 122 exercise 6

Student B Take turns with Student A to describe one of the objects (1–12). Do not use the name of the object in your description. Student A will listen to your description without interrupting and when you have finished talking will write down the number of the object he / she thinks you are describing.

Example: *I'm going to describe my number 2. It's a gadget used for …*

When you have finished, compare your answers.

Unit 10 page 122 exercise 7

Student A Compare the two photographs below, and say how technology has changed the way children play. Remember you have to speak for about a minute.

Student B When your partner has finished speaking, answer this question:

When you were a child did you prefer to play outside or inside? Why?

Talk for approximately 30 seconds.

How has technology changed the way people play?

Student B Compare the two photographs below, and say which skill you think is more difficult to learn. Remember you have to speak for about a minute.

Student A When your partner has finished speaking, answer this question:

Which skill do you think is more useful to have? Why?

Talk for approximately 30 seconds.

Which skill is more difficult to learn?

Unit 7 page 87 exercise 5

Work in pairs. Read these Part 3 prompts. Talk to your partner about how popular these activities would be with students as after-school leisure activities. Talk for about 2 minutes. Then, spend another minute deciding which two to recommend.

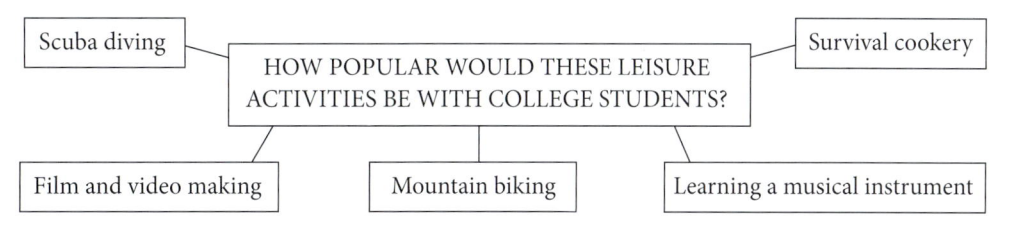

- Scuba diving
- Survival cookery
- Film and video making
- Mountain biking
- Learning a musical instrument

HOW POPULAR WOULD THESE LEISURE ACTIVITIES BE WITH COLLEGE STUDENTS?

Unit 12 page 147 exercise 1

Work in pairs. Student A, ask Student B the questions below.

- What do you spend your money on? Why?
- Do you like shopping on the internet? Why? / Why not?

Student B, ask Student A the questions below.

- Do you have enough free time to do the things you want to do? Why? / Why not?
- How do young people spend their free time in your country?

Unit 12 page 147 exercise 2

Student A Compare the two photographs below, and say why you think the people have chosen to do these activities. Remember you have to speak for about a minute.

Student B When your partner has finished speaking, answer this question:
Which of the people do you most admire? Why?
Talk for approximately 30 seconds.

Why do you think the people have chosen to do these activities?

Student B Compare the two photographs below, and say what you think the people are enjoying about having money to spend. Remember you have to speak for about a minute.

Student A When your partner has finished speaking, answer this question:
Which of these two situations would you most enjoy? Why?
Talk for approximately 30 seconds.

What are the people enjoying about having money?

Grammar reference

Terminology

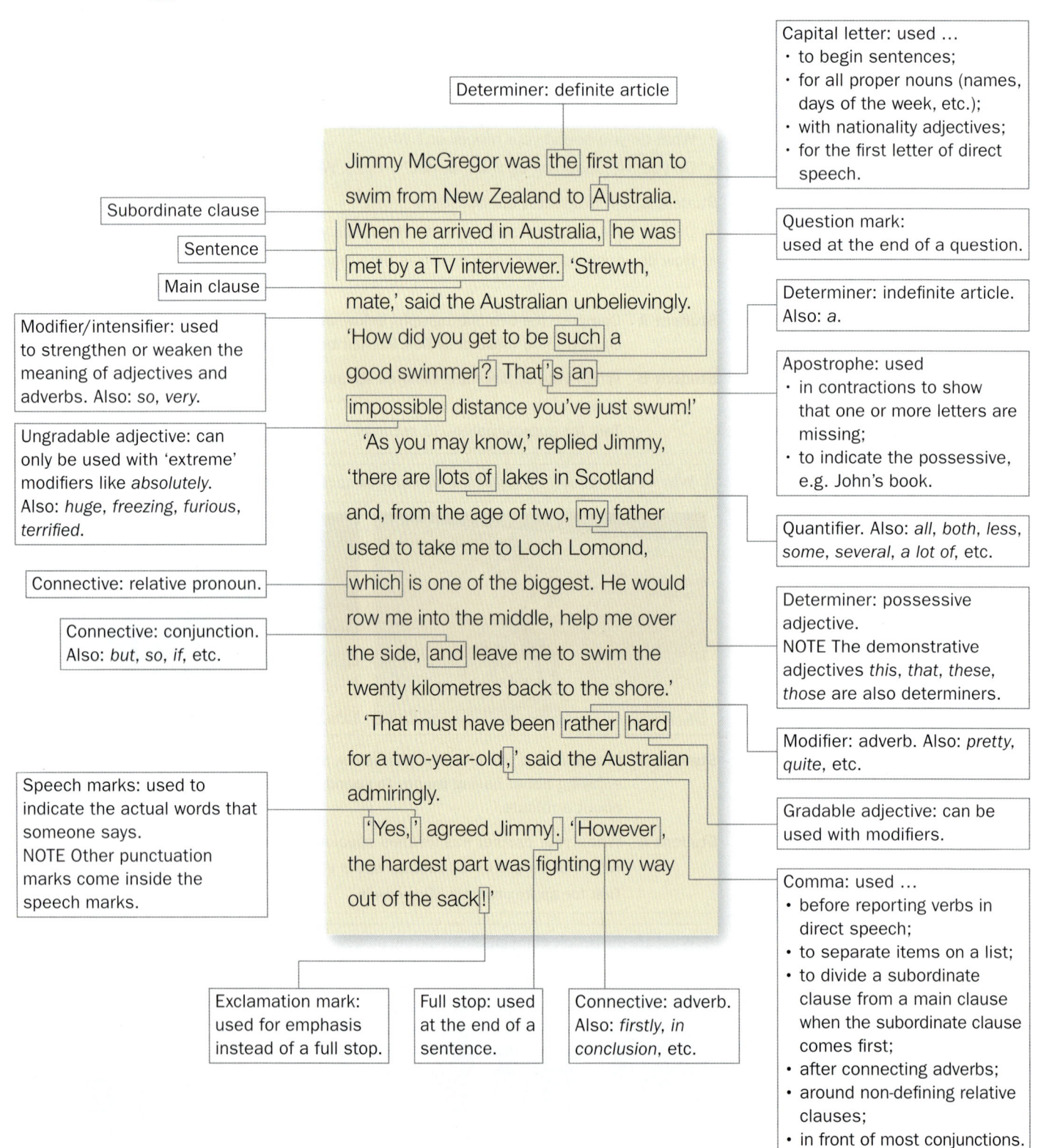

Jimmy McGregor was the first man to swim from New Zealand to Australia. When he arrived in Australia, he was met by a TV interviewer. 'Strewth, mate,' said the Australian unbelievingly. 'How did you get to be such a good swimmer? That's an impossible distance you've just swum!'

'As you may know,' replied Jimmy, 'there are lots of lakes in Scotland and, from the age of two, my father used to take me to Loch Lomond, which is one of the biggest. He would row me into the middle, help me over the side, and leave me to swim the twenty kilometres back to the shore.'

'That must have been rather hard for a two-year-old,' said the Australian admiringly.

'Yes,' agreed Jimmy. 'However, the hardest part was fighting my way out of the sack!'

Determiner: definite article

Subordinate clause

Sentence

Main clause

Modifier/intensifier: used to strengthen or weaken the meaning of adjectives and adverbs. Also: *so*, *very*.

Ungradable adjective: can only be used with 'extreme' modifiers like *absolutely*. Also: *huge*, *freezing*, *furious*, *terrified*.

Connective: relative pronoun.

Connective: conjunction. Also: *but*, *so*, *if*, etc.

Speech marks: used to indicate the actual words that someone says.
NOTE Other punctuation marks come inside the speech marks.

Exclamation mark: used for emphasis instead of a full stop.

Full stop: used at the end of a sentence.

Connective: adverb. Also: *firstly*, *in conclusion*, etc.

Capital letter: used …
- to begin sentences;
- for all proper nouns (names, days of the week, etc.);
- with nationality adjectives;
- for the first letter of direct speech.

Question mark: used at the end of a question.

Determiner: indefinite article. Also: *a*.

Apostrophe: used
- in contractions to show that one or more letters are missing;
- to indicate the possessive, e.g. John's book.

Quantifier. Also: *all*, *both*, *less*, *some*, *several*, *a lot of*, etc.

Determiner: possessive adjective.
NOTE The demonstrative adjectives *this*, *that*, *these*, *those* are also determiners.

Modifier: adverb. Also: *pretty*, *quite*, etc.

Gradable adjective: can be used with modifiers.

Comma: used …
- before reporting verbs in direct speech;
- to separate items on a list;
- to divide a subordinate clause from a main clause when the subordinate clause comes first;
- after connecting adverbs;
- around non-defining relative clauses;
- in front of most conjunctions.

Unit 1

Modal verbs

Obligation

1 *must*

   must + infinitive is used for strong obligations which express the authority of the speaker or writer. It is used

   A for formal rules or laws:
   *Passengers **must fasten** their seat belts for take-off.*

   B for suggestions, advice or recommendations that the speaker or writer feels strongly about:
   *You **must come** to my party. Everyone's going to be there.*

2 *have to*

   have to + infinitive is used for strong obligations which express the authority of a third person, rather than that of the speaker or writer. It is used

   A when the speaker wants to show they are not responsible for imposing the obligation, or does not agree with it:
   *I'll be late home tonight. I **have to work** late. My boss said so.*

   B when the speaker or writer is reminding someone about a rule or law:
   *I'm sorry, but you **have to wear** a seat belt in the back of cars too.*

3 *have got to*

   have got to + infinitive is more informal than *have to*. It is often used

   A for direct commands:
   *You've **got to stop** wasting your money.*

   B for emphasis:
   *I don't care how hard I have to work, I've just **got to pass** the exam this time.*

4 *need to*

   need to is used to express needs or necessities, rather than strict obligations:
   *If we're going to work together, I **need to know** about your background and experience.*

5 Negative forms

   A *mustn't* expresses prohibition (negative rules and laws or strong advice):
   *Drivers **must not exceed** the speed limit.*
   *You **mustn't blame** yourself. It's not your fault.*

   B *do not have to / have not got to* express lack of obligation or necessity:
   *You **don't have to wear** a uniform, but you can if you like.*

   C *do not need to / needn't* + infinitive are used to express lack of obligation or necessity and are similar in meaning to *do not have to*:
   *There are no lessons tomorrow, so I **don't need to get up** early.*
   *You **needn't tell** me your phone number if you don't want to.*

   D *did not need to* + infinitive means 'It was not necessary, so we didn't do it':
   *The train was delayed so we **didn't need to hurry**.*

   E *needn't have* + past participle means 'It was not necessary, but we did it in spite of this':
   *We had to wait for half an hour on the platform because the train was delayed. We **needn't have hurried** after all.*

Permission and prohibition

1 *can / can't*

   This is one of the commonest ways of expressing permission and prohibition:
   ***Can I use** the phone, please?*
   *In Spain you **can't leave** school until the age of 16.*
   NOTE
   May I … ? means the same as *Can I … ?* but is more formal and more polite.

2 Other expressions of permission and prohibition

   A *be allowed to* + infinitive:
   *You're **allowed to buy** lottery tickets when you're 18.*

   B *be permitted to* + infinitive:
   *We were only **permitted to take** photographs in certain places.*

   C *let* + infinitive without *to*:
   *My parents **let me stay out** late at weekends.*

3 Other expressions of prohibition
   You aren't allowed to go abroad without a passport.
   Smoking is not permitted in most cinemas.
   You are not permitted to smoke in this theatre.
   People are forbidden to smoke on the Underground.
   The workers have been prohibited from striking.
   Nigel has been banned from driving for six months.

Present tenses

Present simple

1 The present simple is used to refer to habitual or routine actions:
   *Most people **work** from 9.00 a.m. to 5.00 p.m. and **have** three or four weeks' holiday a year.*
   *My father **leaves** home at 7 o'clock and **commutes** to work.*
   The present simple is also used to refer to facts that are always true:
   *Rivers **flow** to the sea.*
   *Water **boils** at 100°C.*

2 Time expressions used with present simple verbs
   These are some of the expressions of time and frequency used with present simple verbs:
   always, every day / week, etc., *every so often, most weekends, never, occasionally, often, rarely, sometimes, twice a week, usually.*
   *The shops in our town **always close** at 7 o'clock in the evening.*
   *I **never sleep** more than six hours a night.*
   Notice where these words and phrases can be used in sentences:
   - *I **always / hardly ever / never / occasionally / rarely / sometimes / usually** wear bright clothes.*
   - ***Every day / Every so often / Most weekends / Occasionally / Sometimes / Usually** I wear bright clothes.*
   - *I wear bright clothes **every day / every so often / most weekends / occasionally / sometimes / usually**.*

159

Present continuous

1 The present continuous is used to refer to current trends or on-going situations:
We're staying with friends while our house is repaired.
I'm reading War and Peace at present.
The present continuous is also used to refer to actions taking place at the moment of speaking:
Paul's cooking lunch at the moment. Could you ring back this afternoon, please?

2 Time expressions used with present continuous verbs
These are some of the expressions of time and frequency used with present continuous verbs:
at present, at the moment, currently, now, this week, today
Currently, they're working on new antibiotics.
Notice where these words and phrases can be used in sentences:
My sister is currently / now appearing in a new production of a Shakespeare play.
Currently, / At present, / At the moment, / This week, / Today, my sister is appearing in a new production of a Shakespeare play.
My sister is appearing in a new production of a Shakespeare play at present / at the moment / this week / today.
NOTE:
Always can be used with present continuous verbs to mean 'again and again' or 'too frequently'.
I'm always losing my keys.

3 Verbs which are not normally used in the continuous form
The following groups of verbs, which describe states or conditions rather than actions, are not normally used in the continuous form:
- verbs referring to being: appear, seem, exist, consist of, look, mean, resemble
- verbs referring to having: own, belong, contain, hold, possess, have
- verbs referring to opinions: agree, believe, disagree, expect, hope, know, realize, think, understand
- verbs referring to feelings: dislike, fear, hate, like, love, regret, respect, trust
- verbs referring to senses: feel, hear, taste, see, smell

NOTE:
Many of these verbs can also be used to refer to actions. In this case, they can be used in the continuous form. Examples:
I have three brothers. (have = a state verb) / *I'm having a shower.* (have = an action verb)
She expects to get that job. (expect = a state verb) / *She's expecting a baby* (expect = an action verb)

Unit 2

Ability

1 *can* and *be able to*
can and *be able to* are the verbs most commonly used to talk about ability. Sometimes it is possible to use either verb without changing the meaning of the sentence. Sometimes, we have to use *be able to* as there is no appropriate form of *can*.

infinitive	be able to
present	can or am / are / is able to
future	will be able to
past	could or was / were able to
present perfect	have / has been able to
past perfect	had been able to

2 Present ability
To talk about a general ability in the present, both forms are possible, but *can* is more usual.
Gareth can run very fast.
(*Gareth is able to run very fast.*)
To talk about a learned ability in the present, *can* is more usual.
Know how to can be used as an alternative to *can*.
Can you play chess?
Do you know how to play chess?

3 Future ability
To talk about an ability in the future, we use the future form of *be able to*.
Will I be able to play better after I've had some lessons?

4 Past ability
To talk about a general ability in the past, both forms are possible:
Before his accident, Ben could jump really high.
Before his accident, Ben was able to jump really high.
To talk about an ability to do something in the past on one particular occasion, it is not possible to use *could*. We must use the past tense of *be able to* or *manage* (+ infinitive) or *succeed* (+ in + -ing):
Although she had lost a lot of blood, the doctors were able to save the girl's life.
Despite the difficult conditions, the surgeons managed to perform the operation successfully and succeeded in saving the man's leg.
NOTE
If the event was unsuccessful, it is possible to use *couldn't* as well as the past forms of *be able to*, *manage* and *succeed*.
Although he did his best, he couldn't finish it in time.

5 'Conditional' ability
To talk about a hypothetical ability in the present or future, we can use *could* or *would be able to*:
I could probably jump further if I had longer legs.
I would probably be able to play better if I practised more.
To talk about a hypothetical ability in the past, we usually use *could* + *have* + past participle, although we can also use *would have been able to*:
Even if he'd been taller, he couldn't have reached it.
Even if he'd been taller, he wouldn't have been able to reach it.

6 Other structures used to talk about ability
To talk about aptitude and capacity for doing something, we can use *be capable of* + *-ing*:
*He **is** certainly **capable of breaking** the world record.*
To talk about how well we do something, we can use the structure *be good* (*brilliant*, etc.) / *bad* (*terrible*, etc.) *at* + noun or gerund:
*I **have** never **been good at sports**.*
*I **am** particularly **bad at running**.*

Comparative and superlative adjectives and adverbs

Adjectives

1 Regular adjectives with one syllable

Adjective	Comparative	Superlative
tall	taller	the tallest
large	larger	the largest
big	bigger	the biggest

NOTES

A Adjectives ending in two consonants or two vowels and a consonant, add *-er* / *-est*: *long, short, bright, smooth, cool, clean, great*.

B Adjectives ending in *-e*, add *-r* / *-st*: *nice, late, safe, strange, rude, wide*.

C Many adjectives ending in a single vowel + single consonant, double the consonant and add *-er* / *-est*: *fat, thin, flat, sad, wet*.

2 Regular adjectives with two or more syllables

Adjective	Comparative	Superlative
heavy	heavier	the heaviest
modern	more modern	the most modern
important	more important	the most important
common	more common / commoner	the most common / the commonest

NOTES

A Adjectives ending in *-y*, change *y* to *i* and add *-er* / *-est*: *happy, dirty, funny, tidy, busy, early, empty, dry*.

B Most longer adjectives use *more* and *the most*: *comfortable, independent, insignificant, uninteresting*

C Some two-syllable adjectives can form their comparatives and superlatives in two ways; by adding *-er* / *-est* or with *more* and *most*: *clever, pleasant, gentle, narrow, shallow, simple, tired*.

3 Irregular adjectives

Adjective	Comparative	Superlative
good	better	the best
bad	worse	the worst
old	*elder / older	*the eldest / the oldest
far	further / farther	the furthest / the farthest

*only for people; especially people in the family
*I have three brothers. **The eldest**, Tom, is a musician.*

4 Comparative and superlative adjectives in context

A *more* / *-er* + *than*
*I'm **taller than** my brother.*
*My brother's **more serious than** me.*
*I'm **more intelligent than** he is / him.*

NOTES
If the pronoun after *than* is not followed by a verb, use the object pronoun form – *me, him, us, them*, etc.
If the pronoun after *than* is followed by a verb, use the subject pronoun form – *I, he, we, they*, etc.

B *the most* / *-est*
*I'm **the tallest** student in the class.*
*My sister's **the most intelligent** student in her school.*

C *less* + *than* / *the least*
*That film was **less interesting** than the last one I saw.*
*It was **the least interesting** film I've seen all year.*

5 Qualifying comparative adjectives

- Use these words and phrases to refer to big differences: *far, a lot, much, considerably, not nearly as … as*.
*Cars are **considerably faster** and **far more comfortable** than bicycles.*
- Use these words and phrases to refer to small differences: *a bit, a little, slightly*.
*The weather's **a bit hotter** than it was yesterday.*
- Use these words and phrases to refer to no differences: *just, no*.
*It's **no warmer** than it was yesterday.*
*It's **just as cold** today as it was yesterday.*

Adverbs

1 Regular and irregular adverbs

A The majority of comparative and superlative adverbs are formed like this:

Adverb	Comparative	Superlative
slowly	more slowly	the most slowly

B Irregular adverbs are formed like this:

Adverb	Comparative	Superlative
well	better	the best
badly	worse	the worst
little	less	the least
much	more	the most

C Adverbs which are the same as adjectives:

Adverb	Comparative	Superlative
fast	faster	the fastest
hard	harder	the hardest

Other adverbs of this kind include: *far, long, loud, straight*.

2 *The* + comparative + *the*
This construction links two actions or situations – when one thing happens, another thing follows. A comparative expression in the first clause is balanced by a comparative expression in the second clause. Several grammatical patterns are possible here:

- adjective … adjective
The harder a job is, the more rewarding I find it.
- adverb … adverb
The sooner we start, the quicker we'll finish.
- adjective … adverb, or adverb … adjective
The easier a job is, the more quickly I do it.
- *more* (+ noun) … *more* (+ noun)
The more money Jack earned, the more clothes he bought.
- *less* (+ clause) … *less* (+ uncountable noun) / *fewer* (+ plural countable noun)
The less Bob earned, the less food / the fewer holidays he could afford.

161

- *more* (+ clause) ... *less* (+ clause)
  The more you sleep, **the less** you do.
  Other combinations of these patterns are possible.
  Examples:
  The harder Joe worked, **the more** he earned.
  The more he ate, **the fatter** he got.
  NOTES
  A Neither of the two clauses in *the* + comparative + *the* sentences makes sense without the other.
  B In writing, a comma is used to separate the two clauses.
  C Both clauses need a verb.
  D In some expressions with *better*, no verbs are needed.
  Jim: When shall I come round to see you?
  Tim: **The sooner, the better**.

Other comparative constructions

1 *as ... as*
  This construction can be used with adjectives or adverbs to make comparisons between two things or people.
  I'm **as tall as** my brother.
  Trains don't travel **as fast as** planes.
  In negative sentences *so* can be used instead of the first *as*.
  Cats **aren't so friendly as** dogs.

2 Comparative + *and* + comparative
  This construction can be used with adjectives or adverbs to refer to a trend.
  Towards the end of the film, I became **more and more frightened**.
  As the exams approached, I worked **harder and harder**.
  Over the last twenty years, televisions have become **less and less expensive**.

3 Extreme adjectives
Ordinary	Extreme
cold	freezing
angry	furious
hungry	starving

  Most adjectives can be used with *very* or *really* and in the comparative form with *even* for emphasis.
  Yesterday was **very / really cold**, but today is **even colder**.
  NOTE
  really is more informal than *very*.
  Extreme adjectives cannot be preceded by *very* or in the comparative by *even*. If you want to emphasize them, you must use *absolutely* or *really*.
  I was **absolutely / really furious**.
  NOTE
  You cannot use *absolutely* with ordinary adjectives.
  ~~Today is absolutely cold.~~ Today is **absolutely freezing**.

Unit 3
Describing habitual actions

Habitual actions in the present

1 Present simple
  This is the usual way of expressing present habitual actions.
  Whenever I **go** to town, I **spend** too much money.
  tend to + infinitive
  The verb *tend to* + infinitive can be used to refer to usual or generally occurring actions.
  She **tends to get up** late at weekends.

2 Other ways of expressing habitual actions in the present
  A Present continuous + *always*
    This is used mainly to refer to actions which are too frequent. (see Unit 1 Grammar reference)
    He's **always giving** me presents.
    It is also used when you are annoyed with yourself or someone else.
    You're **always complaining** about my cooking.
  B *will* + infinitive
    This can be used instead of the present simple to refer to behaviour which is predictable or typical.
    I'**ll sit** for hours watching TV.
  C *keep* + *-ing*
    This is used for habitual actions which are accidental or annoying.
    I **keep bumping** my head on that tree.

Habitual actions in the past

1 Past simple
  When a past simple verb refers to habitual or repeated actions it can be accompanied by a frequency expression.
  When I worked in London, I **usually got** home at six o'clock.

2 *used to* + infinitive
  This refers to habitual past actions which no longer happen.
  Before I had a car, I **used to cycle** to work.
  It can also be used for actions that did not happen before, but happen now.
  I **didn't use to have** foreign holidays. Now I go abroad every year.
  We **never used to watch** TV at breakfast time.
  NOTES
  A Remember the question form of *used to*.
    Where **did you use to go** for your holidays?
  B Sentences with *used to* do not need frequency adverbs, but they are sometimes included for emphasis.
    I **always used to be** late for school.

3 *would* + infinitive
  This refers to habitual past actions.
  Every summer our parents **would take** us to the seaside.
  Do not use *would* in questions and negative sentences, as its meaning can be completely different.
  NOTE
  There is a difference in meaning between *used to* and *would*.
  A *Used to* can refer to permanent situations as well as habitual actions.
    I **used to be able to see** the church from my bedroom window.

B *Would* can only refer to actions, not situations. You can say:
He'd catch the 7.30 train.
but you cannot say:
He'd work in London.

4 *used to, be used to* and *get used to*
used to has three forms with different meanings.
- *used to* + infinitive
  This refers to habitual past actions (see note 2B above).
  *My father **used to get up** at 5 a.m.*
- *be used to* + *-ing*
  This means 'to be accustomed to'.
  *I must go to bed early. **I'm used to having** ten hours sleep a night.*
- *get used to* + *-ing*
  This means 'to become accustomed to', often to something unusual or strange.
  *If you come to England, you'll have to **get used to driving** on the left-hand side of the road.*
  NOTE
  Other common verbs which follow the same pattern are *look forward to* and *object to*.

Countable and uncountable nouns

Countable nouns

1 Countable nouns are nouns which have singular and plural forms.
computer(s), television(s), man / men, child / children, parent(s)
Singular countable nouns are used with the following:
a / an, the, one, this, that
***The man** over there is wearing **a black hat**.*

2 Countable nouns are used with the following qualifiers:
a few, a lot of, all the, enough, few, lots of, many, most of the, no, none of the, plenty of, several, some, two / three (etc.), *these, those* (etc.)
***Most of the children** had plenty of toys.*

Uncountable nouns

1 Uncountable nouns are nouns that do not have a plural form.
advice, equipment, furniture, information, milk, money, music, paper, research, time, water
Uncountable nouns are used with the following:
a little, a lot of, all the, enough, little, lots of, most of the, no, not much, plenty of, some, the, etc.
*We have **lots of money** left, but **not enough time** to spend it.*

2 Making uncountable nouns countable
To make uncountable nouns countable, use words like these:
piece, bit, box, kilo, piece, loaf, glass, sheet, item, cup, etc.
*I'd like **a cup of coffee** and **two pieces of toast**, please.*
*Would you mind me giving you **a piece of** friendly **advice**?*

3 Nouns which can be countable and uncountable
Some nouns can be countable and uncountable, but the meaning is different depending on the context.
*Look at those fluffy **lambs**.* [*a lamb* (C) = an animal]
*I'm not keen on **lamb**; I just don't like the taste.* [*lamb* (U) = meat from a lamb]
*James got the job because of his **wide experience**.*
[*experience* (U) = knowledge and skill]
*I've just had **a most incredible experience**.* [*an experience* (C) = something that has happened to you, an event]
*Would you like **some wine**?* [*wine* (U) = a drink made from grapes]
*Bordeaux is **a French wine**.* [*wine* (C) = a type of wine]

Unit 4

The future

There are many ways of talking about future time in English. This is a summary of the most common forms and their uses.

1. **Present continuous**
   The present continuous is used to refer to future actions or events which have already been arranged.
   Are you doing anything interesting at the weekend?
   We're spending the summer with our friends in Greece.

2. ***will* future**
   Future simple (*will* + infinitive)
   The *will* future is used to talk about:
   - future facts.
     The sun will rise at 6.30 tomorrow morning.
   - predictions or expectations.
     I expect Helen and John will be late again.
   - strong intentions.
     When Loretta retires, I'll definitely apply for her job.
   - instant decisions about the immediate future.
     The phone's ringing. I'll answer it.
   - offers.
     I'll take you to the airport if you like.

3. **Future continuous** (*will* + *be* + *-ing*)
   This form is used to talk about:
   - events or actions that will be in progress at a specific time in the future.
     This time tomorrow, I'll be travelling through France.
   - predicted or expected trends.
     In the twenty-second century, people will be living to the age of 130.

4. **Future perfect simple** (*will* + *have* + past participle) and **Future perfect continuous** (*will* + *have* + *been* + *-ing*)
   These two forms are used to talk about:
   - actions or events that will already be completed by a particular time in the future.
     By the year 2012, I'll have left school and started work.
   - the continuous nature of actions and events in the future.
     On Saturday we'll have been living here for three years.

   NOTES
   A *Shall* is sometimes used instead of *will* after *I* and *we*.
      In a few days we shall have forgotten about the accident.
   B *Shall* must be used to start questions which are suggestions and offers.
      Shall we phone to see what time the film starts?
      Shall I carry that heavy case for you?

5. ***be going to* + infinitive**
   This is used to talk about:
   - intentions, plans or resolutions.
     After Christmas, I'm going to get a job and save up.
     What are you going to do when you leave school?
   - predictions based on present evidence or knowledge.
     My nose is tickling. I'm going to sneeze.
     My sister's going to have a baby.

6. **Present simple**
   This tense is used to talk about scheduled, timetabled or fixed events.
   The class starts at 9 o'clock tomorrow morning.

7. **Other ways of referring to the future**
   - *be (just) about to* + infinitive
     This is used to talk about actions or events which we expect to happen in the immediate future.
     We'd better hurry – the train is just about to leave.
   - *be on the point of* + *-ing*
     This expression also refers to the immediate future.
     I'm on the point of going out. Could you phone back later, please?
     be likely / unlikely to + infinitive
     This is used to refer to probable or improbable actions or events.
     We're likely / unlikely to see Ian before next week.
   - *be bound to* + infinitive
     This is used to refer to actions or events which you think are certain to happen.
     The police are bound to discover who broke in eventually.

Unit 5

Past time

Past simple

We use the past simple tense when we want to refer to an action or event which is finished and:
- took place at a specific time and place in the past.
  *Jessica **went** to Spain in 2011.*
- took place over a specific period in the past.
  *She **lived** in Spain between 2011 and 2013.*
- was habitual during a specific period in the past.
  *When Jessica **lived** in Spain, she **ate** dinner at about 10 p.m.*

NOTE
A past time reference must either be given or understood from the context.

Past continuous

We use the past continuous to indicate:
- a continuous event in the past (which may or may not be unfinished).
  *Andrew **was working** for his uncle when I first met him.*
- a temporary event in the past which was in progress before another event took place.
  *I'll always remember what I **was doing** when I heard the dreadful news.*
- an event which started before another event in the past and continued.
  *When Neil and Sarah eventually turned up, all the other guests **were already eating** their dessert.*
- simultaneous, continuous actions in the past.
  *While I **was trying** to phone her, she **was trying** to phone me!*
- repeated actions occurring over a period of time in the past.
  *Before I moved into my own flat, I **was always arguing** with my parents.*

Present perfect

1 Present perfect simple
We use the present perfect simple tense when we want to talk about:
- an event which started in the past, continues in the present and may continue into the future.
  *My parents **have been married** for twenty years.*
- a recent event in the past which has relevance to the present.
  *A man **has appeared** in court charged with the murder of the missing person.*
- an event which happened in the past without saying when it happened (because we do not consider this is important).
  ***Have** you **seen** Samantha?*
  *I**'ve read** Hamlet, but I**'ve never seen** it performed.*
- an event which happened in the past but in unfinished time (with expressions like *today, this month, this year*, etc.).
  *I didn't see Josh last week, but I**'ve been out** with him twice already this week.*

2 Present perfect continuous
We use the continuous form
- to emphasize the continuity and duration of the event.
  *The Smiths **have been living** in the same house ever since they got married.*
- to indicate that a continuous activity in the recent past is responsible for a present situation. This activity may or may not be unfinished.
  *I'm not crying – I**'ve been peeling** onions.*

NOTE
The following verbs can be in the present perfect or the present perfect continuous tense with no real change of meaning, although the continuous form is often preferred: *live, wait, drive, smoke, work, stay, study, rain.*
*I**'ve driven** since I was eighteen.*
*I**'ve been driving** since I was eighteen.*

Past perfect

1 Past perfect simple
We use the past perfect simple to indicate a past event or situation which occurred before another past event or situation.
*I**'d been** awake for quite a while before the alarm rang.*
*Although I arrived on time, Mike **had already left**.*

NOTE
A time conjunction sometimes replaces the past perfect to show which of the two past events occurred first. In this case both events can be in the past simple tense.
*Alex **phoned** me **before he left**.*

2 Past perfect continuous
We use the continuous form when we want to emphasize the continuity and duration of an event.
*Richard **had been trying** to get a job for over a year before he was offered his present one.*

Participle clauses

A participle clause contains a present participle (e.g. *seeing*), a past participle (e.g. *seen*) or a perfect participle (e.g. *having seen*). It can be used:
- to indicate two events happening at the same time. It can replace a time clause.
  ***Walking** down the High Street on Saturday, I saw Paul.*
  (replaces *As / When / While I was walking …*)
- to indicate a sequence of events.
  ***Raising** their glasses, they wished Darren a happy birthday.*
- to indicate a reason. It can replace a reason clause.
  ***Not understanding** Albert's question, I was unable to give him an answer.*
  (replaces *Because / Since I didn't understand …*)
  ***Having spent** my money on a car, I couldn't afford a holiday.*
  (replaces *Because / Since I had spent …*)

NOTE
The subject of the participle must also be the subject of the other verb. It is not possible to say '*Having a bath, the phone rang.*'

Unit 6

Gerunds and infinitives

Certain verbs, adjectives and prepositions must always be followed by the gerund; others must always be followed by the infinitive. Some verbs, however, can be followed by either.

Gerunds

Gerunds are verbs that are like nouns. They are formed by adding -ing to the verb and can be used in four ways:

A As the subject of a clause or sentence
Eating out can be expensive.

B As the object of a clause or sentence
One of my interests is **collecting** antiques.

C After some verbs
- After verbs expressing likes and dislikes (see below *The gerund or the infinitive*: B).
  I don't **enjoy seeing** you like this.
- After other verbs such as: admit, appreciate, avoid, can't help, consider, delay, deny, finish, forgive, give up, imagine, involve, keep, mind, miss, postpone, put off, prevent, report, resist, risk, suggest.
  Have you **considered buying** a new one?

D After prepositions
- After all prepositions.
  It's **for opening** bottles.
- After adjective + preposition combinations such as: nervous / worried **about**, bad / good / clever / skilled **at**, sorry / responsible **for**, interested **in**, capable / afraid / frightened / terrified **of**, bored **with**
  I'm **interested in applying for** the job.
- After verb + preposition combinations such as: warn someone **about**, apologize **for**, arrest someone **for**, succeed **in**, congratulate someone **on**, insist **on**, be / get used **to**, look forward **to**, object **to**.
  My little brother **insisted on coming** with me.

The infinitive

The infinitive with *to*
- The infinitive with *to* is always used after certain verbs: afford, agree, arrange, ask, appear, attempt, choose, decide, expect, help, hope, intend, learn, manage, offer, pretend, promise, refuse, seem.
  I can't **afford to go** on holiday this year.
- The infinitive is always used after certain adjectives: amazed, certain, difficult, disappointed, easy, free, glad, happy, likely, pleased, possible, simple, sure, surprised.
  The recipe is **simple to follow**.

The gerund or the infinitive

Some verbs can be followed by the gerund or the infinitive.

A With no change of meaning
The verbs *start, begin, continue* can be followed by either the gerund or the infinitive, without changing the meaning of the sentence.
Jeff **continued to overeat / overeating** despite the doctor's advice.

B With a slight change of meaning
The meaning of the verbs *like, prefer, hate, love* changes slightly, depending on whether the gerund or infinitive follows them.
The gerund is more usual for general statements when the emphasis is on the enjoyment (or not) of the action.
Mary **prefers eating out** to eating at home.
The infinitive is more usual for more specific statements where extra information is given.
Jane **prefers to eat out** because there's no washing-up to do.
NOTE
With the verb *like* + infinitive there is often the added meaning of a preferred alternative.
I like to drive there may imply 'I prefer that means of transport to going by train or coach'.

C With a change of meaning
The verbs *try, stop, regret, remember, forget, mean, go on* can be followed by the gerund or the infinitive, but with a change in meaning.

D Verbs where there is a change of meaning according to whether the gerund or the infinitive is used after them
try
- + gerund = to experiment in order to achieve an objective
  Try going to bed earlier and see if that helps.
- + infinitive = to attempt a difficult action
  Sophie's **been trying to get** a job since she left school, but with no success.

stop
- + gerund = to finish an activity
  Stop talking and get on with your work!
- + infinitive = to interrupt one activity in order to do another
  Roger **stopped** (what he was doing) **to have** a cup of tea.

regret
- + gerund = to be sorry about an action in the past
  Many people **regret marrying** young.
- + infinitive = to be sorry about what you are going to say
  Dr Taylor **regrets to say** that she is unable to see patients without an appointment.

forget / remember
- + gerund = to (not) recall an action
  I distinctly **remember asking** them to come after lunch.
  I won't **forget being** at the Olympic Games as long as I live.
- + infinitive = to (not) do an action you must do
  Ann **remembered to lock** all the doors when she went on holiday, but she **forgot to close** the bathroom window.

go on
- + gerund = to continue an action
  I'll **go on applying** for jobs until I'm successful.
- + infinitive = to finish one activity and start another
  After seven years of study, Andy **went on to become** a doctor.

mean
- + gerund = to involve
  Dieting usually **means giving up** sweet things.
- + infinitive = to intend
  I **meant to send** you a postcard, but I couldn't remember your address.

The verbs of perception *see* (*watch*, *notice*, etc.), *feel*, *hear*, *smell* have a different meaning when they are followed by the infinitive (without *to*) or a participle.
- \+ participle = to experience part of an event
  *I **noticed** a man **acting** in a strange way.*
- \+ infinitive without *to* = to experience the whole event
  *I **heard** my sister **come** in at 1 a.m.*

Unit 7

Passive verbs

1. Verbs that can be used in the passive
   Most transitive verbs can be used in the passive. A transitive verb is a verb which takes an object, e.g. *catch*.
   *The police **caught the thief**.*
   Intransitive verbs cannot be used in the passive. An intransitive verb is a verb which does not take an object, e.g. *fall*.
   *Rodney **fell** and hurt his leg.*

2. Form of the passive
   The passive is formed with the verb *be* in the appropriate tense + the past participle of the main verb. In the case of modals, e.g. *could* and *must*, it is formed with the modal + *be* + past participle. See the table on the next page.

3. Choosing the active or the passive form
   - In an active sentence, the subject is the person or thing that does the action.
     *Barcelona **beat** Manchester United.*
   - In a passive sentence, the subject of the verb is the person or thing affected by the action.
     *Manchester United **were beaten** by Barcelona.*
     When we want to focus on the person or thing affected by the action instead of the performer of the action (the agent), we use the passive.

4. Including the agent (performer or doer)
   When we use the passive we can choose whether to include the agent or not. The agent is the person or thing who / which performs the action.
   *The record **is held by Carl Lewis**.*
   We do not need to include the agent when:
   A the agent is not important. So, we do not need to say:
     *Trespassers **will be prosecuted by the landowner**.*
   B we do not know who the agent is and so would have to use the words *somebody* or *a person*. We do not need to say:
     *My car **has been stolen by somebody**.*
   C when the agent is obvious. So, we do not need to say:
     *The thief **was sentenced** to five years imprisonment **by the judge**.*
   D when the agent has already been mentioned. So, we do not need to say:
     *Some of Stephen King's books **have been written by him** under the pseudonym Richard Bachman.*
   NOTE
   In informal English *get* can sometimes be used instead of *be* to form the passive. The agent is not generally mentioned.
   *Nigel **got stopped** for speeding.*

167

Tense	Subject	Verb *be*	Past Participle
present simple	Letters	are	delivered twice a day.
present continuous	The suspect	is being	questioned by the police.
past simple	The programme	was	first broadcast in 1998.
past continuous	Our hotel room	was being	cleaned when we arrived.
present perfect	My car	has been	stolen.
past perfect	They	had been	warned about the danger.
future	You	will be	paid on Friday.
modal verbs	This meat	must be	cooked for at least an hour.

5 Verbs with two objects
Some verbs can have two objects – a direct object (DO) and an indirect object (IO).
*Lady Markham's late husband **gave the painting** (DO) **to the gallery** (IO).*
*Lady Markham's late husband **gave the gallery** (IO) **the painting** (DO).*
Either of the two objects can be the subject of the passive verb.
***The painting was given** to the gallery by her late husband.*
***The gallery was given** the painting by her late husband.*
When one of the objects is a person, it is more usual for this to be the subject.
***Bobby was given** a new bike for his birthday.*
rather than
***A new bike was given** to Bobby for his birthday.*

6 Passive constructions with the infinitive
When we want to pass on information but we do not know whether the information is true or not, or we do not want to say where the information came from, we can use the passive form of these verbs: *think, believe, report, consider, know, say, expect* + infinitive.
When the information is about a present situation, we use the passive + infinitive.
*The Queen **is thought to be** one of the richest people in the world.*
*Mr Smith **is believed to be staying** with friends.*
When the information is about something in the past, we use the passive + past infinitive (*have* + past participle).
*The ship **is reported to have sunk**. Many people **are thought to have drowned**.*

7 *have / get something done* (causative)
Causative verbs *have something done* and *get something done* are used to refer to actions which are done FOR the subject rather than BY the subject. Causative verbs are used instead of passive verbs to show that the subject causes the action to be done.

1 *have something done*
   *I don't know how to repair cars, so **I'm having mine repaired** at the garage round the corner.*
2 *get something done*
   *I really must **get my eyes tested**. I'm sure I need glasses.*
   ***Get your hair cut**!*

NOTES
A *have something done* is slightly more formal than *get something done*
B *get* is more frequent than *have* in the imperative form
C Non-causative uses of *have* and *get*
   have and *get* are also used to refer to events which happened to someone, but were outside their control:
   *The company was in financial difficulty so I **had my pay reduced**.*
   *The fire spread so quickly that I **got my legs burnt**.*

Unit 8

Reporting speech

Direct speech

We can report what someone has said in two ways.
- We can report their actual words.
- We can report the idea they expressed.

When we report a person's actual words in writing, we use speech marks and an appropriate verb, e.g. *say, tell, ask*.
'I'll be late home tomorrow,' Bob **said**.

Reported speech

When we report the idea and not the actual words a person says we often make changes. These changes are usually to verb tenses, pronouns, word order and time and place references.

1 Reporting statements
 Changes in verb tenses
 When the reporting verb is in the past tense, e.g. *said*, we usually move the tenses in the sentence we are reporting one step back in time.

Direct speech	Reported speech
Present simple	Past simple
'I'm a nurse,' she said.	*She said she **was** a nurse.*
Present continuous	Past continuous
'I'm not going,' he said.	*He said he **wasn't going**.*
Past simple	Past perfect
'Tony did it,' she said.	*She said Tony **had done** it.*
Present perfect	Past perfect
'I haven't read it,' she said.	*She said she **hadn't read** it.*
Past continuous	Past perfect continuous
'I was lying,' he said.	*He said he**'d been lying**.*
will future	Would
'I'll get it,' she said.	*She said she **would get** it.*
Can	Could
'I can speak French,' he said.	*He said he **could speak** French.*
May	Might
'I may be late,' she said.	*She said she **might be** late.*
Must	Had to
'I must go,' he said.	*He said he **had to go**.*

 NOTE
 The past perfect and the modals *might, ought to, could, should* and *would* do not change in reported speech.

2 No changes in verb tenses
 When the reporting verb is in the present tense, e.g. *says*, we do not change the tense of the original verb. For example,
 - when we are reading what someone has said in a newspaper or letter:
   *Darren **says** he**'s been too busy** to write before.*
 - or when we are passing on a message:
   *Lucy **says** she**'ll be** late.*
 - When the reporting verb is in the past tense and we want to emphasize that the statement is still true, we can keep the same tense.
   *'Bill **is** my cousin' She **said** Bill **is** her cousin.*

3 Changes in time and place references
 Some typical changes that may have to be made are:

Direct speech	Reported speech
today	that day
tomorrow	the next day, the following day
yesterday	the previous day, the day before
two days ago	two days before, two days earlier
now	then
here	there
come	go

 Unless time and place words are reported at the same time and in the same place as they were originally said, they change.
 *'Marie **phoned** yesterday.'* (said on Monday)
 *He **said** that Marie **had phoned** two days ago / on Sunday.* (said on Tuesday)

4 Other changes
 Pronouns may change when we are reporting speech. This depends on who is reporting.
 *'I'll give **you** a lift.'* (Jack to Barbara)
 *Jack said **he** would give **me** a lift.* (Barbara to someone else)
 The determiners *this, that, these, those* may change to *the*.
 *'**These** jeans are too tight,' Cyril said.*
 *Cyril said **the** jeans were too tight.*
 The pronouns *this* and *that* may change to *it*.
 *'Give me **that**!' Jayne said.*
 *Jayne told me to give **it** to her.*

5 Reporting verbs
 We can use the verbs *say* and *tell* to report statements. The structure after these verbs is
 - *say* (*that*) + clause:
   *Richard **said (that) he would be late**.*
 - and *tell someone* (*that*) + clause:
   *Richard **told me (that) he would be late**.*
 NOTE The word *that* is frequently omitted in spoken English.

6 Reporting questions
 We make the same changes to verb tenses, time and place references and pronouns as we do when we report statements. We also change the form of the original question into a statement and therefore omit auxiliary verbs (*do, does, did*) and question marks.
 'When are you arriving?'
 *He asked me **when I was arriving**.*
 If there is no question word in the original, we must use *if* or *whether*.
 'Do you understand?'
 *He asked her **if / whether** she understood.*
 To report questions we can use the verb *ask* or the structure *want to know if*.
 *'Are you enjoying yourself?' Mr Jones **asked**.*
 *Mr Jones **wanted to know if** I was enjoying myself.*

7 Reporting advice, commands, requests and warnings
 We can report these kinds of speech using the verbs *advise, tell, ask* and *warn* + personal object pronoun + infinitive.
 - Advice
   'You really should stop!'
   *She **advised me to stop**.*

- Command
  'Don't interrupt me!'
  He **told me not to interrupt** him.
- Request
  'Could you close the door please?'
  She **asked me to close** the door.
- Warning
  'If you tell anyone, I'll …!'
  She **warned me not to tell** anyone.

NOTES

A The structure after *ask* is different depending on whether we are reporting a request or a question.
'Can you remind me, please?' (request)
He asked **me to remind him**.
'Can you come tomorrow?' (question)
She asked **me if I could come** the next day.

B The structure after *tell* is different depending on whether we are reporting a command or a statement.
'Come on! Hurry up!' (command)
She told **us to hurry up**.
'It doesn't start till eight.' (statement)
He told **us (that) it didn't start** until eight.

8 Reporting suggestions
We can report suggestions with the verb *suggest* + clause. For example, to report 'Let's stay in.':
She **suggested that we (should) stay in**.
She **suggested that we stayed in**.
She **suggested staying in**.

NOTE
You cannot use the infinitive after *suggest*.

so / such

We use *so* and *such* to add emphasis.
Everyone was **so** friendly.
They were **such** friendly people.

1 *so*
   so is used with
   - adjectives and adverbs.
     Our journey was **so quick**.
     Our journey went **so quickly**.
   - *much / little* (+ uncountable noun).
     I didn't realize we had **so much time**.
     She didn't realize she had **so little money** left.
   - *many / few* (+ plural countable noun).
     So many people applied for that job, but there were **so few jobs** available.

2 *such*
   such is used with
   - *a* + adjective + singular noun.
     We saw **such a good film** last night.
   - adjective + plural countable noun / uncountable noun.
     Everyone was wearing **such bright clothes**.
     We had **such dreadful weather** on our holiday.
   - *a lot* (*of…*) + plural countable noun / uncountable noun.
     We had **such a lot of things** to do, we didn't know where to start.
     He won **such a lot of money** on the lottery that he could afford a luxury apartment.

Unit 9
Relative clauses

A relative clause is used to add extra information. Instead of giving the information in two sentences, we can combine the two pieces of information in one sentence using a relative clause.
The man was so boring. **He sat next to me** the whole journey.
The man **who sat next to me** the whole journey was so boring.

Relative pronouns

1 A relative clause starts with
  a relative pronoun: *who (whom), which, that, whose where, when, why*
  or no relative pronoun (see 6 below).

2 The choice of relative pronoun depends on whether
   - the relative clause is defining or non-defining.
   - it refers to a person or a thing.
   - it is the subject or object of the relative clause.

	A *Defining*		B *Non-defining*	
	Person	Thing	Person	Thing
1 Subject	who / that	which / that	who	which
2 Object	Ø / who(m) / that	Ø / which / that	who(m)	which
3 Possessive	whose (of which)	whose	whose	whose (of which)

NOTE

A *Who* and *which* are more usual than *that* in writing.
B *Whom* is very formal and is used mainly in writing.

Defining and non-defining relative clauses

1 Defining clauses
  The information given in a defining relative clause is essential to the meaning of the sentence. It makes clear which person or thing we are talking about. For example, if we omit the relative clause in this sentence, we do not know which man the speaker is talking about.
  *The man **who came to the wedding dressed in jeans** is Simon's brother.*
  The defining relative clause gives us this information.

2 Non-defining clauses
  The information given in a non-defining relative clause is not essential to the meaning of the sentence. If we omit the relative clause, it is still clear who we are talking about.
  *Mr White, **who has been head teacher at the school for 40 years**, is retiring at the end of term.*

NOTES

A Defining relative clauses are common in spoken and written English. However, non-defining relative clauses are less common in spoken English.
B In non-defining relative clauses, *which* can refer back to a whole clause.
   *He climbed the mountain wearing only a T-shirt and jeans, **which was a stupid thing to do**.* (The fact that he climbed the mountain wearing only a T-shirt and jeans was a stupid thing to do.)

C Commas are put before and after the non-defining relative clause, unless this is also the end of the sentence.
*We stayed at the Carlton, **which is a five-star hotel in the city centre**.*

3 where, when, why

A *where* can introduce a defining or non-defining relative clause which follows the word 'place' or any noun which refers to a place, for example, 'house', 'restaurant', 'road'.
*Wendy was brought up in **Scotland, where she was born**, but later emigrated to Australia.*
*If you visit Yorkshire, it is worth visiting **the house where the Brontës lived**.*

B *when* can introduce a defining or non-defining relative clause which follows the word 'time' or any noun which refers to a period of time, for example, 'year', 'century', 'winter'.
*June is **the month (when) many couples get married in the UK**.*
*The town is quieter after **lunch, when everyone is having a siesta**.*

C *why* can introduce a defining relative clause after the word 'reason'.
*Do you know **(the reason) why Kate's changed her mind**?*

4 Relative clauses and prepositions

A Informal use
- In spoken English and informal written English, prepositions usually come at the end of the relative clause.
  *The hotel **which we stayed at while we were in London** is very expensive.*
- In informal defining relative clauses the pronoun is usually omitted.
  *The man Ø **I spoke to** gave me different information.*
  *The letter Ø **you refer to** has not been answered to my satisfaction.*

B Formal use
- In formal written English, prepositions usually come before the relative pronoun.
  *The Savoy Hotel, **at which many celebrities stay when they are in the capital**, is very expensive.*
- In formal defining relative clauses with prepositions we use *whom* to refer to people and *which* to refer to things. The pronoun cannot be omitted.
  *The man **to whom I spoke** gave me different information.*
  *The letter **to which you refer** has not been answered to my satisfaction.*
- In formal non-defining relative clauses with prepositions we also use *whom* to refer to people and *which* to refer to things. The pronoun cannot be omitted.
  *The hotel manager, **to whom I spoke about the problem**, suggested I write to you.*
  *The fact that the hotel was undergoing renovation during our stay, **about which we had not been informed**, completely ruined our holiday.*

5 Relative clauses after numbers and certain words

A Non-defining relative clauses can be introduced by a number + *of* + the following words: *all, any, both, each, either, (a) few, many, most, much, neither, none, some*. They are followed by the relative pronoun *whom* for people and *which* for things.
*Dozens of people had been invited, **ten of whom I knew**.*
*I fell asleep during the lecture, **most of which was incomprehensible**.*

B Defining relative clauses can be introduced by the following words: *all, any(thing), every(thing), (a) few, little, many, much, no(thing), none, some(thing)* and superlative adjectives.
We usually use the relative pronoun *that* after these words. When the relative pronoun is the object of the relative clause, *that* is commonly omitted.
*It was **something that could have happened to anyone**.*
*It was **the most difficult exam (that) I've ever taken**.*

6 Omitting pronouns from relative clauses Ø
Omitting relative pronouns is common in spoken or informal written English in

A defining relative clauses when the relative pronoun is the object of its clause.
*The party Ø **I went to last night** didn't finish till late.*
*The tree Ø **the council cut down by mistake** was over fifty years old..*
*Do you know the reason Ø **they've decided to put off the wedding**?*
*August is the month Ø **most people take their annual holiday**.*

B defining relative clauses with a form of the verb *be*, when both the *be* part of the verb and the relative pronoun can be omitted. This is sometimes called a 'reduced' relative clause.
*The man ~~who is~~ **standing on his own over there** is Amy's brother.*
*The car ~~which was~~ **used in the robbery** was discovered abandoned in a nearby field.*

Unit 10

Wishes, regrets and preferences

wish

We use *wish* to talk about situations we would like to change but can't, either because they are outside our control or because they are in the past. The tense of the verb after *wish* does not correspond to the time we are thinking about; it changes. The verb tense is one step back in time (as in reported speech).

1. A wish about a present or future situation is expressed with a past tense:

Situation	Wish
I **am** an only child.	I **wish** I **wasn't** an only child.
I **can't drive**.	I **wish** I **could drive**.
Rod **isn't coming** to the party.	I **wish** Rod **was coming**.

   NOTE
   In formal English we say *I / he / she / it were / weren't*.

2. A wish about a past situation is expressed with a past perfect tense:

Situation	Wish
I'**ve lost** my best pen.	I **wish** I **hadn't lost** it.
I **didn't remember**.	I **wish** I'**d remembered**.

3. Wish … would
   We use *wish … would*:
   - when we want to complain about a present situation:

Situation	Wish
A dog is barking.	I **wish** that dog **would stop** barking!
The road is icy.	I **wish** you **wouldn't drive** so fast.

     NOTE
     We can't say *I wish I would …* Referring to ourselves we have to say *I wish I could …*

   - when we are impatient for an event outside our control to happen:

Situation	Wish
You're waiting for the bus.	I **wish** the bus **would come**.

     NOTE
     It is not possible to use *wish … would* with the verb *be* unless we are complaining. We say 'I *wish* it *were* Friday' and not 'I *wish* it *would be* Friday'.

Other structures to express wishes and regret:

A If we want a future event to happen or not happen, and this event is possible and not just a desire, we use the verb *hope* + present simple.
   I **hope** I **pass** my exams.

B *If only* can often be used in place of *wish* to express a slightly stronger sense of regret.
   I **wish** Sue **was** here / **If only** Sue **was** here, she'd know what to do.

C I'd rather
   We use *would rather* to express a preference
   1. about our own actions.
      - If we are referring to a present situation, we use *would rather* + infinitive without *to*).
        I'**d rather be** rich than poor.
      - If we are referring to a past situation, we use *would rather* + perfect infinitive).
        I'**d rather have lived** 100 years ago than now.
   2. about someone else's actions.
      - If we are referring to a present situation, we use *would rather* + past simple).
        I'**d rather** you **came** tomorrow / I'**d rather** you **didn't come** on Wednesday.
      - If we are referring to a past situation, we use *would rather* + past perfect).
        I'**d rather** you **hadn't told** me / I'**d rather** you **had kept** it to yourself.

D It's time
   We use the expressions *it's time* and *it's high time* to show that we think something should happen soon. We use the past tense to refer to the present or the future:
   My hair is rather long. **It's time** I **got** it cut.
   He's over thirty. **It's high time** he **settled down** and **got** himself a proper job!
   We use the expression *it's time* + *to* infinitive to show that the moment for something to happen has come:
   It's 5 o'clock. **It's time to go** home. (We normally finish at 5 o'clock.)

Unit 11

Conditional sentences

There are four main types of conditional sentence. Each type has a distinctive pattern of verb tenses, and its own meaning.

Zero conditional

Form
If + present + present simple imperative
Meanings
This type of sentence is used for conditions which are always true.
If Mike reads on the train, he feels sick. (Every time Mike reads on the train, the same thing happens: he feels sick.)
This type of sentence is also used for scientific facts.
If you put paper on a fire, it burns quickly.
It is also used to give instructions.
If the phone rings, answer it.
In zero or present conditional sentences *when* or *whenever* can be used instead of *if*.

First conditional

Form
If + present simple + future *will*
Meaning
This type of sentence is used to predict likely or probable results in the future, if a condition is met.
If we don't leave now, we'll miss the train.
If we leave now, we won't need to hurry.
First conditional sentences are often used to express persuasion, promises, warnings and threats.
If you pass your exams, we'll give you a job.
If you don't turn that music down, you'll go deaf.
Some modal verbs can be used instead of *will*.
If we leave now, we may catch the train.
If you come to London again, you must call and see us.

Second conditional

Form
If + past simple + would / could / might
Meaning
This type of sentence is used to speculate about imaginary or improbable situations; the implication is that the conditions will not be met.
You'd feel healthier if you did more exercise.
If you went to Africa, you'd have to have several injections.
(It's not likely you'll go to Africa, but it is possible.)
Second conditional sentences can also refer to unreal situations
If people didn't drive so fast, there wouldn't be so many fatal accidents. (Actually, people do drive fast and there are a lot of fatal accidents.)
If I were taller, I'd play basketball. (Being taller is impossible for me.)
Second conditional sentences are often used to express advice
If I were you, I wouldn't drive so fast.

might / could
Might and *could* can be used instead of *would* in the main clause of second conditional sentences to show uncertainty.
If you did more exercise, you might feel healthier.

Third conditional

Form
if + past perfect … would / might / could have + past participle
Meaning
This type of sentence looks back at the past and speculates about possibilities which didn't happen.
If I'd had your address, I'd have sent you a postcard. (I didn't have your address, so I didn't send you a postcard.)
You might not have crashed into the bus if you'd been driving more slowly.
NOTE
When the *if* clause comes before the main clause, it is followed by a comma. When the *if* clause comes after the main clause, there is no comma between the clauses.

Mixed conditional sentences

Form
if + past perfect … would / could / might
Meaning
This type of sentence, which is a mixture of a third conditional sentence and a second conditional sentence, links a completed past action with a present result.
If I hadn't broken my leg, I would go on holiday with you.
I'd have a better job now, if I'd worked harder when I was at school.

Other ways of introducing conditions

unless
Unless can sometimes be used instead of *if not*.
Unless we leave now, we'll miss the train. (If we don't leave now, we'll miss the train.)
as long as
As long as is used to emphasize a condition.
I'll lend you the money you need as long as you promise not to waste it.
provided (that)
Provided (that)… and *Providing (that)* … mean 'on condition that' and are slightly more formal than *if*.
You can come on holiday with us provided (that) you do some

173

of the cooking.

Unit 12
Probability and possibility

Expressing near certainty

If we are almost certain that something is or is not the case, and this certainty is based on evidence, we can make statements using *must* or *can't*.

NOTES

Can't (not *mustn't*) is the negative of *must*.

1 To talk about a present situation we use *must* or *can't* + infinitive without *to*.
   *My doctor **must be** married. She wears a wedding ring.* (I am almost certain she is married.)
   *Angus **can't have** a lot of money. He's been out of work for over a year.* (I am almost certain he doesn't have a lot of money.)
   We can also use the continuous form of the verb.
   *Virginia **must be wondering** where I am. I said I'd be there at 3 p.m. and it's now 5 p.m.*
   *John **can't be coming**. He would be here by now if he was.*

2 To talk about a past situation we use *must* or *can't* + *have* + past participle.
   *Sandra **must have passed** her driving test because I saw her driving a car on her own.* (I am almost certain she has passed her test.)
   *Fiona and Neil **can't have enjoyed** their holiday because they haven't said anything about it.* (I am almost certain they didn't enjoy their holiday.)
   We can also use the continuous form of the verb.
   *I'm sorry I'm late. You **must have been waiting** for ages!*
   *You **can't have been listening** very carefully because I did say tomorrow, not today.*

Expressing possibility

If we are not certain that something is the case but we think it is possible, we can make statements using *may / might* or *could*.

1 To talk about a present situation we use *could, may, might* + infinitive without *to*.
   *Paula **could / might / may be** on holiday.* (Perhaps she's on holiday.)
   *Claude **could / might / may not want to come** with us.* (It's possible he doesn't want to come with us.)
   We can also use the continuous form of the verb.
   *Julie **could / might / may be visiting** her mother.*

2 To talk about a past situation we use *may, might, could* + *have* + past participle.
   *Freda **could / may / might / have overslept**.* (It's possible that she's overslept.)
   The lorry driver couldn't have caused the accident. The lorry driver **may / might not have caused the accident.*
   *(It's possible he didn't cause the accident.)
   We can also use the continuous form of the verb.
   *The missing girl **may have been wearing** a blue skirt.*
   NOTES
   A There is no real difference in meaning between *may, might* and *could* in affirmative sentences.

B The negative forms of *may* and *might* are *may not* and *might not*. These are not usually contracted.

C The negative form of *could* is *couldn't*. Its meaning is similar to *can't*, which means it can only be used to express near certainty NOT possibility:
*He **can't / couldn't** be lying.* (I am almost certain he isn't lying.)

Articles

The definite article *the*

Three of the main uses of the definite article are to refer to:

A something that has been mentioned before.
   Bill: *I've got a dog.*
   Ben: *What's **the dog**'s name?*

B something there is only one of in a particular context.
   ***The Queen** spent three days in Wales.*
   *Soon after we'd taken off, **the pilot** welcomed us on board.*

C something the speaker and listener both know about.
   ***The film** was really good – thanks for recommending it.*

It is also used in these ways:

D with superlative constructions.
   *She's **the fastest runner** in Europe.*

E with adjectives used as nouns referring to groups of people.
   *There's one law for **the rich** and another for **the poor**.*

F with the names of oceans, seas, rivers, mountain ranges.
   ***the** Atlantic, **the** Thames, **the** Alps*

G with the names of some countries and groups of islands.
   ***the** United States, **the** United Kingdom, **the** West Indies*

The indefinite article *a / an*

These are the main uses of the indefinite article:

A to refer to something for the first time.
   *I've got **a dog**.*

B to refer to a person or thing (but not a special person or thing).
   *Can I have **a drink** please? Tea, coffee, beer, I don't mind.*

C to refer to a person's job.
   *Alan is **a telephone engineer**.*

D with numbers.
   ***a** hundred, **a** million*

Zero article (Ø)

These are the main contexts in which no article is used:

A with plural countable nouns with general meaning.
   *Ø **Professional footballers** are paid too much money.*

B with uncountable nouns with general meaning.
   *He used to drink a lot of Ø **coffee**, but now he drinks only Ø **tea**.*
   *They fell in Ø **love** while they were in Spain.*

C with the names of towns, cities, states and most countries.
   *Ø **New York**, Ø **Texas**, Ø **Greece***

D with nouns for certain places or situations.
   *Suzy went into Ø **hospital** yesterday.*
   *on Ø **deck**, at Ø **home**, on Ø **holiday**, to Ø **church**, at Ø **school**, at Ø **university**.*

Overview of exam tips

Reading and Use of English

Part 1
- Read the text quickly for general understanding before you look at the four options for each gap.
- Look at the four options A, B, C and D and the words on either side of the gap. There may be a grammatical reason why some choices are not possible.
- Don't leave any questions unanswered. If you are not sure, make a sensible guess.

Part 2
- First, read the text quickly to get a general idea of the topic.
- Use the words on either side of the gap to help you decide what kind of word is missing.
- Missing words are typically prepositions, pronouns, conjunctions, adverbs and verbs. They will not usually be nouns or adjectives.
- It's a good idea to write your answers on the exam paper to check they make sense, before you transfer them to the answer sheet.

Part 3
- First, read the text quickly to get a general idea of the topic.
- When you read the text for a second time, use the words on either side of the gap to help you decide what kind of word is missing.
- When you have chosen your answers, read through the whole text to check it makes sense.

Part 4
- Think about what part of speech the key word is. This will help you to work out the correct grammar for the gapped sentence.
- Think carefully about the grammar of the gapped sentence. It may be active or passive and the key word may need a dependent preposition.
- You can use contractions, but remember they count as the number of words they would be if they were not contracted. For example, *didn't* and *I'll* are counted as two words, *can't* is counted as one.
- Check your final answers for spelling mistakes.

Part 5
- Read the whole text through quickly before you start the task. Don't stop to think about individual words you don't know.
- Read each question carefully and decide what information is required.
- Choose the option you think is correct. Then check your answer by trying to eliminate the other three options.

Part 6
- Read the gapped text quickly. Then read the missing sentences and underline any reference words such as names, pronouns and times.
- Check that any reference words and other language connectors in the sentence you've chosen fit the context of the gap.

Part 7
- Underline key words and phrases in the questions before you read the text. Check you understand what they mean. Then, think of other words which have a similar meaning, or how the underlined words and phrases could be paraphrased.
- Some people find it useful to read all the texts quickly for gist first. Other people might prefer to read each text quickly, trying to find at least one answer which matches the information in the text. Try both methods and see which you prefer.
- If you can't find an answer quickly, go on to the next question and come back to it.

Writing

Part 1 - Essay
- Before writing an essay, make a paragraph plan. This should include an introduction which is as interesting as you can make it.
- It is important that you plan how you are going to answer the question and organize the information before you start writing.
- First, decide if you agree or disagree with the statement. Then think of one or two ideas for each of the points under 'Things to write about', remembering to add your own idea.

Part 2 – Email / letter
- Note down some ideas for all the questions before you start writing your answer.

Part 2 – Article
- Think of an interesting title for your article. It could be a statement or a question, but it should tell the reader what the article is about.

Part 2 – Review
- Once you have decided which place you are going to review, quickly note down your answers to both questions in the task. Do this before you start writing.

Part 2 – Letter / email
- Remember to begin your letter in an appropriate way and give your reason for writing in your first sentence.

Part 2 – Report
- Try not to repeat the exact wording of the task in your introduction.
- Remember to use headings in your report. You can also make recommendations in your final paragraph, even if the task does not require you to do so.

Listening

Part 1
- Before you listen to the recording, read the question and the three options. As you listen for the first time, mark the option which you think is correct.

Part 2
- Read the sentences you have to complete before the recording starts. Decide what kind of information you need to listen for.
- When you listen for the first time, complete as many sentences as you can. Don't worry if you can't complete all of them at this stage. The second time you listen, complete the rest of the sentences and check the ones you have already completed.

Part 3
- Before you listen for the first time, read statements A–H and underline any key words and phrases.
- The second time you hear the recording, make your final choice of answer. Remember you will not use three of the letters.

Part 4
- Before you listen for the first time, read the questions and the three options carefully, underlining key words.
- As you listen for the first time, mark or make a note of the options which you think are possible.

Speaking

Part 1
- Give full answers to the questions. Don't just answer with a few words or short sentences.

Part 2
- When you're comparing the photographs, look for similarities and differences between them.
- This part of the test assesses how well you can speak for longer periods. It is important that you keep talking for a minute.
- When it is not your turn to speak, it is important to listen to what your partner is saying. This will help you to make your own 30-second comment when they have finished speaking.
- Remember to compare the photographs before you answer the second part of the question.

Part 3
- Make sure you give your partner the opportunity to speak. If they don't say anything, ask them what they think.
- Remember to give reasons and explanations for your answers.

Part 4
- Listen carefully to what your partner says. The examiner may ask you the same question, so you should be prepared to agree or disagree with what your partner says.

Whole speaking test
- If you don't know your partner, introduce yourself before the exam starts. This will make you feel more relaxed.
- If you don't understand what the examiner wants you to do, you can ask them to repeat the instructions.
- If you don't understand what your partner has said, ask them politely to repeat. You get marks for how well you interact with your partner.
- Try to treat the exam as if it were a class speaking activity. If you are more relaxed, you will perform better.

Writing guide

Essay (Part 1)

Part 1 of the Writing paper is always an essay. You have no choice here.

How should I approach the task?

> In your class, you have been talking about the way animals are treated in modern society. Now, your teacher has asked you to write an essay.
>
> Write an essay using all the notes and giving reasons for your point of view.
>
> Write your **essay** in 140–190 words.
>
> **Essay question**
> Should animals be used in scientific experiments to try out new products to be used by humans?
>
> **Notes**
> Things to write about:
> 1. testing cures for humans
> 2. animal suffering
> 3. _____ (your own idea)

Who will read my essay? You should assume that only a teacher will read your essay.

What information should I include? A good essay includes clearly-stated opinions supported by well-chosen examples and convincing reasons for each of the points in the Notes, including your own idea.

What is the purpose of the essay? Essays are usually set by teachers for students. They give students the opportunity to express opinions on subjects which may be controversial, in a logical, structured way.

What style should I use? Essays are formal pieces of writing. Opinions should be expressed in a clear and logical way. Use discourse markers (*On the other hand,* / *Firstly,*) to make clear how your different points are related.

How should I structure an essay?

It is very important that essays are clearly structured. This means writing in paragraphs and making sure each paragraph includes a 'topic sentence'. Topic sentences express the main idea in a paragraph and are followed by 'supporting sentences' which expand on the idea in the topic sentence.

The first paragraph of your essay should introduce the subject and outline the main arguments related to it.	In many countries, experiments are carried out on animals to test drugs, medicines and beauty products such as shampoo or shower gel. Scientists say they need to use animals, but many ordinary people believe these experiments are cruel. I will discuss both points of view and express my own opinion.
State what you intend to do in your essay.	
The second paragraph should provide more detail in support of one side of the argument.	Scientists argue that cures for human diseases would not be found if animal experiments were banned. They claim that it is safer to test new medicines on animals before giving them to humans, and maintain that the animals they use in their work do not suffer.
The third paragraph should present the other side of the argument.	On the other side of the argument, many people believe that animals feel pain in the same way as humans, and the mistreatment of innocent creatures, like monkeys or mice, for scientific research is cruel and immoral. They believe that human volunteers should be used instead.
The concluding paragraph should clearly express your own opinion. Always back up your opinion with a clear reason.	In my opinion, there is no justification for using animals to test beauty products. However, I believe that it may be necessary to use animals for testing drugs because these experiments may save human lives.

What phrases can I use?

Stating an aim	• I will discuss both points of view and express my own opinion.
Expressing personal opinions	• In my opinion, … • I (do) believe that … • On balance, it seems to me that …
Reporting other people's opinions	• Scientists argue / claim / say / maintain that … • Many people believe / think that … • According to (experts), …
Expressing different sides of an argument	• On the one hand, … • On the other hand, … / On the other side of the argument, …
Expressions which introduce a contrast	• However, … , but …, nevertheless, … • while …, although …, whereas … • Having said that, … • Despite this, … / Despite the fact that … • In spite of …
Expressions which add information and ideas	• In addition to this, … • What is more, … • Apart from that, … • As well as that, … • Besides (this), …
Introducing a reason or explanation	• because / since … • Because of this, … • This is because … • The (main) reason for this is …
Introducing an example	• for instance, … • for example, … • such as …
Summarizing / Concluding phrases	• In conclusion, … / To conclude, … • To summarize, … / To sum up, …
Other useful phrases	• In fact, … • (For me) the question is …

writing guide

Formal letter / email (Part 2)

How should I approach the task? You have seen the following advertisement on your university noticeboard.

> Looking for work this summer?
>
> Do you speak a foreign language?
>
> Do you know your town well?
>
> Are you a good communicator?
>
> We are looking for information guides to help foreign tourists who are visiting your town.
>
> If interested, please apply in writing to the address below.
>
> Write your **letter** in 140–190 words.

What is the purpose of a formal letter or email? There can be many purposes: to ask for or give information, to apply for a job, to make a booking (e.g. for a holiday), to make a complaint, etc.

Who will read it? The person or organization you are contacting, or who has contacted you. This will probably be someone you do not know well, if at all.

What style should I use? A formal style is appropriate when you are writing to someone you do not know or do not know well, or when making an application or complaint. Be polite. Use indirect expressions, formal linking phrases and set phrases wherever appropriate. Avoid being too familiar, or using contractions and colloquial language.

What information should I include? You should include all the information you are asked for or need to give.

How should I structure a formal letter / email?

Begin a formal letter / email in one of these ways:
- *Dear Mr / Mrs / Miss / Ms Lodge* – use the person's title and surname if you know it.
- *Dear Sir/Madam* if you don't know the person's name, or whether they are a man or a woman.

Say why you are writing. Clearly state the subject or context.

Organize all the essential information in a clear and logical way.

Say how you expect the other person to respond to your letter if this is appropriate.

Finish your letter in one of these ways:
- *Yours sincerely*, if you have started your letter with the name of the person you are writing to.
- *Yours faithfully*, if you have started your letter with *Dear Sir/Madam*.

> Dear Sir/Madam,
>
> I saw your advertisement for information guides on the university noticeboard yesterday, and I am interested in applying.
>
> I have almost completed my second year at the university, where I have been studying history, and, as my exams will be finished in a few weeks' time, I will soon be free to do other things. I am looking for part-time or full-time work from then until mid-October, and the job you are advertising sounds ideal.
>
> As I have lived here all my life, I know the city very well. I also speak English to upper-intermediate level as well as being able to communicate in basic French and Italian. I imagine that the job will involve helping foreign tourists to find places in the city by giving clear directions and recommending good places to eat and stay. If that is the case, I believe that I am perfectly capable of doing that.
>
> I hope you will consider my application and I look forward to hearing from you.
>
> Yours faithfully,
> Miguel Sanchez

What phrases can I use?

Saying why you are writing
- I am writing to complain about / enquire about / apply for …
- I would like to request further information about …
- I would be most grateful if you could send me details of …
- In response to your letter of 26 February, I am writing to …

Organizing information
- Firstly, … • Secondly, … • In addition, … • Furthermore, … • Lastly, …

Asking for action
- I would be grateful if you could … • Please could you …
- It would be helpful if you would … • I hope you will …

Closing the letter
- I look forward to hearing from you.

Informal letter / email (Part 2)

How should I approach the task? You have received an email from a British friend. Read this part of the email and then write your email to Jo.

> Some friends of mine would like to visit your country for a couple of weeks and I was thinking you would be the best person to ask for advice. They would like to know the best time of year to come and which places they should visit when they are there.
>
> Thanks a lot,
>
> Jo

Write your **email** in 140–190 words.

What is the purpose of an informal letter or email? They can serve many purposes: to exchange news, to request or give information, to ask for or make suggestions or recommendations, etc.

Who will read it? The person you are contacting or who has contacted you.

What style should I use? An informal style is appropriate when you are writing to a friend. Slang and colloquial expressions are sometimes appropriate; contractions are always appropriate.

What information should I include? You should include all the information you are asked for.

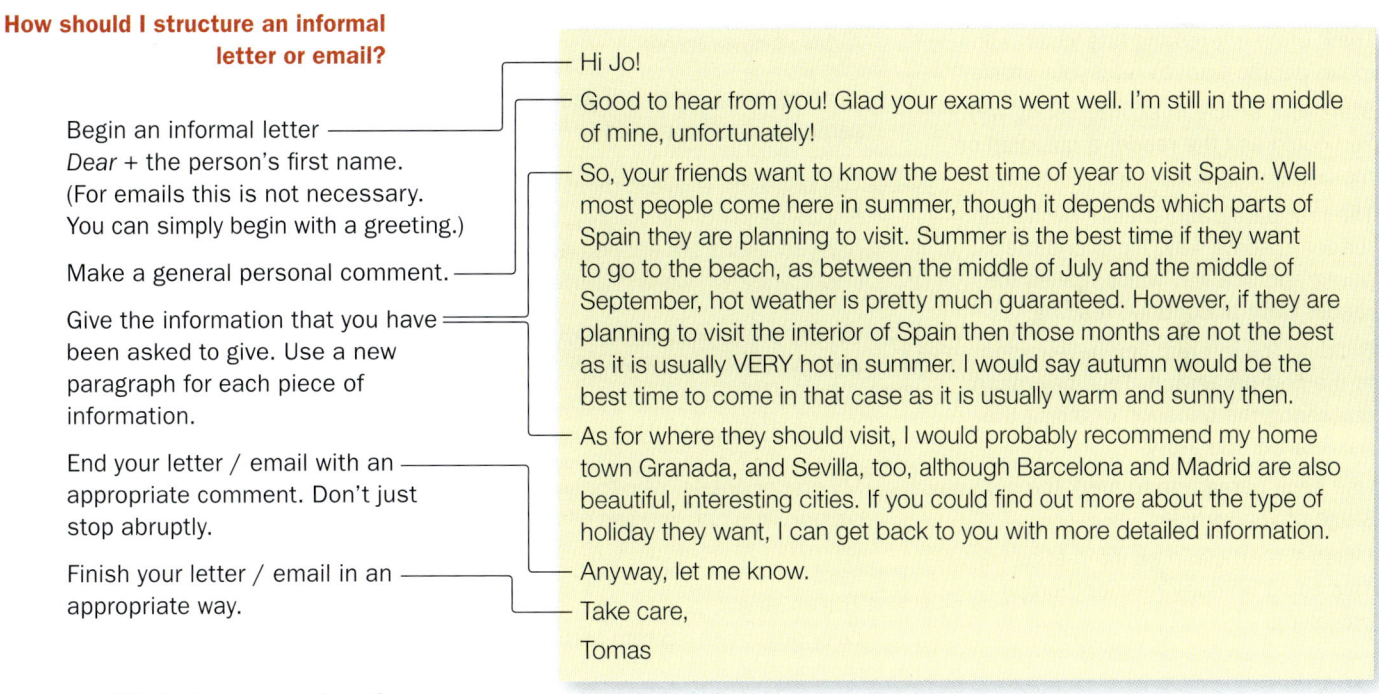

How should I structure an informal letter or email?

Begin an informal letter *Dear* + the person's first name. (For emails this is not necessary. You can simply begin with a greeting.)
— Hi Jo!

Make a general personal comment.
— Good to hear from you! Glad your exams went well. I'm still in the middle of mine, unfortunately!

Give the information that you have been asked to give. Use a new paragraph for each piece of information.
— So, your friends want to know the best time of year to visit Spain. Well most people come here in summer, though it depends which parts of Spain they are planning to visit. Summer is the best time if they want to go to the beach, as between the middle of July and the middle of September, hot weather is pretty much guaranteed. However, if they are planning to visit the interior of Spain then those months are not the best as it is usually VERY hot in summer. I would say autumn would be the best time to come in that case as it is usually warm and sunny then.

— As for where they should visit, I would probably recommend my home town Granada, and Sevilla, too, although Barcelona and Madrid are also beautiful, interesting cities. If you could find out more about the type of holiday they want, I can get back to you with more detailed information.

End your letter / email with an appropriate comment. Don't just stop abruptly.
— Anyway, let me know.

Finish your letter / email in an appropriate way.
— Take care,

Tomas

What phrases can I use?

Letter / email openings
- *How are you?*
- *Thanks for your letter / email. It was good to hear from you.*
- *I'm sorry I haven't written for such a long time but …*

Saying why you are writing
- *You asked me to recommend some (places to stay in my country) …*
- *I've managed to find out some information about (language schools) for you.*
- *About your planned visit, …*

Letter / email endings
- *Write back soon.*
- *Look forward to seeing you soon.*
- *Give my regards to your parents.*

Signing off
- *Love* or *All the best* or *Take care* – if you are writing to a friend.
- *Best wishes* or *Kind regards* – if you don't know the person very well.

Article (Part 2)

How should I approach the task? You have seen this announcement in an English-language magazine for young people.

> **You Write – We Print**
>
> Family celebrations are often memorable occasions. Write an article describing a family celebration that you remember well. The three most interesting articles will be published in our next issue.
>
> Write your **article** in 140–190 words.

Who will read the article? Readers choose articles that interest them or are relevant to them in some way, and ignore those that look dull or irrelevant.

What information should I include? You may have to describe personal experiences or express opinions and ideas which people of your age can identify with. What you write need not be true.

What is the purpose of the article? To inform readers about a particular topic in an entertaining way.

What style should I use? Magazine articles, especially for young adult readers, are often written in a light-hearted style. The title and opening paragraph should capture the readers' attention.

How should I structure an article?

Think of an interesting title which will make people want to read your article. — **A day I'll never forget**

Start your article in an interesting way. You could ask the reader a question or make a strong statement. — Have all the members of your family ever met together in the same place at the same time? It happened to me quite recently and it was a remarkable event.

The first paragraph should involve the reader in some way. Try to end the paragraph in a way which makes the reader want to continue reading. — The occasion I have in mind took place last summer. It was my grandparents' fiftieth wedding anniversary, and my brother Tim decided to organize a surprise party for them. He phoned everyone in the family and told us his plan. Most importantly, we weren't allowed to say anything to our grandparents.

Build on the interest you have raised in the first paragraph. This may mean answering the question or telling the next part of the story. — On the eve of the anniversary, we arrived at Tim's house at midday. By three o'clock, there were over a hundred people there, including cousins, uncles and aunts I hadn't seen for years. Everyone was excited as they waited for the 'happy couple' to arrive.

Use each paragraph to mark the next stage of your article. — My grandparents, who thought they were visiting my brother, arrived at four o'clock. You can imagine what happened when they found us all waiting for them. I have never seen anyone look so surprised and so happy.

Finish the article in an interesting way. This could be humorous or thought-provoking. — The celebrations went on until the next morning. Now, we're looking forward to celebrating their sixtieth anniversary.

What phrases can I use?

Addressing the reader directly
- Have you ever …?
- What do you think about …?
- You may be wondering why / what / how …

Expressing a strong opinion
- There's nothing worse than …
- You may not agree with me, but I think …
- What I believe is …
- What is most important (is) …

Describing a personal experience
- It happened to me when …
- This is what happened when …
- The occasion I have in mind is …
- I'll never forget the time …
- I must admit, …

Conversational expressions
- You can imagine …
- If you ask me, …
- Another thing is that …
- To be honest, … / To tell the truth, …
- Believe it or not, …
- The thing is, …

Review (Part 2)

How should I approach the task? You have seen the following announcement in an international music magazine.

> Do you like music concerts? Write a review of a concert you've been to. Include information on the music and atmosphere, and say whether you would recommend the artist or band to other people. The best reviews will be published next month.
>
> Write your **review** in 140–190 words.

Who will read a review? A review will usually be read by readers of a magazine or newspaper.

What is the purpose of a review? A review is intended to give information to the reader which will help them decide whether to attend an event, go to see an artist / band, buy an album, read a book, see a film, etc.

What style should I use? Use a style similar to an article, which is likely to interest the reader.

What information should I include? Give essential information about the event, artist / band, album, book, film, etc. Say what you liked and didn't like. Make a recommendation to the reader.

How should I structure a review?

- State the name of the film, play, concert, etc. at the start of the review.
- Introduce the topic of the review in the first paragraph.
- Give the positive and negative features in separate paragraphs.
- Finish with a final recommendation.

Happy Shoppers at Cardiff Coal Exchange

Happy Shoppers are four guys from Bristol. They became quite famous last year when one of their songs was played on a popular TV show. Yesterday, I saw them play live to a big audience at the Coal Exchange in Cardiff.

On the plus side, the music was great. Happy Shoppers have an original sound, with elements of hip-hop and rock. Their music is very catchy, and people really enjoyed dancing to it.

On the other hand, the band didn't really entertain the audience as much as they could have. The singer never spoke between songs and didn't encourage the audience to sing along, which was a pity. Also, his voice was poor. But he did apologize, saying that he had a cold.

Overall, I'd recommend going to see Happy Shoppers, especially if you like dancing. I'm sure they will learn how to entertain the audience more as they get more experience.

What phrases can I use?

Giving background
- *This show stars …*
- *The book was written by …*
- *The film is about …*

Expressions which introduce a contrast
- *On the plus side, …*
- *On the negative side, …*
- *On the one hand, …*
- *On the other hand, …*

Recommending
- *Overall, I'd recommend …*
- *All in all, the (film) was …*
- *I wouldn't hesitate to recommend …*
- *I wouldn't encourage anyone to …*

Report (Part 2)

How should I approach the task?

> A group of students from Australia is coming to stay in your town for two weeks as part of an exchange programme. The organizer has asked you to write a report suggesting places the group should visit and activities they could take part in during their stay.
>
> Write your **report** in 140–190 words.

What is the purpose of a report? A report is intended to give information, evaluate something or make suggestions and recommendations.

Who will read it? Usually the person or people who have asked for the report. This may be a teacher, an official body (e.g. a town council) or your boss, for example.

What style should I use? Reports are usually written in a formal, impersonal style, avoiding overuse of the pronoun 'I'.

What information should I include? Give only essential information and recommendations. Avoid unnecessary detail. Make a number of points, giving some description and explanation. Conclude with a personal recommendation if required.

How should I structure a report?

Use clear headings to help the reader see how the report is organized. Introduction and Recommendations or Conclusion are often appropriate.

Give each section in the report its own paragraph. Use numbers or bullets to make them stand out. Where appropriate, divide sections into paragraphs.

Use your conclusion to summarize briefly. Make sure that you express your personal recommendation if this is asked for in the question. Make points clearly and directly.

Introduction
This report will consider what a group of exchange students from Australia could do while they are staying in our town. Several visits and other activities will be suggested.

Places to visit
Since our town is well-known as a cultural centre, many foreign visitors find the following particularly interesting places to visit:
– the cathedral   – the palace
– the market, where local craftsmen sell traditional products

Activities
In the past, students from abroad have said they would like to meet and do things with students here. For this reason, joint activities between our visitors and our college students should be considered. The following could be organized:
– a sports competition   – a party

I suggest a variety of visits and activities for the visitors during the fortnight. During their first week, they could visit the cathedral and the palace and go to the market, which is held on Saturdays. Also, a basketball and / or football competition could be held against students at our college. At the end of their second week, we could organize a farewell party at the college.

Conclusion
I am sure that a combination of sightseeing and socializing, as suggested, would give students a very positive experience.

What phrases can I use?

Stating aims
- The aim of this report is to …
- This report will consider / examine / compare …
- This report is intended to …

Giving reasons
- Since / As (our town is well-known), …
- For this reason / these reasons, …

Making suggestions or recommendations
- In view of this, I (would) recommend / suggest (that) …
- We / I suggest (that) …
- They / We could …

Audioscript

🔊 **1.01**

1
Narrator You hear a man telling a friend about an email he has received.
Woman So tell me exactly what happened.
Man Well, I got one of those emails that looked as if it came from my bank. It said I was at risk of identity theft and told me I had to log on and verify my account information. I was really worried.
Woman So what did you do?
Man Well, I was about to reply to give them the information they wanted, but then I thought I ought to check with my bank first. So I rang my branch and they said they never sent emails like this. But it looked so realistic – it had my bank logo on it and it had links to real websites.
Woman I've heard of that before. Apparently it's a very common scam which everyone needs to be aware of.

2
Narrator You hear someone talking about her first impressions of someone.
Woman The first time I met Ben was at a party. We were introduced to each other by Charlie, a mutual friend, and we chatted for a few minutes – you know, we exchanged the usual pleasantries: 'Where do you live?'; 'What do you do?'; 'How do you know Charlie?' – that sort of thing. Then he started talking about his job – he seemed very self-centred and that put me off a bit, but I didn't think much about it. A couple of weeks later, he phoned me and asked if I'd like to meet for a drink. I ummed and ahhed a bit and then I said, 'Yeah, why not?' So we met and he was really nice. He even said he was sorry if he'd come over as a bit arrogant at the party.

3
Narrator You hear a conversation between a young man and an older relative.
Young man I wonder if I could ask your advice.
Older man Sure. How can I help?
Young man Well, I'm going for a job interview next week and I'm thinking about how to do my best. They've already got my CV, so they know about my qualifications, and obviously I must look my smartest at the interview and sound as intelligent as I can.
Older man Do you know all about the company?
Young man Not yet, but I'll be doing a bit of research at the weekend so that I can ask sensible questions about the kind of work I'd be doing if I got the job.
Older man Good idea. So what are you worried about?
Young man I want them to see what I'm really like – you know, I don't want to have to pretend to be someone I'm not.
Older man That's fine. Just be yourself. I'm sure they appreciate that.

4
Narrator You hear someone describing how he heard about winning a competition for a mobile phone.
Man Last year, I got an email telling me I'd won a mobile phone in a competition. I couldn't remember going in for a competition, but that didn't matter. I had to email my debit card details, so they could charge me for the cost of shipping the phone to me. Like an idiot, I made a basic mistake by giving them my card details and the address for the phone to be delivered to. Needless to say the phone never arrived, but my bank statement showed that money was being taken out of my account.

5
Narrator You hear two friends talking about tennis.
Speaker 1 Hello, Anna! Where are you going?
Speaker 2 To play tennis, believe it or not. Can't you tell from what I'm wearing?
Speaker 1 Well you do look as though you're going to play something, but I didn't know you played tennis.
Speaker 2 I've only just started – I don't have my own racket yet.
Speaker 1 Well, you look very smart. We must have a game some time?
Speaker 2 Do you play tennis, then?
Speaker 1 Yes, I do. In fact, I've been playing since I was eleven or twelve.
Speaker 2 Really? Are you a good player?
Speaker 1 I used to be very good, but I haven't played much recently.
Speaker 2 Great – I'll give you a ring to arrange a time.

6
Narrator You hear someone talking about a bad experience on a social networking site.
Man I had a pretty nasty experience on a social networking site. It started when I got a series of offensive messages, then whoever it was said they were going to pass on private information about me if I didn't give them money. At first I thought it might be someone in my group at college, but I didn't recognize the information on the person's profile. It was obviously a fake identity. I did think about going to the police, but in the end I decided to ignore the whole thing and not make a fuss. And fortunately, after a week or two it stopped. So, if you want my advice, you shouldn't put confidential information about yourself on social networking sites.

7
Narrator You hear a message on a telephone answering machine.
Woman Hi, Mary! It's Alice. I'm just ringing to say sorry for something that happened yesterday. I was in town doing some last-minute shopping and someone on the other side of the road called my name. When I looked round, I didn't see anyone I recognized – just a police officer and hundreds of shoppers. Anyway, I didn't think any more about it. Then, about half an hour later, I was on the bus coming home, when I suddenly remembered – your brother Jeremy joined the police last year, didn't he? It must have been him who called to me, but I just didn't recognize him in his uniform. Please apologize to him for me when you see him. Thanks. Bye.

8
Narrator You hear a politician talking about his appearance.
Man If you want my opinion, I think appearance is very important if you want to convince people that you are a serious politician. That's why I always wear a suit and tie if I'm on official business – especially if I'm in a meeting, being interviewed on television, or talking to members of the public. I know there are politicians – especially the younger ones – who think it's cool to dress down – you know jeans, open-necked shirt and trainers, but for me that's just too informal. Of course, at home with my family, I dress informally, too, but never when I'm at work. It projects the wrong image.

🔊 **1.02**

Examiner Good morning! My name is Gail Evans and this is my colleague John White. And your names are?
George My name is George Pappas.
Adriana My name is Adriana Calligaris.
Examiner Can I have your mark sheets, please? Thank you. Where are you from George?
George I am from Patras – it's a fairly large town in the south west of Greece.
Examiner And you?
Adriana I'm from Granada.
Examiner First, we'd like to know something about you. What do you enjoy doing in your spare time George?
George I read quite a lot, but I'm also very keen on all kinds of sport. I play football, basketball and tennis, so sport takes most of my spare time.
Examiner And Adriana?
Adriana I like sport, too.
Examiner Do you play any sports?
Adriana I used to play tennis.
Examiner George, who do you spend your spare time with?
George My team mates if there's a match or a practice. I spend the rest of my spare time with college friends or my family. I have two brothers and a sister and we all get on very well.
Examiner Tell us something about one of your close friends.
George OK. My best friend is called Anatol. We're in the same class at college, but we've been close friends since we were about 12. Actually, we have completely different characters. I'm sociable whereas Anatol's rather shy – especially with people he doesn't know well. When I first met him, he seemed very unfriendly, but now we get on extremely well.
Examiner Adriana, I'd like to ask you about your clothes. What kind of clothes do you feel most comfortable in?
Adriana T-shirt, jeans and trainers.
Examiner Are there occasions when you wear smart clothes?
Adriana Yes, there are.
Examiner When was the last time you wore smart clothes?
Adriana Last weekend.
Examiner George, do you ever wear smart clothes?
George Yes, sometimes, for example for special family occasions like weddings, and for interviews. But I prefer T-shirts and jeans like Adriana.
Examiner Thank you.

🔊 **1.03**

Examiner What did you do last weekend?
Candidate I went to the cinema.

Examiner How long have you been studying English?
Candidate I've been studying English for 4 years.

Examiner How do you spend your spare time?
Candidate I swim quite a lot.

Examiner Who do you spend most of your spare time with?
Candidate I spend most of my spare time with my friends.

Examiner What kind of clothes do you like wearing?
Candidate I'd have to say casual clothes.

Examiner Tell us something about one of your close friends.
Candidate My best friend is called Antonio.

🔊 **1.04**

Where are you from?
Describe the area where you live.
Tell me some of the things you enjoy doing with your family.
Do you have any holiday plans for next year?
What did you do on your last birthday?
What is your favourite way of travelling?

🔊 **1.05**

Examiner In this part of the test, I'm going to give each of you two photographs. I'd like you to talk about your photographs on your own for about a minute, and also to answer a question about your partner's photographs. George, it's your turn first. Here are your photographs. They show people studying in different places. I'd like you to compare the photographs and say how you think the people feel about studying in these different places. All right?

🔊 **1.06**

George In this picture the students are studying in a lecture hall – probably in a university or college. In the other picture the students are studying in a classroom. The lecture hall is much bigger than the classroom and there are many more students in the hall than the classroom. Some of the students have to sit a long way away from the lecturer whereas in the classroom they are a lot nearer. The main difference between the two places is that you can ask the teacher questions in the classroom but you can't interrupt a lecturer if there is something you don't understand. I imagine that the students who are in the lecture hall feel less involved than the ones in the classroom because they are just listening and taking notes while in the classroom the students would feel more involved because they can participate in the lesson and do more active activities, like speaking for example.
Examiner Thank you. Adriana, which of these places would you prefer to study in?
Adriana I'd much rather study in a classroom than in a lecture hall. Personally, I find it hard to hear and see if I'm in a big room, so unless I'm sitting right at the front I find it difficult to follow what the lecturer is saying and I switch off. And of course, if you switch off you could miss something really important. I also find sitting still for an hour very difficult, and just listening and taking notes is boring. In the classroom you can move about and there is the opportunity to work with other people.
Examiner Thank you.

🔊 **1.07**

a The lecture hall is much bigger than the classroom.
b Teachers aren't nearly as strict as they used to be.
c It's just as hard to spell a word in English as to pronounce it.
d Class sizes are considerably smaller these days.

185

1.08

a My sister's only a bit older than me. She's a lot cleverer than me, though.
b This car's not nearly as expensive as that one. And it's far cheaper to run.
c This lecture is just as hard to follow as yesterday's. Physics is by far the most difficult subject I've studied. It's much harder than chemistry.
d Italian is no more difficult to learn than Spanish.

1.09

Narrator You will hear a man talking about 'hyper-parenting'. For questions 1–10, complete the sentences with a word or short phrase. You now have forty-five seconds to look at Part 2.

Presenter Life for Cathy Hagner and her three young children is set to permanent fast-forward. Their full school day and her 9 a.m. – 2 p.m. job are busy enough. But it's at 4 p.m., when school is out for the day that the pace really quickens. Cathy frantically drives Brendan, twelve, and Matthew, ten, from soccer field to basketball court while dropping off eight-year-old Julie at piano lessons. Often, the exhausted family doesn't get home until 7 p.m. – just in time for a quick supper before the children have to do their homework.
Cathy, who lives in a small town outside Buffalo in New York State, acknowledges the stress such a way of life causes the whole family and has wondered whether it is worth it. But she defends herself by saying that she knows lots of families whose children do even more than hers do.
This is the world of hyper-parenting. A world in which middle-class American – and, increasingly, British – parents treat their children as if they are competitors eternally racing towards some unidentified finishing line. A world in which children are rushed from activity to activity in order to make their future CVs as impressive as possible. A world in which raising the next top sportsperson, musician, artist, whatever, has apparently become a more important goal than raising a happy, well-balanced child.
US child psychiatrist Dr Alvin Rosenfeld, co-author of *Hyper-Parenting: Are You Hurting Your Child by Trying Too Hard?*, explains why hyper-parenting has become such an issue. He says, 'Parents have been led to believe that they can somehow programme their children for success if only they do all the right things. It starts even before they are born, when pregnant women are warned of dire consequences if they don't eat the right foods. Then, they are told that playing a baby Mozart could speed its development, so they play Mozart and it just goes on from there. It's a very winner-takes-all view of society and it's making a lot of parents – and children – very unhappy.'
Childhood expert, William Doherty of the University of Minnesota, informs us that doctors across the country are reporting a growing trend in children suffering frequent headaches due to exhaustion and stress.
In the UK, too, GPs and child experts are reporting similar symptoms of stress. With two working parents now the norm, many children have to go to clubs at the end of the school day through necessity. But competitive pressures are also fuelling an explosion of private-sector extra-curricular activities, including sports, language, music and maths classes for children as young as four.
Pyschiatrist, Terri Apter, admits that there is definitely a new parenting trend under way which says that parents have to uncork all their child's potential at a young age. They are concerned that they are letting down their children if they don't. She goes on to say that it isn't an entirely new phenomenon, that there have always been pushy parents, but that what was previously seen as eccentric behaviour was now much more the norm. Mothers see their children's friends doing lots of extra-curricular activities and they believe they have to follow suit. It all becomes very competitive.
Terri Apter has seen at first hand the harmful effects of hyper-parenting. She is currently studying a group of British and American eighteen-year-olds, many of whom are having enormous difficulty adjusting to the freedom of college life. She explains that a lot of them are so used to having their time completely filled up by their parents that, when they leave home they lack the most basic self-management skills and simply don't know what to do with themselves. The answer, she says, is for parents to lighten up and take a sensible middle road – allowing time for free play as well as structured activity. She sums up: 'Everyone wants their child to shine, but going to art or jazz classes is not necessarily any more beneficial than giving young children time and freedom to play by themselves. Or just to sit and think.'

1.10

Narrator You will hear part of a radio phone-in programme on the subject of people's use of digital technology. For questions 1–7, choose the best answer (A, B or C). You now have one minute to look at Part 4.

Presenter In this evening's programme, we're starting with a subject which has got many of you worried. We'll be discussing young people and digital technology. It's something that worries not only parents but young people themselves. On our studio panel, we have Evan Matthews, a child psychologist, Joanne Carter, a secondary school head teacher, and Liz Winslett, who has three teenage children and is a student counsellor. Our first caller this morning is James Benson. What is your question, James?

James Thank you. I'd like to ask you what you think about my parents' recent behaviour. They're getting more and more obsessed about the amount of time I spend with what they call my 'virtual friends'.

Evan Hi, James. Can you tell me who these friends are?

James They're mainly people I've met on social networking sites.

Evan And how much contact do you have with them?

James Well, on a normal day, I'll update my status as soon as I wake up. Then I'll check to see if anyone's sent me any messages on my mobile.

Evan And how long does that usually take?

James About five minutes if I have to reply to any messages.

Joanne What about later in the day?

James Well, if I don't have to go to college, I'll spend a couple of hours chatting to friends in the morning and maybe another two in the evening.

Joanne Hmm, that does seem rather excessive.

James I suppose so, but it's what I'm used to. But actually, what Mum and Dad really object to is seeing me texting my friends – especially at mealtimes. They say it's rude and antisocial.

Joanne And what do you think?

James I just think it's completely normal for people of my age.

Joanne How many texts do you send a day?

James About fifty or sixty.

Joanne OK – and do you understand why your parents are getting so annoyed?

James Not really. It's just a bit of fun. I think adults take these things too seriously.

Liz Can I ask you, James, do you have any other interests outside your virtual world?

James No, not now. I used to play tennis with my dad most weekends. But he always seems too busy these days.

Presenter OK, James, I think we get the idea of what your life is like. I'd now like to ask our panel to comment on what they've heard. Can I start with you Evan?

Evan OK, James. I have to say I have great sympathy with your parents and completely understand their point of view. They feel they're losing you to your virtual friends. My advice to you would be to spend less time on your phone and try to spend at least a couple of hours a day when you're not at college doing things with real people.

Presenter Thank you. Joanne?

Joanne Here's what I suggest, James. First, I think you should accept that you have an addiction then I suggest you try to cut back your contact with digital friends by a few minutes every day, so that by this time next year your life is in more balance. Try to get back to playing tennis with your dad like you used to. And try to spend more time with real people – you'll soon get used to it. You won't lose any genuine friends and you won't have your parents nagging you all the time.

Presenter Thanks. And lastly, Liz Winslett.

Liz Right, James. I imagine your addiction is probably a very temporary one. I would guess that in a month or two you'll get bored with your virtual life and just slip back into your old life – that's if my own son's experience is anything to go by. In other words, I think you're going through a phase.

Presenter Thank you all very much – and thank you, James, for your intriguing question.

James Thanks.

1.11

give in
give out
give away
give back
give up on

1.12

I really ought to give it back.
I really ought to give the DVD back.
One of the supermarkets is giving them away.
One of the supermarkets is giving free samples away.

1.13

Examiner Now, I'd like you to talk about something together for about two minutes. I'd like you to imagine that you are on a committee which has been asked to come up with ideas for stopping young people from smoking. Here are some of the suggestions and a question for you to discuss. First, you have some time to look at the task. Now, talk to each other about the advantages and disadvantages of each suggestion.

1.14

Sophie I think these are really good ideas, so let's take them one at a time, shall we?

Christian OK. Well, for a start, I think they should raise the price of cigarettes. That way young people would probably smoke less.

Sophie We don't want them to smoke less. We want them not to smoke at all. If it was up to me, I'd raise the smoking age to twenty.

Christian Twenty? I'm not sure about that. You might stop young people from buying cigarettes, but if you did that, they would just get their older friends or even their parents to buy cigarettes for them. They do that now, don't they?

Sophie That's true. What about banning advertising? Do you think that would make a difference?

Christian Yes, it might. Seeing pictures of good-looking people smoking and looking happy must make smoking very attractive to some young people.

Sophie Yeah, so if we stopped them from seeing those images, it might help.

Christian The other thing I think they should do is have an advertising campaign to show people how smoking can damage their health.

Sophie They've tried that before, haven't they, and they found it didn't make much difference. It's like the health warnings on cigarette packets which say things like 'Smoking kills'. They don't seem to stop people smoking.

Christian You're right. I think they tried it with teenagers – and teenagers do all kinds of things that damage their health – and they don't seem to care. What they should do is have a campaign in every primary school.

Sophie You're probably right – it's definitely worth a try and we've got to try everything. Do you think providing people with alternatives would be a good idea – such as patches that you stick on your arm or special chewing gum?

Christian Anything's worth a try. Have you heard about electronic cigarettes?

Sophie Yes, that's a really weird idea, isn't it?

Christian Yes, it is, but I know someone who tried them – and it's worked quite well so far.

Examiner Thank you.

1.15

Examiner Now you have about a minute to decide which two ideas would be most likely to stop young people from smoking.

1.16

Sophie Well, they are all quite good ideas, aren't they?

Christian Yes, but we've already decided that raising the age when people can buy cigarettes won't work, haven't we?

Sophie Yes, they just get other people to buy them. We need to think of a way of stopping young people actually wanting to smoke in the first place.

Christian That's true, but the thing is that all the ideas have been tried before, haven't they?

Sophie Yes, but something needs to be done, doesn't it?

Christian You're right – they've got to do something.

Sophie So, can we decide on two ideas?

Christian Shall we suggest a health campaign in primary schools and a complete ban on cigarette advertising?

Sophie OK! That sounds sensible.

Examiner Thank you.

1.17

Examiner Now, I'd like you to talk about something together for about two minutes. I'd like you to imagine that you are on a committee which has been asked to come up with ideas for stopping young people from smoking. Here are some of the suggestions and a question for you to discuss. First, you have some time to look at the task. Now, talk to each other about the advantages and disadvantages of each suggestion.

Sophie I think these are really good ideas, so let's take them one at a time, shall we?

Christian OK. Well, for a start, I think they should raise the price of cigarettes. That way young people would probably smoke less.
Sophie We don't want them to smoke less. We want them not to smoke at all. If it was up to me, I'd raise the smoking age to twenty.
Christian Twenty? I'm not sure about that. You might stop young people from buying cigarettes, but if you did that, they would just get their older friends or even their parents to buy cigarettes for them. They do that now, don't they?
Sophie That's true. What about banning advertising? Do you think that would make a difference?
Christian Yes, it might. Seeing pictures of good-looking people smoking and looking happy must make smoking very attractive to some young people.
Sophie Yeah, so if we stopped them from seeing those images, it might help.
Christian The other thing I think they should do is have an advertising campaign to show people how smoking can damage their health.
Sophie They've tried that before, haven't they, and they found it didn't make much difference. It's like the health warnings on cigarette packets which say things like 'Smoking kills'. They don't seem to stop people smoking.
Christian You're right. I think they tried it with teenagers – and teenagers do all kinds of things that damage their health – and they don't seem to care. What they should do is have a campaign in every primary school.
Sophie You're probably right – it's definitely worth a try and we've got to try everything. Do you think providing people with alternatives would be a good idea – such as patches that you stick on your arm or special chewing gum?
Christian Anything's worth a try. Have you heard about electronic cigarettes?
Sophie Yes, that's a really weird idea, isn't it?
Christian Yes, it is, but I know someone who tried them – and it's worked quite well so far.
Examiner Thank you … Now you have about a minute to decide which two ideas would be most likely to stop young people from smoking.
Sophie Well, they're all quite good ideas, aren't they?
Christian Yes, but we've already decided that raising the age when people can buy cigarettes won't work, haven't we?
Sophie Yes, they just get other people to buy them. We need to think of a way of stopping young people actually wanting to smoke in the first place.
Christian That's true, but the thing is that all the ideas have been tried before, haven't they?
Sophie Yes, but something needs to be done, doesn't it?
Christian You're right – they've got to do something.
Sophie So, can we decide on two ideas?
Christian Shall we suggest a health campaign in primary schools and a complete ban on cigarette advertising?
Sophie OK! That sounds sensible.
Examiner Thank you.

1.18

adventurous
conservative
conventional
unconventional
extraordinary
fashionable
imaginative
normal
strange
surprising
traditional
unusual

1.19

Narrator You will hear five short extracts in which people are talking about bringing up children. For questions 1–5, choose from the list (A–H), what each speaker says. Use the letters only once. There are three extra letters which you do not need to use. You now have thirty seconds to look at Part 3.
Speaker 1 I'd say that men and women are as good as each other at looking after children and loving them. I grew up without my dad around. At the time it seemed normal enough, but now I have kids of my own, I realize that mothers and fathers help us in different ways. As a dad myself, I know there's a bond between children and their dads that's just as important as having a mum around, and from experience I'd say that only a man can really do that job.
Speaker 2 If you're thinking about the day-to-day care of children, I'd say that fathers and mothers can be equally successful. I know several families where the mother is the main breadwinner and the father looks after the kids – and it works perfectly well. But I'm sure that the physical relation between a baby and its mother creates an emotional tie which there's no substitute for, and of course this won't change because men will never be able to have children.
Speaker 3 Mothers and fathers are different and always will be, but both are essential. It's far too much work for one person to look after a family on their own, so it's important for the father to help out right from the start. The key thing is to always put the interests of the children first. I know that I have a special relationship with them as a mum, but I can see that my kids need their dads around, too.
Speaker 4 The idea that men are worse at looking after children is rubbish. Dads can do everything just as well as mums. Women are only better at childcare because, at the moment, they spend more time with their kids than men do. It's like my mum – she doesn't understand how to use email, but if she worked in an office like me she'd know exactly what to do – it's just a question of familiarity.
Speaker 5 When I was a kid, my father made more effort to spend time with us than most fathers would have done, which wasn't what real men were supposed to do. Whenever he wasn't at work, he dedicated all his time to me and my sisters. Other than my mum, people didn't really recognize how special he was. My father wasn't like everyone else, so people just ignored him. Nowadays, most men are involved with their kids like he was.

1.20

Examiner In this part of the test, I'm going to give each of you two photographs. I'd like you to talk about your photographs on your own for about a minute, and also to answer a question about your partner's photographs. Claudia, it's your turn first. Here are your photographs. They show two offices. I'd like you to compare the photographs and say how you think the relationships are different in the two offices. All right?
Claudia In this picture all the employees are sitting at their own computers, so they almost certainly can't see each other. This probably means that they don't talk to each other very often except in their breaks. It looks like a very big office, maybe with hundreds of employees, so it could be a call centre of some kind. In this picture the manager may work in a separate office so the chances are he or she is quite remote from the staff. He or she may not even know all the employees' names, but probably has to check regularly how hard they are working. By contrast, the other picture shows a small open office with just a few employees. I should think that these employees have good relationships with each other, and you can see that they all look quite happy. Their manager may be in this office, but you can't tell who it is. I'd say he or she knows the names of all the staff, and probably doesn't need to check how hard they're working. In offices like these I imagine it's possible to have regular meetings so that problems and difficulties can be sorted out before they get worse.
Examiner Thank you. [Pause] Kostas, which of these places would you prefer to work in? Why?
Kostas I'd much rather work in the office on the right because everyone looks so happy and relaxed. I guess the atmosphere in the other office might be very tense. I think I'd find this office quite a stressful place to work in. I think it's probably a call centre and these places have a bad reputation as places to work. I know from experience that I work better if I'm relaxed. I'm also quite a sociable person, so I'd enjoy the social side of any job I did. I think it would be easier to make friends with colleagues in this office.

1.21

Narrator You will hear a man talking about his experiences of eating in other countries. For questions 1–7, choose the best answer (A, B or C). You now have one minute to look at Part 4.
Interviewer This afternoon we have in the studio John Reginald, a former diplomat and now a full-time writer. His first book, an autobiography, has the title *A Strong Stomach*. Why this title, John?
John Reginald Well, food really can be a tricky issue. Obviously, as a diplomat you attend many official dinners and you have to learn to negotiate your way through a minefield of rules of etiquette – what is acceptable in one culture can be quite inappropriate in another. But the main thing I discovered very early on is that basically you really have to be prepared to eat whatever is set in front of you. And, believe me, this does sometimes necessitate having a strong stomach, hence the title.
Interviewer Can you give us some examples?
John Reginald The one that springs to mind happened at my first official dinner when I was in the Middle East. The main dish was a sheep's head and as the guest of honour I was presented with the eyeball, which over there is regarded as a delicacy.
Interviewer Oh, dear! Did you manage to eat it?
John Reginald I really didn't have much choice. If I hadn't eaten it, I would have offended my hosts. As simple as that.
Interviewer So was that the worst thing you've ever been served?
John Reginald It was among the worst, certainly. But there have been many others. I had dried bat once when I was in the Pacific – that wasn't very nice, either – dry and leathery! It wasn't so much the taste, which was bad enough, but the fact that it was almost impossible to swallow. But I think top of the list is probably snake blood, which was served to me at a meal in Thailand.
Interviewer What makes something repulsive to eat?
John Reginald If I can see what it actually is, it's worse. If I am obviously eating a part of an animal which is recognizable as such then that makes it harder to eat. If what is on your plate is an eyeball then you can't pretend that you are eating something else. For some people smell is the most important factor, but I don't have a very good sense of smell, fortunately, and yes, taste is important as well. I once ate raw turtle eggs. They were fishy, in an extremely unpleasant way.
Interviewer So what advice would you give to someone in a situation where something is put in front of them that they don't want to eat?
John Reginald I'd say: one, don't not eat it. You need to be polite. It could be one of their national dishes. Two, take it easy; eat too fast and you might find that you get some more and, three, pretend you're eating something you like.
Interviewer I have to say that I found your book very amusing. From the title I thought it was going to be some sort of medical textbook, so I was pleasantly surprised. Is there another book in the pipeline?
John Reginald Yes, but the next one will be totally different. My editor wanted me to do a follow-up – again based on my experiences – things that almost led to diplomatic incidents. And I had thought about doing a sort of guide book for businessmen who travel abroad – etiquette in different countries – but I've recently become interested in the origins and rationale behind the consumption of food in different countries so that's what it'll be about.

1.22

Examiner Now, I'd like you to talk about something together for about two minutes. I'd like you to imagine that your teacher has asked you for your ideas on different ways of getting to know a country and its culture. Here are some of the ways of getting to know a country and its culture and a question for you to discuss. First, you have some time to look at the task. Now, talk to each other about how much you can learn about a country and its culture from these experiences.
Candidate A Shall I start?
Candidate B Yes, if you like.
Candidate A Personally, I think you can probably learn quite a lot about a country if you're doing voluntary work there. You're likely to be working alongside local people for a start …
Candidate B I guess so but I'm not sure how much you'd learn about the country. You'd probably be working with poor people or disadvantaged people. They're not representative of the whole country.
Candidate A Yes, that's a good point. OK, let's move on to sightseeing.
Candidate B If you ask me I believe you can get a good general impression of the history of a country from sightseeing 'cos you are seeing lots of historical monuments. Do you agree?
Candidate A Yeah and you usually have a guide who tells you all about the history too. But you don't really get to meet the people, do you?
Candidate B No, you're right. 'Cos you're usually in a big group of people from your own country. Learning a language?… In my opinion, you can learn a lot about a country from learning a language. For a start, if you know a language you can communicate with the people. I don't think you can really know a country if you don't speak the language. What do you think?

Candidate A I agree.
Candidate B Au pair? I'm not sure I know what an au pair is …
Candidate A It's someone who goes to live in a country so they can study the language. They stay with a family and look after the children and in exchange they get their food and accommodation and time off to go to classes.
Candidate B Ah, right. Well, I'd say you could learn a lot through doing that. You'd be living with a typical family, seeing how they live and improving your language …
Candidate A Not necessarily. They could be recent immigrants and speak their own language all the time.
Candidate B Oh! I suppose so. Right the last one, backpacking. Have you ever done that abroad?
Candidate A Yes, I backpacked around Asia for six months a few years ago.
Candidate B And did you learn a lot about the countries you visited?
Candidate A Yeah, quite a lot. You tend to use public transport so you get to meet ordinary people and you can take your time to look around places. But if you don't speak the language – as I didn't – then the experience is limited.
Examiner Thank you.

1.23

Examiner Now, you have about a minute to decide which two experiences you think you would learn the most from.
Candidate B I think we more or less agreed that you might not learn a lot from voluntary work.
Candidate A Yes.
Candidate B And sightseeing. I think we both thought that you'd learn a lot about the culture and history of a place but you wouldn't have many opportunities to meet the people.
Candidate A Yes. So we've got three left to choose from. Personally, I'd choose learning a language and backpacking.
Candidate B I'd agree with you on learning a language but I'd have to disagree with you on backpacking.
Candidate A Would you? Why?
Candidate B Because, as you said, if you don't speak the language then you can't really communicate with the people.
Candidate A Why would you choose working as an au pair?
Candidate B Well, I know you said that you might end up working with recent immigrants, but I'm sure you'd be able to change families if that happened.
Candidate A That's very true. I take your point.
Candidate B Shall we agree on learning a language and working as an au pair, then?
Candidate A OK, you've convinced me.
Examiner Thank you.

1.24

I don't know about that.
Absolutely!
I agree with you up to a point.
Sorry, but I have to disagree with you there.
I'm not sure I agree with you there.
I couldn't agree more.

1.25

Narrator You will hear part of a radio programme about factors which determine success. For questions 1–10, complete the sentences with a word or short phrase. You now have forty-five seconds to look at Part 2.
Radio DJ The idea that thinking is superior to feeling is an attitude that many psychologists today would consider out-of-date. They would argue that emotional intelligence is just as important as IQ when determining a person's overall success. Let me give you two examples of research which backs up this theory. When ninety-five graduates from Harvard University were followed into middle age, the men with the highest intelligence test scores in college were not found to be particularly successful – in terms of salary, productivity or status – compared with those who had scored lower. IQ, it would seem, contributes only about 20% to the factors that determine life success, leaving 80% to other forces. So, what are these other forces? Peter Salovey of Yale University would argue that emotional self-control is one of the most important. He conducted an experiment with a class of four-year-olds. He gave each of them a sweet, and told them they could eat it immediately. However, if they could resist eating the sweet until the experimenter came back into the classroom, he would then give them two sweets.
For what seemed like an endless 15 minutes, most of the children waited. However, about a third of the children were unable to wait. They grabbed the sweet almost immediately after the experimenter left the room.
When the same children were followed up as teenagers, those who at four had been able to resist temptation were, as adolescents, more socially competent, self-reliant, dependable and confident. They also had dramatically higher scores on IQ tests. However, those who at four had been unable to resist temptation were more indecisive, more socially isolated and less confident. This experiment suggests that emotional self-control is an important contributor to intellectual potential, quite apart from IQ itself. Another ability that can determine not just academic but job success is optimism. In a study of insurance salesmen, psychologist Martin Seligman, showed the relation between optimism and high work performance. Selling insurance is a difficult job and three quarters of insurance salesmen leave in their first three years. Given the high costs of recruiting and training, the emotional state of new employees has become an economic issue for insurance companies. Seligman's study found that new salesmen who were natural optimists sold much more than salesmen who were pessimists, and were much less likely to leave in the first year. Why? Because pessimists think failures are due to some permanent characteristic in themselves that they cannot change, whereas optimists believe they are due to something temporary that can be changed. They believe they can succeed next time round.

1.26

Examiner Now I'd like you to talk about something together for about two minutes. I'd like you to imagine that the principal of your college has asked you to give a talk to the other students on the best ways to relieve stress. Here are some activities people do to relieve stress and a question for you to discuss. First you have some time to look at the task.
Now, talk to each other about how effective each of the activities is in relieving stress.

1.27

Examiner Do you agree that living in a city is more stressful than living in the country?
Maria I've never actually lived in the country, but I imagine it would be.
Examiner Why?
Maria Well, for several reasons: first of all, because many cities nowadays are huge, people spend a lot of time just getting to and from their workplace. This is stressful as they usually have to travel on crowded trains or buses, or if they go by car, they may spend hours stuck in traffic jams. They can never be sure that they will get to work on time so this makes their daily commute to work stressful.
Examiner Do you agree, Pierre?
Pierre Yes, I do. And apart from the reasons that Maria gave I'd also like to add that, since people live much closer together in cities, there is a greater possibility of tension between them. Just to give a few examples: people work and sleep at different times, so there is bound to be conflict here; some people don't think of their neighbours and play loud music or have their televisions up too high and because the walls of most modern buildings are quite thin you can hear everything.
Examiner Maria, do you think people today are more or less stressed than they were in the past?
Maria That's difficult to say. I think people today think that they are more stressed than people were in the past, yes, but whether they are or not is another matter.
Pierre There was an interesting programme on TV where a family lived life for a couple of months as they would have lived it in the 1940s. I can remember being surprised that at the end of the series the woman said she found modern life more stressful than life in the 1940s. She said it was because women had a simpler role in life then – to be wives, mothers and housewives. Nowadays, they have to be all those things not to mention work as well.
Maria I agree, but I think one of the main reasons why people feel more stressed today is because society is more materialistic. People want more things. Things cost money. In order to make more money you have to work more. That means you have less time to do the other things you either want to do or have to do. And that is what makes you stressed.
Pierre Also, I think technology has made life today more stressful. In the past people worked a nine-to-five job and then went home and switched off. But nowadays, if you work in business, for example, you are on call almost twenty-four hours a day and even when you are on holiday you are expected to check your emails.
Examiner Is it always a good thing to be relaxed? Can you think of any occasions when it might be a bad thing to be too relaxed? Pierre?
Pierre Too relaxed? Hmm …
Examiner Maria?
Maria Well, you can't be too relaxed in certain jobs, at least not all of the time. For example, pilots need to be alert during take-off and landing. They can be relaxed the rest of the flight unless something happens and there is an emergency, of course. In fact, there are many jobs where you can be relaxed a lot of the time but need to be alert and concentrating hard at other times: surgeons, for instance, and air-traffic controllers. Not only are people's lives in their hands but also, in the case of pilots, their own lives, too.
Pierre It's not a good idea to be too relaxed during an interview, either, because you might give the impression that you don't really care if you get the job or not.
Maria And we mustn't forget about when people are driving. I heard that most accidents happen when people are driving near their homes. Because they are familiar with the route, they are too relaxed and not paying enough attention to the road and that's when accidents happen.

1.28

Candidate A Well, for several reasons: first of all, because many cities nowadays are huge, people spend a lot of time just getting to and from their workplace.
Candidate A This is stressful as they usually have to travel on crowded trains …
Candidate B I'd also like to add that, since people live much closer together in cities, there is a greater possibility of tension between them.
Candidate B Nowadays, they have to be all those things not to mention work as well.
Candidate A I agree, but I think one of the main reasons why people feel more stressed today is because society is more materialistic.
Candidate B Also, I think technology has made life today more stressful.
Candidate A For example, pilots need to be alert during take-off and landing.
Candidate A In fact, there are many jobs where you can be relaxed a lot of the time but need to be alert and concentrating hard at other times: surgeons, for instance, and air-traffic controllers.
Candidate A Not only are people's lives in their hands but also, in the case of pilots, their own lives, too.
Candidate A And we mustn't forget about when people are driving.

1.29

but also
for example
forget about
not only
one of

1.30

First of all, because many cities nowadays are huge, people spend a lot of time just getting to and from their workplace. People work and sleep at different times so there is bound to be conflict here.

1.31

Examiner Which do you think would be more stressful – being self-employed or working in a large company?
What could companies do to make work and the workplace more relaxing for their employees?
What kind of holiday would you find stressful?

2.01

Examiner Now, I'd like you to talk about something together for about two minutes. I'd like you to imagine that a secondary school is planning some after-school leisure activities for its students. Here are some of the activities that are being considered and a question for you to discuss. First, you have some time to look at the task.
Now, talk to each other about how popular each of these activities might be with students.
Candidate A There are some quite interesting things to do here, aren't there? I'd find designing websites really exciting.
Candidate B Okay, but we've got to think about what most students would enjoy, so let's think about them one at a time. What about martial arts – do you think that would be popular?
Candidate A Yes, probably, but only with a few people. Karate's like fighting, and most people I know wouldn't be interested in that.
Candidate B Yes, but it's also a way of keeping fit, so it might be popular with more people than you

think. If you ask me, I'm sure appreciating modern music would be really popular, although I suppose it depends on what they mean by modern music.

Candidate A Yes, I don't think people would be interested if it was modern classical music.

Candidate B No, I think you're right. But if it was modern pop music, I bet it would attract a lot of interest. But I don't quite know how you would appreciate it.

Candidate A No, that sounds a bit serious, doesn't it? I know one or two of my friends would really love to debate social and political issues, but I can't imagine most people I know showing any interest in those kinds of subjects at all – I'm absolutely certain they'd find debates really boring.

Candidate B You said you'd enjoy website design, didn't you?

Candidate A Yes, I did – and I know loads of other people who'd love it. You can do so many things with computers now.

Candidate B What kind of website would you like to design?

Candidate A I'd love to design one with lots of animation.

Candidate B Really? How about researching local history? I know one or two of my friends who might quite like that.

Candidate A No, I'm afraid that wouldn't interest me at all. I've never been very keen on history of any kind.

Examiner Thank you. Now you have about a minute to decide which two activities would be most popular with students you know.

Candidate B Well, I'd suggest the modern music and website design. I think they'd be the most popular out of the five activities we've talked about.

Candidate A I agree about the website design, but I think we should have something not related to technology – so what about suggesting debating social and political issues or maybe karate as an alternative.

Candidate B Even though we've said they would probably be minority interests?

Candidate A Yes. Students could only take part in one activity at a time, so we should have something for people who aren't interested in technology.

Candidate B You could be right. I think most of us spend long enough on computers as it is, don't we?

Candidate A We certainly do. So have we made our decision?

Candidate B Yes, we'll go for website design and debating social and political issues.

Candidate A Okay.

Examiner Thank you.

2.02

I enjoy swimming but only in an outdoor pool.
I like to be doing something active.
I was going to say playing football, too.
I could name a lot of things I like doing.
I like reading and going out with friends best.

2.03

1

Narrator You will hear people talking in eight different situations. For questions 1–8, choose the best answer (A, B or C). You hear someone being interviewed.

Man Definitely jazz – any kind, really – traditional or modern. I don't exactly know what it is about it that appeals to me. It's not just the music; it's the atmosphere in the clubs and the people you meet at concerts. I quite like other kinds of music as well: blues, soul, world, even some classical. But I have to say, I'm not that keen on pop. It all sounds the same to me these days – a sure sign that I'm getting middle-aged.

2

Narrator You hear someone describing an event she went to.

Woman It was amazing. My friend and me were right at the front. We were in the most expensive seats. But even there it was almost impossible to hear anything. As soon as they came on and started playing, everyone went mad. You could just about hear the bass and the drums from time to time, but the words were completely inaudible. We could see their mouths opening and closing, but nothing seemed to come out.

3

Narrator You hear someone describing something she finds annoying.

Woman It's everywhere you go these days. I was on the train on the way to work last week. A girl came and sat next to me. I was trying to read a report and all I could hear was this repetitive drumming noise – sort of disco music, I suppose. I just couldn't concentrate. I've got a friend who listens when he goes jogging. That's OK, because he's not disturbing anyone. But in public places they're a real nuisance – a blatant case of noise pollution if you ask me.

4

Narrator You hear the presenter of a radio programme talking.

Man I've got an email here from Mrs Johnson. She'd like to have *Love Hurts* played for her son Michael. Mum sends you her love, Michael, wherever you are. She's asked me to tell you that she loves you very much and says please, please, please contact her before your birthday – she doesn't want to lose touch with you. Just a phone call would do. You don't have to tell her where you are if you don't want to. So, for Michael Johnson, here's *Love Hurts* from your Mum.

5

Narrator You hear someone talking about their favourite situation for listening to music.

Man I had a CD player fitted in the boot a few months ago. It takes six CDs at a time. So you get your favourite CDs, put it on random, and off you go. The good thing about random is you don't know which CD or which track you're going to hear next. You get to listen to different kinds of music without having to stop or take your hands off the wheel. And you can have the volume turned up as high as you like. It's brilliant on long journeys.

6

Narrator You will hear someone talking about a common human experience.

Woman It's very strange, you just have to hear a certain sound or catch a whiff of a particular smell and everything comes flooding back. I mean, I can remember exactly where I was when I heard Madonna's first hit. It was a winter evening. I was in my mother's kitchen making myself a cheese sandwich. I only have to hear that first guitar chord and I'm back in my mum's kitchen. Another example is the smell of suntan lotion. It always takes me straight back to a holiday in Spain when I was four years old.

7

Narrator You hear a man talking about somewhere he has just been.

Man It's something I've always been terrified of, but it was absolutely killing me. In the end it got so bad, I just had to have it seen to. Actually, it only needed filling, which wasn't as bad as having to have it taken out. Anyway, I was sitting there in the chair, feeling very nervous, waiting for the drill, when this wonderful Indian music started playing. It was incredible – my anxiety completely disappeared and I relaxed my whole body.

8

Narrator You hear someone talking about the beneficial effects of music.

Woman We now use music to help them recover – especially if they're here for a long stay. Experimenting with different kinds of music, we've found that certain sounds have the power to change moods and emotional states for the better. Many of them come to us shattered, angry and full of pain, both physical and mental. They've had their lives reduced to a bed and a locker. We try to bring peace to their body and their mind.

2.04

Narrator You will hear five short extracts in which people are talking about how they use the internet. For questions 1–5, choose from the list (A–H) which main use each speaker describes. Use the letters only once. There are three extra letters which you do not need to use. You now have thirty seconds to look at Part 3.

1

Speaker 1 I find it really useful to help me with school work – especially when we're doing geography or history projects. I know people of my parents' generation used to spend hours in the school or the town library finding the information they needed. My dad said the information was almost always out of date. The internet is fantastic – I've always found what I'm looking for. The only problem is that sometimes there's just too much stuff to get through. One of my friends said she'd once spent five hours looking for information. You've just got to know when to stop.

2

Speaker 2 I'm addicted to my computer mainly as a way of keeping in touch with people. It's just so easy to talk to your friends. At the moment I'm chatting to my older brother who's in Thailand – he's told me incredible stories about what he's getting up to. It's almost as good as the phone and it doesn't cost anything. I've started talking to a few people I don't know, but I haven't made any new friends like that. I think it's a bit scary – the idea that you can get to know someone like this and then call them your friend. You don't really know anything about these people – I mean, everything they say could be lies.

3

Speaker 3 I use it for various things – you know, the obvious ones like emailing, getting the latest news, but at the moment mostly for buying things. The thing is, I really don't enjoy going shopping in town any more. It takes me half an hour to get there on the bus and the shops are always really crowded. I buy all kinds of things from websites – like last week, I bought a DVD, a new pair of jeans and some make-up. It's so quick and easy – you just click on what you want, put it in your basket, go to the checkout and pay with your card. And most things don't take long to arrive. I said I'd show my brother how to do it tomorrow.

4

Speaker 4 Music, definitely. It has to be music. That's about all I use it for really, apart from occasionally checking the sports results. It's fantastic if you're into music of any kind. I go on some of the music sites and download all kinds of music files straight to my smart phone. It's so easy these days. I can't afford to pay, but I don't download anything that you're supposed to pay for. I know some people do. The music industry's trying to crack down on the illegal downloading. They say they're losing sales because people aren't buying CDs any more, or paying for downloads. I reckon they're fighting a losing battle.

5

Speaker 5 I use it for all kinds of stuff, but at the moment mainly catching up with programmes I couldn't watch first time round for some reason. It's incredibly useful to be able to do that. Most of them you can still get for up to a week after they're first broadcast. The quality's not quite as good on my laptop, but at least you don't have to wait for ages until they repeat the broadcast. And of course, you can pause programmes and fast forward them so you can avoid the adverts.

2.05

Examiner In this part of the test, I'm going to give each of you two photographs. I'd like you to talk about your photographs on your own for about a minute, and also to answer a short question about your partner's photographs. Xavier, it's your turn first. Here are your photographs. They show different advertisements. I'd like you to compare the photographs and say which advertisement is more effective. All right?

Xavier Hmm, I think they're both very effective advertisements. I'd certainly notice them if I saw them in the street. I like the advert for women's clothes because of its size – the way it goes from the top of the building to the bottom – it looks so powerful. But the problem for me, is that people may be more impressed by the size of the advert than by what it's advertising. When you've looked at the woman and the clothes she's wearing, you see the name Gap, but to my mind that's less interesting than the shape and size of the advert. For me, the main reason the advert for Nike sports gear is more effective is that it makes you think. You say to yourself things like "That guy looks really strong. He must be good at his sport" – then you notice the name Nike in the bottom corner and you think "Maybe he's good at his sport because he wears clothing and shoes made by Nike". Of course, you probably don't go straight out and buy yourself Nike sports gear, but the name may stay in the back of your mind when you next go shopping. In my opinion it's a very successful advert.

Examiner Thank you. Carmen, which do you prefer?

Carmen I'd say the Nike advert's more effective, too. To be honest, I don't think much of the ad on the building. It's a clever idea to use a building like this, but to me the clothes are not interesting enough. I also think the word Gap is a bit lost where it is. It might have been better at the top of the wall.

Examiner Thank you.

2.06

mass media
press conference
eyewitness
newsagent's
soap opera
current affairs
talk show
headline
remote control
foreign correspondent

2.07

Manoulis I come from Athens in Greece.

Examiner First we'd like to know something about you. Clara, what kind of weather do you like best?

Clara I like hot, sunny weather best.

Examiner Why?

Clara	Because I like doing things outside, like going to the beach with my friends or just sitting in an open-air café having a cola and chatting to them. Things like that.
Examiner	Manoulis, how do you spend your free time when the weather is bad?
Manoulis	If it's cold and wet I don't usually go out. I stay at home and maybe watch a DVD, play my guitar or listen to music in my room. But if the weather has been bad for a few days I'll probably go out – shopping or to the cinema – 'cos I'll be bored staying at home.
Examiner	Clara, what's your home town like?
Clara	I live in Barcelona. It's a very cosmopolitan city. Parts of the city are very modern but it also has a historic old quarter with narrow streets. You can find all sorts of small shops, bars and restaurants there. It's a vibrant city with plenty to do and see.
Examiner	Manoulis, how has your town changed in recent years?
Manoulis	It looks much nicer than it used to because the local council have cleaned all the old buildings. And the town centre has been pedestrianized so it's much nicer to go shopping there now. They've also built another multi-storey car park, so parking in the town centre is easier than it used to be.
Examiner	Thank you.

2.08

Speaker 1	I stay at home and maybe watch a DVD, play my guitar or listen to music.
Speaker 2	You can find all sorts of small shops, bars and restaurants there.

2.09

Speaker 1	After I got home I made something to eat, watched TV and then did my homework.
Speaker 2	Can you get me some milk, sugar and rice, please?
Speaker 3	I'll have the prawns for starters, the duck for the main course and ice cream for dessert.

2.10

Narrator	You will hear part of a radio programme about the effects of air travel on the environment. For questions 1–7, choose the best answer (A, B or C). You now have one minute to look at Part 4.
Presenter	Hello. This week we will be looking at ways in which we can reduce our 'carbon footprint'. By 'carbon footprint' we mean a measure of the impact that human activities have on the environment in terms of the amount of greenhouse gases they produce. These days it's easy to work out how big one's own personal 'carbon footprint' is provided you have internet access. You can simply go online and put in the following information: how much your annual household fuel bill is, how often and how far you travel and a calculator will work it out for you. Your secondary carbon footprint is determined by your buying habits. Basically, if you buy food or items produced locally, then your carbon footprint will be smaller than if you buy produce which has to be flown or shipped from the other side of the world. There are of course ways of reducing our carbon footprint: we can car share to work, travel by bus or train rather than by car; we can buy local fruit and veg or wine. If you live in the UK then buy your wine from European countries rather than Australia, for example, and avoid items that have been made in China or India. Let's start by looking at the effect of air travel on the environment. Sue Hendry, how have you been addressing this?
Sue Hendry	Well, I quit flying a year ago. For too long I'd been saying 'they', that is, governments, must do something about global warming rather than 'we' or 'I'. Then I suddenly realized that I can't expect things to change if I'm not prepared to change myself. How could I look my children in the eye in twenty years' time and say, 'I could have done something, but I chose not to.' The arguments against flying are obvious: Do you know that a return flight from London to Australia equals the emissions of three average cars for a year? And a return domestic flight from London to Edinburgh produces eight times the carbon dioxide you would use if you took the train?
Presenter	Nigel Hammond, what's the present situation in the travel industry?
Nigel	There has been a huge rise in the number of people flying from UK airports. The cheap flights offered by budget airlines have meant that many people think nothing of popping over to the continent for the weekend. Long-haul destinations are becoming increasingly popular too. But the biggest rise has been in short-haul flights both domestic and to places like Spain, France and Italy.
Sue Hendry	I think the problem is that, although most people know that flying contributes hugely to global warming, they are not really prepared to do anything about it. So they'll feel a bit bad while they're sitting on the plane, but the moment they get to their destination, it'll be long-forgotten.
Presenter	So, what solutions are there?
Nigel	There are a variety of possible solutions. One is to put up the tax on aviation fuel but this has been tried already and didn't work. Another is to limit the number of flights people can take a year. I like that idea, but I'm not sure how practical it would be. Still, I definitely think it would be worth giving it a go. And then there is 'carbon offsetting' whereby people plant trees. But if the trees are cut down or there's a fire, then you've lost your offset.

2.11

Examiner	In this part of the test, I'm going to give each of you two photographs. I'd like you to talk about your photographs on your own for about a minute, and also to answer a short question about your partner's photographs. Nadia, it's your turn first. Here are your photographs. They show people doing household tasks in different decades. I'd like you to compare the photographs and say how you think technology has changed people's lives.
Nadia	Both photos show people working in a kitchen. In this photo a woman is washing clothes whereas in the other photo a man is cooking. The kitchens are very different. This one is very old um er not modern but the other one is modern. There are a lot of machines which do things for you or help you do things more quickly. In this picture the woman is washing clothes by hand because she doesn't have a washing machine. She's using a … well a kind of machine to get the water out of the clothes. It looks hard work and I guess it was very … took a long time. The man looks quite relaxed probably because he has lots of things to help him. I think there's a dishwasher and a … machine where you heat up food, for example. Doing household tasks is much easier these days because of technology.
Examiner	Tomas, which of these household tasks do you prefer to do?
Tomas	To be honest, I hate washing clothes even with a washing machine. I much prefer cooking. I suppose for some people cooking is em a thing that's not very enjoyable to do the same as doing the washing up or cleaning but for other people it's … well it's a … very nice activity. You can be creative and if you practise you can improve. Cooking a nice meal gives you much more … is more … well it's nicer to do than having a em lot of clean clothes. For me, anyway.
Examiner	Thank you.

2.12

Narrator	You will hear someone giving a talk about gadgets. For questions 1–10, complete the sentences with a word or short phrase. You now have forty-five seconds to look at Part 2.
Presenter	Our lives today are dominated by gadgets. According to a recent survey British people spend nine hours a day on average using some form of electronic gadget: most time was spent on the computer (around four hours), followed by the television (90 minutes), the phone (around 40 minutes), and the microwave (10 minutes). The same survey revealed that one third of British people also considered their ability to use gadgets as their most valuable life-skill. Other life-skills such as cooking, DIY and gardening were ranked next with speaking a foreign language coming way behind. We have, it seems, become a nation both obsessed with and passionate about technology. This would seem to be supported by the long queues for the latest Apple iPad, which started three days before the item was even on sale, to the High Street stampedes for the latest Nintendo game. And even though we are living in a difficult economic climate, it seems the price tag for the latest piece of gadgetry hardly matters. The important thing is to be the first among your friends to have it. So why do we have this obsession with gadgets? A lot of technology purchases are a case of 'keeping up with the Joneses' – someone you know gets the latest TV or smart phone, for instance, and you feel you are missing out if you don't get one, so you do. I wonder how many bread machines, which everyone seemed to have in the 1990s, are now lying unused at the back of kitchen cupboards? And is our obsession something new? Well no it isn't something new. Admittedly in the 1950s there wasn't the range or number of gadgets that there are today, but there was still the same excitement when any new gadget appeared. My grandparents told me that they were the first in their street to have a television and at the coronation of Queen Elizabeth II in 1953 all the neighbours were invited in to watch the ceremony. This, apparently, was not unusual. The 1950s in the UK was a decade when most women did not go out to work but stayed at home to raise their families. Most of their day was taken up with cleaning, cooking, washing and other household tasks. Items which had been luxuries before the war now became affordable for many families. With the introduction of the modern vacuum cleaner into most middle-class homes in the 1950s, and the precursor to the modern washing machine around the same time, a woman's workload was substantially reduced and women had more leisure time than ever before. Most women nowadays would not be pleased to be given a household gadget except for possibly a cappuccino coffee maker as say a birthday gift, but in those days it was received with delight. Until recently, it was always assumed that men were more gadget-obsessed than women – but it seems that today's women are just as interested in gadgets as men. The main difference between the sexes seems to be in the design – a lot of women, for example, want a phone that will perform, say, five basic functions: calling, texting, taking photos, storing photos and accessing the internet. For men, the more functions there are the better.

2.13

labour-saving
mass-produced
home-made
user-friendly
cold-blooded
hard-wearing
last-minute
low-fat
sugar-free
high-risk
short-sleeved
part-time

2.14

Examiner	Now, I'd like you to talk about something together for about two minutes. I'd like you to imagine you are moving to a new town and you would like to make some new friends. Here are some actions you could take and a question for you to discuss. First, you have some time to look at the task. Now, talk to each other about how these actions might help people to make new friends.
Candidate A	Okay, well, to start with I think lots of people find it difficult to make new friends in situations where there are lots of people they don't know, at a party, for example. I know I do. So inviting people to a party wouldn't help people like me.
Candidate B	Really?
Candidate A	Yes, I don't like being somewhere with a lot of people I've never met before.
Candidate B	Oh, don't you, I do. I find it really exciting – in fact, I've made some really good friends at parties, so having a party I could invite new people to would really help me.
Candidate A	People are different, though, aren't they? I mean, many people tend to make new friends on education courses or at sports clubs – places where they go to actually do something active.
Candidate B	I suppose so, but nobody actually does an education course to make new friends, do they?
Candidate A	No, probably not, but people do make new friends once they're there, don't they? Especially if it was part-time, an evening course maybe.
Candidate B	Yes, of course.
Candidate A	You must have made one or two friends while you were on a course, haven't you?
Candidate B	Yes, I have, but when I'm studying, my mind is on the course, not on the other students.
Candidate A	Is that right? I think that's quite unusual. I can concentrate on the course and pay attention to other students. What about working as a volunteer for a charity organization?
Candidate B	Yes, I think that's a really good idea. If you're a volunteer you're probably working with other volunteers who have similar ideas to you. You're working for other people, aren't you? So it's important to get on with your colleagues, isn't it?

Candidate A Yes, I hadn't thought of it like that. You're not doing it for money so you're not competing with other people in any way, are you?
Candidate B And social networking sites?
Candidate A I've never made any good friends myself that way.
Candidate B I know what you mean. People can seem to be good friends, can't they?
Candidate A They can.
Candidate B But then if you meet them, they're often a disappointment.
Candidate A Yes, I've had a couple of disappointments like that.
Candidate B Oh yeah?
Candidate A Yes, it wasn't important, but it shows how wrong you can be about a person when you haven't met them, doesn't it?
Candidate B And in any case I can't see how joining a new networking site would help you to make new friends if you moved to a new place.
Examiner Thank you. Now you have about a minute to decide which two actions would be most likely to help people to make new friends.

2.15

The theory part of the driving test isn't difficult, is it? [rising intonation]
The theory part of the driving test isn't difficult, is it? [falling intonation]

2.16

Narrator You will hear people talking in eight different situations. For questions 1–8, choose the best answer (A, B or C). Question 1. You will hear a woman talking about an invitation she turned down.
Woman I was at my boyfriend's house a couple of weeks ago, and his mother asked me if I'd like to stay for lunch. I said I was expected home, but it was a complete lie – I'd actually told my parents I'd be out all day and not to expect me home before the evening. The thing is, I'd eaten at his house before and the food was terrible. But you can't tell the truth in situations like that, can you?
Narrator Question 2. You hear a man being interviewed about his job.
Interviewer So why do you think the general public don't trust people like you?
Man I think there are two main reasons. Firstly, we're famous for breaking our promises, aren't we? When we want people to vote for us, we pretend that we can make everything right. We say things like 'This time next year you'll all have more money in your pocket'. And sometimes it's impossible to make these things happen – it's then that people accuse us of telling lies. The second reason is to do with the party system – we all have to say we agree with our party leader, whether we really do or not.
Narrator Question 3. You hear a woman talking about meeting a neighbour in town.
Woman I'm not really keen on lying, but I was in town the other day and I bumped into one of my neighbours. She said she'd heard that my sister and her husband had split up, and she wanted to know if it was true. I kept a straight face and said I'd no idea. It was a lie, of course – I mean I'd known about it for ages, but I wasn't going to give our family secrets away to someone I hardly knew. The trouble is, she'd have wanted to know all the details, and everyone would have known by the weekend.
Narrator Question 4. You hear a woman talking about a party she went to.
Woman I have to admit, life would have been dull if I hadn't told the occasional lie. Not wicked ones – just little lies that don't hurt anyone. I remember once at a party, I got stuck with this really boring boy. All he could talk about was football. After about twenty minutes, I was really fed up, so I told him my cousin played for England – his eyes nearly popped out of his head. He wanted to know my cousin's name, and could I introduce him. When I said it was David Beckham, I thought he was going to faint with excitement. It's not true – I just wanted to see his face.
Narrator Question 5. You hear a man talking about an accident he was involved in.
Man On the way back, I was really tired. I should have stopped for a quick nap, but I didn't. I kept going 'cos it was late and I wanted to get home. It was easy driving – there was hardly any traffic on the road. But unfortunately, I nodded off for a second, went off the road and scraped the car against a tree. There wasn't much damage to the car – and I was fine after that. As soon as I got home, I told my dad that I'd hit a tree, but what I didn't say was that I'd nodded off.
Narrator Question 6. You hear a woman talking about a phone call she answered.
Woman The other day, the phone rang, and my brother asked me to answer it. He thought it was probably his friend Barbara and he didn't want to speak to her. He asked me to say he wasn't in. Actually, it wasn't Barbara – it was another friend of his: Annie. Anyway, I just said he was out. Later, when I told him who it was, he was absolutely furious. His exact words were: 'If I'd known it was Annie, I'd have spoken to her.' That's one of the problems about lying for someone else, isn't it?
Narrator Question 7. You hear two people talking about something which one of them has bought.
Woman Didn't you think it was a bit strange, someone offering you such a bargain at a motorway service area?
Man Not really. It looked exactly like the real thing. And anyway, I've needed a new one for ages – mine hasn't kept proper time since I dropped it in the bath.
Woman So when did you realize you'd been tricked?
Man As soon as I took it out of its case, I knew it was a fake. When I turned it over it said Made in Toyland on the back!
Narrator Question 8. You hear a woman talking about something she did for her sister.
Woman My sister was on holiday last summer. She was expecting her exam results towards the end of August and she asked me to open her letters and telephone her with the results as soon as they arrived. She'd only been away about a week when the letter came – I was so excited, I just ripped it open without thinking. I couldn't believe it. She'd failed. I didn't know what to do. I couldn't tell her. She rang the next day and I said the letter hadn't come. I mean, if I'd told her the result, it would have ruined her holiday.

2.17

Officer How's the Miller Case going, Inspector?
Inspector Well, Ma'am ... I've just finished interviewing our three main suspects. That's Simon Prince, Margaret McKenzie and Timothy Carlyle. There was no forced entry to the house, no broken windows or doors, so we concluded that the murderer and the victim must have known each other.
Officer Tell me about Prince. He found the body, didn't he?
Inspector That's right and contacted us. He heard the shot. He's Miller's neighbour and has known him for years.
Officer What's his financial situation?
Inspector He was a financial director until two years ago. He lost his job and things have gone very wrong for him since. He's got a lot of debts.
Officer So, we have a motive – money. What else do we know about him?
Inspector He's got a few bad habits. He's a heavy drinker. He has a gambling problem. His wife divorced him last year. He's in quite a state – unshaven, unwashed, no smart clothes.
Officer Right ... one unhappy man. What about Margaret McKenzie?
Inspector She's the housekeeper. She worked for Miller for about three years. I got the impression she didn't like him much. I don't think her wages were very high and she's got three children.
Officer Husband?
Inspector In prison – for burglary – he's a master at blowing up safes, apparently.
Officer Interesting ... Miller's safe was blown, wasn't it?
Inspector That's right.
Officer OK. Anything else? Does she have any bad habits? Drinking? Drugs?
Inspector None that we know about. Well, she smokes cigarettes, but that's about all.
Officer Timothy Carlyle?
Inspector He was Miller's best friend. They'd known each other for years. He's got a reasonable job in a bank, but I don't think he earns a lot, so perhaps money could have been a motive ...
Officer ... or jealousy ... of a successful friend?
Inspector Maybe.
Officer Married or single?
Inspector Single and very presentable looking – always very smart, shirt and tie, hat and briefcase.
Officer Seeing anyone?
Inspector Not that he'd admit to, although I get the feeling he was lying when I asked him that question.
Officer Interesting ... Why would he lie about that? What about bad habits?
Inspector He drinks a bit, I think. Nothing serious.

2.18

Officer Congratulations, Inspector. I hear you've made an arrest.
Inspector That's right.
Officer Perhaps you could fill me in?
Inspector Of course. We made a detailed study of the crime scene. There were two glasses on the coffee table and a half empty bottle of whisky. This suggested that the victim must have known his murderer.
Officer And that the murderer was a drinker.
Inspector That's right. This ruled out McKenzie and pointed to either Prince or Carlyle who both drink. There was, however, a cigarette in the ashtray. We found no cigarettes belonging to Miller in the house, so we assume he was a non-smoker. The only smoker amongst our suspects is McKenzie. We also found a lady's scarf on one of the chairs again pointing to the housekeeper. Also, the Hoover was still in the room and it was plugged in! That said to me she must have been in the house at the time of the murder, otherwise it would have been put away.
Officer Then of course there was the fact that explosives were used ...
Inspector ... and McKenzie's husband is in prison for using explosives.
Officer So you arrested Margaret McKenzie.
Inspector Yes, we did. But ... there's something else ...
Officer The whisky glasses ...
Inspector ... and the hat. There was a man's hat on the table.
Officer Simon Prince's?
Inspector No ... I decided it can't have been his ... it was too smart.
Officer Timothy Carlyle?
Inspector That's right. He and McKenzie were in it together ... for the money.

2.19

Narrator You will hear five short extracts in which people are talking about money. For questions 1–5, choose from the list (A–H) what each speaker says. Use the letters only once. There are three extra letters which you do not need to use. You now have thirty seconds to look at Part 3.
Speaker 1 For some people it's a harmless enough activity. They can have the odd bet, buy the occasional lottery ticket and it doesn't do them any harm. But for me it was like the money didn't have any value; it was just about winning. As soon as I had cash I'd gamble it away. Fortunately, I was one of the lucky ones; I got help and my family were very supportive. And I don't have a problem with it any more ... I don't think it's considered a problem by society in the same way that drug addiction is, for example, but I think it should be.
Speaker 2 Some people say that drugs are largely to blame for most criminal activity these days and that if they legalized hard drugs it would make a huge difference to the crime figures. But I hope they never do 'cos then I'd be out of a job! I'm not an addict myself. I don't do drugs. That's for idiots and that's not why I became a dealer. It was simply a case of making a living. OK, I know that in the eyes of the law I'm a criminal but if I don't do it someone else will. That's how I see it. It's an easy way to make money, but unless I get caught, I've got no intention of doing an ordinary job. There's just not enough money in it.
Speaker 3 When I was at university, I took out a loan to help me pay my way, and by the time I graduated I owed £4,000. To be honest, I wasn't really bothered at first as I expected to get a good job straight away and be able to pay it back quite quickly. However, I still haven't got a proper job and now I owe £3,000 on my credit cards on top of the bank loan, and I've got absolutely no idea what I'm going to do. I realize it's entirely my own fault, but I think credit card companies and banks are also to blame. It's just too easy to get credit nowadays.
Speaker 4 Money was always a problem. When I met John he had a good job but he lost it shortly after we got married. However, I had a job and I thought we could make ends meet. Then I got pregnant and had to give up work to look after the baby. John still couldn't find a job and by this time there was another one on the way. We couldn't afford to buy nice things for the kids or go out or do anything. That's when we started arguing, and from then on things just got worse. In the end, we split up. I think if we hadn't had money problems, we might still be together.
Speaker 5 If you owe money, you worry about how on earth you are going to pay it back. If you can't afford to buy your kids presents for Christmas you get stressed and upset. Even when you've got enough money, you think you need more. I got caught up in the rat race, just trying to earn more and more. I was working too hard, and if I hadn't done something about it I'd have found myself having a heart attack when I was still in my forties. Now, I realize there are far more important things in life than money.

OXFORD
UNIVERSITY PRESS

Great Clarendon Street, Oxford, OX2 6DP, United Kingdom

Oxford University Press is a department of the University of Oxford.
It furthers the University's objective of excellence in research, scholarship,
and education by publishing worldwide. Oxford is a registered trade
mark of Oxford University Press in the UK and in certain other countries

© Oxford University Press 2015

The moral rights of the author have been asserted

First published in 2015

2019 2018 2017 2016 2015

10 9 8 7 6 5 4 3 2 1

No unauthorized photocopying

All rights reserved. No part of this publication may be reproduced, stored in a retrieval system, or transmitted, in any form or by any means, without the prior permission in writing of Oxford University Press, or as expressly permitted by law, by licence or under terms agreed with the appropriate reprographics rights organization. Enquiries concerning reproduction outside the scope of the above should be sent to the ELT Rights Department, Oxford University Press, at the address above

You must not circulate this work in any other form and you must impose this same condition on any acquirer

Links to third party websites are provided by Oxford in good faith and for information only. Oxford disclaims any responsibility for the materials contained in any third party website referenced in this work

ISBN: 978 0 19 450283 2

Printed in China

This book is printed on paper from certified and well-managed sources

ACKNOWLEDGEMENTS

The authors and publisher are grateful to those who have given permission to reproduce the following extracts and adaptations of copyright material: p.31 Adapted extract from "Raising the next Tiger Woods is now more important than raising a happy, well-balanced child" by Polly Ghazi, The Guardian, 21 February 2001. Copyright Guardian News & Media Ltd 2001. Reproduced by permission. p.36 Adapted extract from The Fix by Damian Thompson, © 2012 Damian Thompson. Reprinted by permission of HarperCollins Publishers Ltd. p.39 Adapted extract from "Kicking the habit" by Andy Darling, The Guardian, 4 December 2007. Copyright Guardian News & Media Ltd 2007. Reproduced by permission. p.40 Adapted extract from "Are You Superstitious?" by Dr. Allan N. Schwartz, www.mentalhelp.net, 10 April 2012. Reproduced by permission of Dr. Allan N. Schwartz. p.46 Adapted extract from "UF Researcher: Distant Space Travel Better Conducted As Family Affair" by Cathy Keen, http://news.ufl.edu, 14 February 2002. Reproduced by kind permission of University of Florida. p.59 Adapted extract from "Are you a tourist or a traveller?" by Anthony Peregrine, www.telegraph.co.uk, 3 August 2012. © Telegraph Media Group Limited 2012. Reproduced by permission. p.74 Adapted extract from "Army ants and chimps give researchers some food for thought" by Marc Abrahams, www.guardian.co.uk, 17 September 2012. Copyright Guardian News & Media Ltd 2012. Reproduced by permission. p.83 Adapted extract from "Welcome to the 'weisure' lifestyle" by Thom Patterson, CNN, 11 May 2009. © 2009 Cable News Network, Inc. All rights reserved. Used by permission and protected by the Copyright Laws of the United States. The printing, copying, redistribution, or retransmission of this Content without express written permission is prohibited. p.85 Adapted extract from "Playing music should be fun!" by Stefan Joubert, www.londonmusicinstitute.co.uk, 13 October 2011. Reproduced by permission of Stefan Joubert, virtuoso guitar mentor and instructor from www.stefanjoubertguitarschool.com. p.88 Extract from "Use Your Vacation Time Wisely" by Dona DeZube, http://excelle.monster.com, 06 July 2010. Reproduced by kind permission of Monster Worldwide. p.99 Extract from Strange Places, Questionable People by John Simpson, Pan Books. Copyright © John Simpson 2008. Reproduced by permission of Pan Macmillan UK. p.109 Adapted extracts from History of the Americas by Tom Leppard, Alexis Mamaux, Mark Rogers, and David Smith (Oxford University Press, 2011), reprinted by permission of Oxford University Press. p.143 Adapted extract from Second Chances. 100 Years of The Children's Court: Giving Kids A Chance To Make A Better Choice by Center on Juvenile and Criminal Justice (CJCJ), 1999), San Francisco, CA, www.cjcj.org. Reproduced by permission.

Although every effort has been made to trace and contact copyright holders before publication, this has not been possible in some cases. We apologize for any apparent infringement of copyright and if notified, the publisher will be pleased to rectify any errors or omissions at the earliest opportunity.

The publisher would like to thank the following for their kind permission to reproduce photographs: Alamy pp.9 (young man a/Miguel A. Munoz), 9 (man b/Image Source), 9 (woman green top e/ACE STOCK LIMITED), 9 (asian woman f/Image Source Plus), 9 (man j/Image Source Plus), 9 (woman glasses m/Image Source), 9 (asian man hat n/Alex Segre), 9 (asian man sea o/PhotoAlto sas), 9 (man white background r/Rob Wilkinson), 9 (woman necklace s/Blend Images), 9 (young man black t-shirt t/Radius Images), 13 (Design Pics Inc.), 18 (nurse/RTimages), 18 (traffic warden/Graham Harrison), 18 (postman/john angerson), 20 (Hugh Threlfall), 21 (teacher/devilmaya), 21 (catwalk/CatwalkFashion), 21 (gymnast/Blend Images), 24 (Fresh Start Images), 25 (Ian Shaw), 26 (thislife pictures), 27 (group study/Striking Images), 27 (lecture hall/dpa picture alliance), 30 (PjrNews), 33 (man computer/MARKA), 37 (fStop), 42 (Michael Dwyer), 45 (business meeting/ONOKY – Photononstop), 48 (Alexey Zarubin), 50 (father with two children/My Planet), 50 (father with baby/Wave Royalty Free/Design Pics Inc), 50 (mother and son swing/Johner Images), 53 (big office/imagebroker), 53 (small office/Blend Images), 57 (fast food outdoors/Africa), 57 (fast food indoors/david pearson), 57 (rickshaw/Johnny Jones), 57 (scooter/David Coleman), 59 (beach/JAM WORLD IMAGES), 59 (machu pichu/Alex Bramwell), 61 (PhotoAlto), 63 (oranges/Funky Stock – Paul Williams), 63 (crickets/Mar Photographics), 63 (honey/mark follon), 63 (oyster/MBI), 64 (dbimages), 65 (Andrew Watson), 67 (Kathy deWitt), 70 (Wavebreak Media ltd), 75 (Arco Images GmbH), 80 (Wavebreak Media ltd), 81 (photographer/Cultura RM), 83 (BESTSTOCK), 84 (Radius Images), 85 (Juice Images), 87 (Jeff Gilbert), 89 (reading/I love images/Education), 90 (man laptop/Ambient Excellence), 90 (woman library/Didier ZYLBERYNG), 90 (woman writing/Susan E. Degginger), 93 (radio/Eddie Gerald), 97 (sports advert/Robert Landau), 97 (clothes advert/Imagestate Media Partners Limited – Impact Photos), 98 (Tomas Abad), 102 (Chris Jobs), 105 (fire/David R. Frazier Photolibrary, Inc.), 109 (RGB Ventures LLC dba SuperStock), 110 (Jacques Jangoux), 112 (beach/Editorials), 112 (winter/Design Pics Inc.), 115 (GeoPic), 116 (Derek Pratt), 117 (tire/Redorbital Photography), 117 (living room/Design Pics Inc.), 118 (scarves/Adam van Bunnens), 118 (cutlery/Radius Images), 119 (machine c/INTERFOTO), 119 (machine b/Everett Collection Historical), 119 (machine d/INTERFOTO), 121 (kantapong phatichowwat), 124 (tv/Gino's Premium Images), 124 (kettle/Paul Springett 03), 124 (fridge/Gl0ck), 124 (microwave/Mile Atanasov), 129 (arms crossed/PhotoAlto), 130 (older man b/PhotoAlto sas), 130 (man beard/moodboard), 134 (Juliet Brauner), 137 (Tony Eves), 139 (Steve Vidler), 140 (Jordan Rooney), 141 (graffiti/Nic Cleave Photography), 143 (Jeff Gilbert), 147 (transport/Paul MacCrimmon), 149 (red nose a/razorpix), 150 (marathon/Keith Douglas), 153 (painter/Eye Ubiquitous), 153 (student/Alpha and Omega Collection), 154 (caucasian family/MarioPonta), 155 (corkscrew/milos luzanin), 155 (nail file/Zoonar GmbH), 155 (timer/David Cook/blueshiftstudios), 155 (scales/Gary Vogelmann), 155 (bird table/Mouse in the House), 155 (flip flops/Winston Link), 156 (bird table/Mouse in the House), 156 (timer/David Cook/blueshiftstudios), 156 (nail file/Zoonar GmbH), 156 (scales/Gary Vogelmann), 156 (corkscrew/milos luzanin), 156 (flip flops/Winston Link), 156 (hoop and stick/Old Visuals), 156 (videogames/Blend Images), 156 (elderly woman/Ian Shaw), 157 (restaurant/ONOKY – Photononstop); 157 (basketball/Ashok Saxena), BBC Motion Gallery p.99; CartoonStock pp.51 (Mike Flanagan www.CartoonStock.com), 88 (Ron Coleman www.CartoonStock.com); Comic Relief pp.149 (red nose b), 149 (red nose c), 149 (red nose d/Tom Dymond), 149 (red nose e); Corbis UK Ltd pp.18 (pilot/Johnėr Images), 21 (singer/Siphiwe Sibeko/Reuters), 36 (Tim Hill/Food and Drink Photos), 39 (Radius Images), 45 (friends/Dreampictures/Image Source), 45 (father and son/Jade/Blend Images), 47 (John Lund/Tom Penpark/Blend Images), 49 (Wolff & Tritschler), 54 (red carpet/Levente Mihaly/Demotix), 66 (Owen Franken), 69 (Oivind Hovland/Ikon Images), 74 (Don Parsons/Visuals Unlimited), 78 (Jordan Siemens), 79 (Andy King/Sygma), 89 (gym/Nancy Honey/cultura), 117 (lantern/Per Magnus Persson/Johnr Imag), 157 (senior running/Gareth Brown); Fotolia pp.9 (woman beanie g/bevangoldswain), 18 (fast food worker/Lisa F. Young), 73 (Minerva Studio), 105 (snow/Chris Gloster), 124 (hairdryer/Julián Rovagnati); Getty Images pp.9 (woman c/Fuse), 9 (asian man h/Jade), 9 (girl curly hair p/Rafael Elias), 9 (man glasses q/Carlina Teteris), 11 (interview/Robert Daly), 11 (cv cartoon/dane_mark), 12 (PhotoAlto/Antoine Arraou), 13 (MistikaS), 14 (kimberrywood), 15 (AID/a.collectionRF), 16 (man hurdling/PeskyMonkey), 16 (man hurdling close up/PeskyMonkey), 16 (painting/Peter Barritt), 17 (Tara Moore), 18 (police officer/Darryl Estrine), 21 (museum/Manchan), 21 (surgeon/Dana Neely), 29 (13spoon), 31 (Ariel Skelley), 32 (Transcendental Graphics/), 33 (woman shoes/Eileen Bach), 33 (coffee machine/IGphotography), 33 (man street/Fabrice LEROUGE), 33 (playing videogames/Jupiterimages), 33 (woman office/Thomas Barwick), 34 (Sebastian Pfuetze), 35 (Gustav Dejert), 38 (T-Immagini), 40 (mirror/Soren Hald), 40 (umbrella/WIN-Initiative), 40 (cracks/GSO Images), 41 (PhotoAlto/James Hardy), 45 (nurse and patient/Luis Alvarez), 45 (teacher and student/MachineHeadz), 46 (Jayme Thornton), 54 (footballer/XiXinXing), 54 (businesswoman/Howard Kingsnorth), 54 (scientist/CZQS2000/STS), 58 (Martin Harvey), 62 (Keren Su), 63 (avocado/Foodcollection RF), 68 (Martin Harvey), 70 (Kyle Monk), 72 (dumayne), 77 (Tara Moore), 81 (chatting/Cavan Images), 81 (baking/Factoria Singular), 81 (videogames/Jupiterimages), 81 (guitar/Jessie Jean), 90 (woman long hair laptop/David Malan), 90 (Gallo Images), 93 (subway/sturti), 93 (watching tv/Noel Hendrickson), 93 (newspaper/Charlotte Steeples Photography), 94 (Baran Ozdemir), 101 (Thomas Barwick), 105 (flood/Visual News Pakistan), 105 (cattle/Sami's Photography), 106 (Susana Gonzalez/Newsmakers), 112 (park/Nicolas McComber), 117 (house/Arpad Benedek), 117 (crayons/Ian Smith), 122 (woman/SSPL/National Railway Museum), 122 (man/Doris Rudd Designs, Photography), 125 (Paul Avis), 128 (Courtesy of Gisela Capitain, Cologne and Stuart Shave/Modern Art, London. Photo by Jeff J Mitchell/Getty Images/Martin Boyce, Turner Prize 2011, BALTIC Centre for Contemporary Art in partnership with Tate), 129 (two men/stevecoleimages), 129 (two women/Westend61), 130 (boy e/Caroline Schiff), 130 (red hair d/PraxisPhotography), 130 (elderly woman f/Universal Stopping Point Photography), 130 (woman c/Rob Lewine), 131 (Nick David), 132 (Image Source), 141 (homeless/2012 AFP), 141 (job centre/Jason Alden/Bloomberg), 141 (debt/Christine Glade), 146 (MoneyImages), 147 (high street/Bruno De Hogues), 150 (concert), 150 (bungee jumping/IMAGEMORE Co, Ltd.), 153 (acrobats/Bertrand Rindoff Petroff), 153 (teacher/Thomas Roetting), 154 (man/antonio arcos aka fotonstudio photography), 154 (mother/Liam Norris), 154 (asian family/Blend Images – Jade), 155 (football advert/JOERG KOCH/AFP), 155 (egg slicer/Lew Robertson), 155 (oven gloves/Dorling Kindersley), 155 (barstool/www.jupiterimages.com), 156 (oven gloves/Dorling Kindersley), 156 (barstool/www.jupiterimages.com), 156 (egg slicer/Lew Robertson), 156 (driving/Mark Bowden), 157 (amusement park); Modern Art Gallery p.128 (Courtesy of Gisela Capitain, Cologne and Stuart Shave/Modern Art, London. Photo by Jeff J Mitchell/Getty Images/Martin Boyce, Turner Prize 2011, BALTIC Centre for Contemporary Art in partnership with Tate); Oxford University Press pp.9 (woman bandana d/Tetra Images), 9 (woman plait i/Oxford University Press/Mark Bassett), 9 (woman red hair k/Westend61), 9 (red hair man l/Westend61), 50 (mother and child toys/MIXA), 95 (Johner Images), 112 (flowers/Corbis), 155 (whisk/Ingram), 155 (screwdriver/Dennis Kitchen Studio, Inc.), 155 (binoculars/Photodisc), 156 (whisk/Ingram), 156 (screwdriver/Dennis Kitchen Studio, Inc.), 156 (binoculars/Photodisc); Rex Features pp.23 (Morten Nordby), 126 (life of pi/Moviestore), 126 (jurassic park/Moviestore Collection), 126 (king kong/SNAP), 155 (real life advert/SEVGI/SIPA); Ronald Grant Archive p.126 (toy story); Science Photo Library p.119 (machine a/SHEILA TERRY); Serviceplan Group p.155 (shark advert/Faber Castell); Société des Produits Nestlé S.A p.123; Superstock Ltd. pp.45 (wife and husband/Exotica), 81 (tai chi/Flirt), 89 (concert/imagebroker.net#sthash.BKCVv8uu.dpuf), 113 (Sami Sarkis/age fotostock), 118 (chair/Thorsten Marquardt/Mauritius), 129 (woman/age fotostock), 155 (bus advert/Marka); Zooid Pictures p.117 (present)

Illustrations by: Andy Parker p.145 (living room); 145 (woman), 145 (young man), 145 (older man), Oxford University Press pp.148 (woman), 148 (cat), 148 (tortoise); Spike Gerrell p.60; Tim Kahane pp.86 (football), 86 (tennis), 86 (running), 86 (basketball), 86 (cycling), 86 (golf), 86 (motor sports), 86 (boxing)